Pocket Guide *to* Legal Writing

DELMAR CENGAGE Learning

Options.

Over 300 products in every area of the law: textbooks, online courses, CD-ROMs, reference books, companion websites, and more – helping you succeed in the classroom and on the job.

Support.

We offer unparalleled, practical support: robust instructor and student supplements to ensure the best learning experience, custom publishing to meet your unique needs, and other benefits such as Delmar Cengage Learning's Student Achievement Award. And our sales representatives are always ready to provide you with dependable service.

Feedback.

As always, we want to hear from you! Your feedback is our best resource for improving the quality of our products. Contact your sales representative or write us at the address below if you have any comments about our materials or if you have a product proposal.

Accounting and Financials for the Law Office • Administrative Law • Alternative Dispute Resolution • Bankruptcy • Business Organizations/Corporations • Careers and Employment • Civil Litigation and Procedure • CLA Exam Preparation • Computer Applications in the Law Office Constitutional Law • Contract Law • Court Reporting • Criminal Law and Procedure • Document Preparation •Elder Law • Employment Law • Environmental Law • Ethics • Evidence Law Family Law • Health Care Law • Immigration Law • Intellectual Property • Internships Interviewing and Investigation • Introduction to Law • Introduction to Paralegalism Juvenile Law • Law Office Management • Law Office Procedures • Legal Nurse Consulting Legal Research, Writing, and Analysis • Legal Terminology • Legal Transcription Media and Entertainment Law • Medical Malpractice Law • Product Liability Real Estate Law • Reference Materials • Social Security • Sports Law • Torts and Personal Injury Law • Wills, Trusts, and Estate Administration • Workers' Compensation Law

---

DELMAR CENGAGE Learning
Executive Woods, 5 Maxwell Drive
Clifton Park, New York 12065

For additional information, find us online at:
www.cengage.com/delmar

Pocket Guide *to* Legal Writing

WILLIAM H. PUTMAN

DELMAR
CENGAGE Learning™

Australia • Brazil • Japan • Korea • Mexico • Singapore • Spain • United Kingdom • United States

Pocket Guide to Legal Writing
William H. Putman

Vice President, Career Education Strategic Business Unit:
Dawn Gerrain

Director of Editorial:
Sherry Gomoll

Editor: Shelley Esposito

Editorial Assistant:
Brian Banks

Director of Production:
Wendy A. Troeger

Production Editor:
Betty L. Dickson

Director of Marketing:
Wendy Mapstone

Marketing Specialist:
Gerard McAvey

Cover Design:
Rose Design

For product information and
technology assistance, contact us at **Cengage Learning
Customer & Sales Support, 1-800-354-9706**

For permission to use material from this text or product,
submit all requests online at **www.cengage.com/permissions**
Further permissions questions can be emailed to
permissionrequest@cengage.com

Library of Congress Control Number: 2005014491

ISBN-13: 978-1-4018-6597-9

ISBN-10: 1-4018-6597-6

Delmar
Executive Woods
5 Maxwell Drive
Clifton Park, NY 12065
USA

Cengage Learning is a leading provider of customized learning solutions with office locations around the globe, including Singapore, the United Kingdom, Australia, Mexico, Brazil, and Japan. Locate your local office at **www.cengage.com/global**

Cengage Learning products are represented in Canada by Nelson Education, Ltd.

To learn more about Delmar, visit **www.cengage.com/delmar**

Purchase any of our products at your local bookstore or at our preferred online store **www.ichapters.com**

Printed in China
9 10 11 18 17 16

DEDICATION

This book is dedicated to P.Y., whose love, inspiration, and guidance made this text possible. Thank you.

Contents

Chapter 3
Grammar

47

Chapter 4 69
Punctuation

Chapter 5
Legal Citation

Chapter 5 — page 89

Chapter 6   135
Computer and Internet Research Web Sites

Chapter 7   149
Preparing to Write—The Writing Process for Effective Legal Writing

---

Chapter 10
Court Briefs

Acknowledgments

I wish to gratefully acknowledge and express my deep appreciation to a number of individuals who took time and effort to assist in the development of this book. Without their expertise, suggestions, and support, this text would not have been possible. I am particularly indebted to the following individuals:

- ▶ Sheila McGlothlin, a paralegal, for her support in the overall development of the text.
- ▶ Vicki Zelle, an attorney and former paralegal, for her review and contributions.
- ▶ Shelley Esposito, Brian Banks, and all of the individuals at West Legal Studies who helped with the development of this text. Their encouragement, suggestions, patience, and support were essential to completion of the text.

Finally, I would like to thank the reviewers who provided valuable comments and suggestions for the text:

Holly Enterline
Southwest Tennessee Community College

Hank Arnold
Aiken Technical College

Kim Neal
Kaplan University

Scott Rockley
Lansing Community College

Elizabeth Brantlinger Agnus
St. Joseph's College

Deborah Keene
Lansing Community College

Elizabeth Mann
Greenville Technical College

About the Author

William Putman received his Juris Doctor degree from the University of New Mexico School of Law and has been a member of the New Mexico Bar since 1975. For ten years, he was an instructor in the Legal Assistant Studies Program at Albuquerque Technical Vocational Institute, a community college, and in the Paralegal Studies Program at Santa Fe Community College.

He authored the textbooks *Legal Analysis and Writing, Legal Research, Analysis and Writing,* and *Legal Research*. For two years, he wrote the legal writing column in *Legal Assistant Today* and published several articles on legal analysis and writing in the magazine.

Chapter **1**

Sentences and Paragraphs

Contents

1.1 SENTENCES

A sentence is the fundamental building block of writing. A sentence is usually a statement that conveys an idea or ideas. Good writing skills include knowledge of the basics of proper sentence construction. When reviewing sentences and paragraphs, you may use the checklist presented in Exhibit 1-1 at the end of the chapter.

1.1 A STRUCTURE/PATTERN

A sentence is usually a statement in which the actor (the subject) performs some action or describes a state of being (the predicate).

For Example:

Subject	Predicate
John	wrecked the car.
John	is ill.

The predicate is composed of the verb and object of the verb, such as a direct object. An object of the verb may be required to receive the action of the verb.

> ■ *For Example:*
>
> **Subject**   **Predicate**
> John   wrecked the car.

The car is a direct object that receives the action of the verb *wrecked*.
   At a minimum, a sentence must have a subject and a predicate. In its simplest form, a sentence requires a noun and a verb.

> ■ *For Example:*
>
> Judges rule.

Make sure your sentences have at least a subject and a predicate. In addition to a subject and a predicate, a sentence may have words that modify (describe or qualify) other words, such as adjectives and adverbs.

> ■ *For Example:*
>
> John wrecked the *red* car. *Red* is an adjective that modifies (describes) the noun *car.*
> The judge ruled *harshly. Harshly* is an adverb that describes the verb *ruled.*

Sentences may also include various phrases and clauses. Those are discussed in the next section.

1.1 B   PHRASES AND CLAUSES

1. **Phrases**   A phrase is a group of words that lacks a subject or predicate or both. Therefore, it is not a sentence. A phrase usually functions in a sentence as an adjective, an adverb, or a noun. There are several types of phrases:
   a. *Absolute Phrase*—modifies a clause in a sentence.

> ■ *For Example:*
>
> *Her fingers flying,* Mary quickly demonstrated how to assemble the switch.

   b. *Appositive Phrase*—describes or renames the noun it modifies.

> ■ *For Example:*
>
> Mary, *the top student in her class,* was awarded the scholarship.

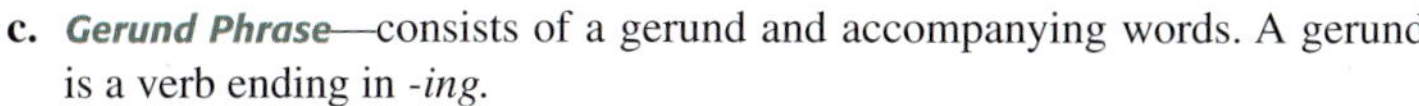

c. *Gerund Phrase*—consists of a gerund and accompanying words. A gerund is a verb ending in *-ing*.

> ◘ *For Example:*
>
> Tom, *having finished his nap,* went back to work.

d. *Infinitive Phrase*—consists of an infinitive and accompanying words. An infinitive is the word *to* followed by a verb.

> ◘ *For Example:*
>
> It is important *to take continuing education classes.*

e. *Participial Phrase*—consists of a participle and accompanying words. A participle is a verb that may be used as an adjective.

> ◘ *For Example:*
>
> The paralegal, *hired to perform research,* was paid an excellent salary.

f. *Prepositional Phrase*—begins with a preposition and ends with a noun or noun substitute. A preposition is a word that expresses a relationship between the word or words that follow and other words in the sentence. Some common prepositions are *about, after, at, before, by, for, from, in, of, on, over, through, up,* and *with.*

> ◘ *For Example:*
>
> *After Mary completed the brief,* she went to lunch.

2. Clauses A clause is a group of words that includes a subject and a predicate. There are two types of clauses:

▶ *Independent clause*—Also referred to as a *main clause,* an independent clause can stand alone as a complete sentence. Every sentence has a main clause.

> ◘ *For Example:*
>
> Elsa studied very hard.

▶ *Dependent clause*—Also referred to as a *subordinate clause,* a dependent clause cannot stand alone as a sentence.

> ◘ *For Example:*
>
> After Elsa studied very hard.

There are three types of dependent clauses: adjective, adverb, and noun.

   a. *Adjective Clause*—a dependent clause that modifies a noun or pronoun. Adjective clauses begin with a relative pronoun (such as *that, who, whom,* or *which*) or a relative adverb (*when* or *where*). An adjective clause usually follows the word it modifies.

> ◻ *For Example:*
>
> The paralegal, *who is an expert in estate planning,* conducted the initial meeting with the client.
> Tyrone, *who was exhausted from the previous evening,* left the meeting.

   b. *Adverb Clause*—a dependent clause that modifies a verb, an adjective, an adverb, a phrase, or an independent clause. The clause is introduced with a subordinating conjunction such as *although, because, if, unless,* or *when.*

> ◻ *For Example:*
>
> Omar left the meeting *when he was finished.*
> Don't talk *unless you are spoken to.*

   c. *Noun Clause*—a dependent clause that functions as a subject, direct object, or subject compliment. A noun clause usually begins with a relative pronoun or *how, that, what, whether,* or *why.*

> ◻ *For Example:*
>
> I don't care *who is responsible.*
> *When he prepares it* is of no consequence to me.

1.1 C   TYPES AND CLASSIFICATIONS

1. Types   There are four basic types of sentences—simple, compound, complex, and compound-complex

   a. *Simple Sentence*—A simple sentence is composed of an independent clause and no subordinate clauses. It is composed of only one subject and verb structure.

> ◻ *For Example:*
>
> Barb writes songs.
> Hector decided to do his work.

   b. *Compound Sentence*—A compound sentence is composed of two or more independent clauses. The clauses are usually linked by a semicolon or a coordinating conjunction such as *and, but, or, nor, yet, for,* or *so.*

> ■ *For Example:*
>
> Carol played the flute, and Ann played the piano.
> Abdul waited in the entry way, yet Rick continued to read.

   c. *Complex Sentence*—A complex sentence is composed of an independent clause and one or more dependent clauses.

> ■ *For Example:*
>
> He made a mistake when he asked Peter to attend.
> Do not cross the bridge before you come to it.
> Although Irina was busy, she took time to help the courier.

   d. *Compound-Complex Sentence*—A compound-complex sentence is composed of at least two independent clauses and one or more dependent clauses. The dependent clause is italicized in the following examples.

> ■ *For Example:*
>
> Lenny hurried *whenever he was late,* and he often forgot to shave.
> He got a lot of work done, *although he was sloppy;* but he often missed deadlines *when he was tired.*

2. Classifications   Sentences are classified according to one of four functions—declarative, interrogative, imperative, and exclamatory.
   a. *Declarative Sentence*—A declarative sentence makes a statement.

> ■ *For Example:*
>
> Drew is ready to go to court.
> The sun will rise before the moon sets.

   b. *Interrogative Sentence*—An interrogative sentence asks a question.

> ■ *For Example:*
>
> Is Drew ready to go to court?
> Will the sun rise before the moon sets?

   c. *Imperative Sentence*—An imperative sentence gives a command.

> ■ *For Example:*
>
> Open the window.
> Please follow the citation rules.

   d. *Exclamatory Sentence*—An exclamatory sentence expresses emotion. Exclamatory sentences end with an exclamation point.

> *For Example:*
> Stop fighting!
> Come here right now!

1.1 D   BASIC RULES AND PROBLEM AREAS

The following subsections introduce basic rules and problem areas involving sentences and sentence structure. You should keep these topics in mind when drafting or reviewing sentences.

1. **Subject/Verb Distance**   The subject and verb should be kept as close together as possible. A sentence is easier to understand when the subject and verb are close together. Intervening words, clauses, or phrases disrupt the action and make the sentence difficult to understand. In the following examples, intervening words and phrases are italicized.

> *For Example:*
> Rob, *apparently upset and in a bad mood,* hit James.
> The argument that the good faith exception applies *because the officers were acting in good faith and the warrant was defective due to magistrate error* is supported by the facts.
>
> **Revisions:**
> Apparently upset and in a bad mood, Rob hit James.
> The argument that the good faith exception applies is supported by the facts. The officers were acting in good faith, and the warrant was defective due to magistrate error.

2. **Sentence Length**   Although there is no rule governing sentence length, a shorter sentence is easier to understand. The length of a sentence will vary according to the nature of the information it must convey. A good average for sentence length is 20 to 25 words. If you find that your sentences are too long, eliminate extra words or break the sentence into shorter sentences.

> *For Example:*
> The evidence should be suppressed because the warrant did not authorize unannounced entry, and there were no exigent circumstances at the scene that provided justification for the officers' actions of entering the residence unannounced.
>
> **Revision:**
> The evidence should be suppressed because the warrant did not authorize unannounced entry. In addition, the circumstances at the scene did not provide justification for unannounced entry.

3. Sentence Variety   Often when a rough draft is completed, all of the sentences are similar. They may be approximately the same length and organized in the same way. This can be tedious for the reader. There are several ways to add variety to your writing.

   a. *Sentence Openings*—A standard sentence begins with a subject that is followed by a verb, then an object. To provide variety in writing, some sentences should not follow that format. Variety can be accomplished by moving words, phrases, or clauses before the subject.

> *For Example:*
>
> Karen has refused to issue stock dividends even though the corporation
>   has an accumulated cash surplus of $500,000.
> Steve completely controls the business because he is the majority
>   shareholder.
> Larry told them the dividends would be issued soon, when he was questioned about corporation profits.
>
> **Revisions:**
> Because Steve is the majority shareholder, he completely controls the
>   business.
> Even though the corporation has an accumulated cash surplus of $500,000,
>   Karen has refused to issue stock dividends.
> When questioned about corporation profits, Larry told them the dividends
>   would be issued soon.

   b. *Sentence Length*—Do not make all of the sentences the same length. If all sentences are the same length, the writing can be choppy, different to follow, and boring.

> *For Example:*
>
> On December 5, Nick Stevens was skiing Bright Light. Bright Light is an intermediate ski run at Blue Sky Resort. At the midway point, the run takes a sharp turn. After the turn, the run plunges steeply downhill. Mr. Stevens encountered the turn. The sun was shining directly in his eyes. He did not see that the run was completely covered with ice. Due to the sun's glare, he did not see the ice hazard. He immediately lost control and hit a tree. He broke his left arm and leg.

   By combining and varying the length of these sentences, the paragraph can be made less choppy.

> *For Example:*
>
> On December 5, Nick Stevens was skiing Bright Light, an intermediate ski run, at Blue Sky Resort. At the midway point, the run takes a sharp turn and plunges steeply downhill. When Mr. Stevens encountered the turn,

   c. *Excessive Words, Phrases, and Clauses*—Sentences should not include excessive words, phrases, or clauses that add little to the meaning. Check each sentence for words that can be eliminated. Simplify the finished product.

     (1) Redundant words.　Redundant words repeat the description of another word. The following is a list of some commonly used redundant pairs. Any one of the terms can be used; use of both terms is not appropriate.

alter/change	end/result	merged/together
and/moreover	exact/same	null/void
cease/desist	few/in number	sole/exclusive
descend/down	full/complete	specific/example
due/owing	join/together	true/correct
each/every		

     (2) Excessive words, phrases, and clauses.　Sentences should not be cluttered with excessive unnecessary words, phrases, and clauses. Often the sentence can be corrected by eliminating or rephrasing the unnecessary material.

Inflated phrases
In order to accomplish his goal, he had to go to school.
Gamal missed the meeting *due to the fact that* he was late.
Olivia decided that she would have to try again *in the event that* Jerry
    failed to appear.

Revisions:
To accomplish his goal, he had to go to school.
Gamal missed the meeting *because* he was late.
Olivia decided that she would have to try again *if* Jerry failed to appear.

Failure to use a pronoun:
Mr. Thompson directed several musical productions. *The Singing Tree* was
    Mr. Thompson's most complex and popular stage play.

Revision:
Mr. Thompson directed several musical productions. *The Singing Tree* was
    his most complex and popular stage play. (The pronoun *his* replaces
    Mr. Thompson.)

The following is a list of common wordy phrases with a concise substitute.

Wordy Phrase	Concise Substitute
along the lines of	like
at the present time	now
by means of	by
due to the fact that	because
for the reason that	because
in as much as	since
in order to	to
in the event that	if
in the vicinity of	near
until such time that	until

(3) **Excessively complex sentences.**   Some sentences are unnecessarily
    complex and clumsy. They can be remedied by rewriting the sentence.

For Example:
Mr. Calligan, *who is an experienced electrician,* went to the construction
    site *with the expectation that* all of the ducting *would be* in place.
There is another possible solution *to the problem, which* is to rewrite the
    proposal.
It would not be unwarranted to expect that we will encounter further prob-
    lems on the project.

> **Revisions:**
> Mr. Calligan, an experienced electrician, went to the construction site expecting all of the ducting to be in place.
> Another possible solution is to rewrite the proposal.
> We can expect to encounter further problems on the project.

4. Run-on Sentences   A run-on sentence occurs when two independent clauses are joined incorrectly. Each sentence should contain one main idea. You may be tempted to pack more than one idea into a sentence—usually when the ideas are related. If a sentence you are reviewing is very long, it may be a run-on sentence, and you may be attempting to convey too many ideas in the sentence.

> ⊡ *For Example:*
>
> Thomas does not dispute the fact that the court properly resorted to estimating a plant quantity for the 1991 grow, his dispute concerns the basis for the court's estimation. (That sentence conveys two related ideas: what he does not dispute and what he does dispute. Each idea should be presented in separate sentences.)
>
> **Revision:**
> Thomas does not dispute the fact that the court properly resorted to estimating a plant quantity for the 1991 grow. His dispute concerns the basis for the court's estimation.

There are two types of run-on sentences: a fused sentence and a comma splice.
   a. *Fused Sentence*—A fused sentence occurs when two independent clauses are joined with no punctuation and no coordinating conjunction.

> ⊡ *For Example:*
>
> Mr. Stevens encountered the turn the sun was shining directly in his eyes.

   b. *Comma Splice*—A comma splice occurs when two independent clauses are joined by a punctuation mark without a coordinating conjunction.

> ⊡ *For Example:*
>
> Mr. Stevens encountered the turn, the sun was shining directly in his eyes.

   c. *Correcting a Run-on Sentence*—A run-on sentence can be corrected in four ways:
   ► add a comma and a coordinating conjunction
   ► place a period between the clauses, making separate sentences
   ► add a semicolon, colon, or dash
   ► restructure the sentence

(1) Revision with a comma and coordinating conjunction.   A run-on sentence can be corrected by adding a comma and the appropriate coordinating conjunction (*and, but, or, nor, for, so,* or *yet*) to combine the clauses into one sentence.

For Example:

Mr. Stevens encountered the turn, *and* the sun was shining directly in his eyes.

(2) Revision by making separate sentences.   The revision can be accomplished by placing a period between the clauses and making separate sentences. That is a good strategy to use when the clauses are long or when they are not closely related.

For Example:

Thomas does not dispute the fact that the court properly resorted to estimating a plant quantity for the 1991 grow, his dispute concerns the basis for the court's estimation.

Revision:

Thomas does not dispute the fact that the court properly resorted to estimating a plant quantity for the 1991 grow. His dispute concerns the basis for the court's estimation.

(3) Revision with a semicolon, colon, or dash.   If the independent clauses are closely related, you can use a semicolon to revise the run-on sentence. The use of a semicolon is discussed in detail in Chapter 4.

For Example:

When Mr. Stevens encountered the turn, the sun was shining directly in his eyes he did not see that the run was completely covered with ice.

Revision:

When Mr. Stevens encountered the turn, the sun was shining directly in his eyes; he did not see that the run was completely covered with ice.

(4) Revision by restructuring the sentence.   Another way to revise a run-on sentence is to restructure the sentence by making one of the independent clauses a dependent clause.

For Example:

The sun was shining directly in his eyes he did not see that the run was completely covered with ice.

> **Revision:**
> Because the sun was shining directly in his eyes, he did not see that the
> run was completely covered with ice.

5. **Sentence Fragments**   A sentence fragment is an incomplete sentence. Every
   sentence in any writing must be a complete sentence; therefore, no writing
   should include sentence fragments. A sentence may be incomplete because it
   lacks a subject, a verb, or both.

> ◘ *For Example:*
>
> The top student in her class. (*The top student in her class* is an appositive
>   phrase.)
> Her fingers flying. *(Her fingers flying* is an absolute phrase.)

Often the fragment includes a subject and a verb, but it is an incomplete sentence
because it is a dependent clause.

> ◘ *For Example:*
>
> Because she is an expert in the area.
> Who is an expert in the area.

Although these examples have a subject (*she* and *who*) and a verb (*was* and *is*),
they are incomplete sentences because they begin with a subordinating conjunction (*because* in the first sentence) and a relative pronoun (*who* in the second sentence). The words at the beginning of the examples should alert the writer that
these are not complete sentences.
   Sentence fragments may be corrected in the following ways:

▶ combine the fragment with an adjacent sentence
▶ eliminate the subordinating conjunction or relative pronoun
▶ rewrite the fragment to include the missing subject, verb, or both

   a. *Combine the fragment with an adjacent sentence*—The fragment may be
      corrected by combining the fragment with the sentence it refers to, usually
      an adjacent sentence.

> ◘ *For Example:*
>
> Because she is an expert in the area.
> Who is an expert in the area.
>
> **Revisions:**
> Sarah conducted the meeting because she is an expert in the area.
> Sarah, who is an expert in the area, conducted the meeting.

b. *Eliminate the subordinating conjunction or relative pronoun*—An easy solution is to make a dependent clause a complete sentence by eliminating or
changing the beginning word.

> **For Example:**
>
> Because she is an expert in the area.
> Who is an expert in the area.
>
> **Revisions:**
> She is an expert in the area. (The subordinating conjunction, *because,* is
>   eliminated.)
> She is an expert in the area. (The relative pronoun, *who,* has been changed
>   to *she.*)

c. *Rewrite the fragment to include the missing subject, verb, or both*—Another way to correct a fragment is to turn it into a sentence by supplying
the missing element(s).

> **For Example:**
>
> The top student in her class.
> Her fingers flying.
>
> **Revisions:**
> Liza, *the top student in her class,* was awarded the scholarship.
> *Her fingers flying,* Mary quickly demonstrated how to assemble the switch.

6. Mood Shifts   Mood indicates whether the actor in a sentence is making a
statement; asking a question; giving a command; or expressing a wish, a condition contrary to fact, a request, or a recommendation. The **indicative mood**
is used for statements of fact, opinions, or questions.

> **For Example:**
>
> He is an excellent performer.

The **imperative mood** is used for commands and direct advice.

> **For Example:**
>
> Go to the store.
> Give me the instruction manual.

The **subjunctive mood** is used to express a wish, state a condition contrary to
fact, or make a request or recommendation.

> **For Example:**
>
> Jacinta wished she had not told Dashon she would go.
> We recommend that you adopt the listed terms and conditions.
> If you would only do what I say, you would not have these problems.

You should avoid improper mood shifts in your writing.

> **For Example:**
>
> Read the instruction manual, and you should follow it carefully. (The sentence shifts from the imperative to the indicative mood.)
>
> **Revision:**
> Read the instruction manual and follow it carefully.

7. **Active/Passive Voice**   The word *voice* refers to the relationship of the subject and its verb; voice is either active or passive. Voice tells the reader whether the subject of the sentence is the actor or is acted upon (receives the action).
   a. *Active Voice*—The general rule is that you should draft sentences using active voice. When active voice is used, the subject of the sentence is the actor.

> **For Example:**
>
> **Active voice:**
> The automobile hit the child.
> The construction workers built the dam.
>
> **Passive voice:**
> The child was hit by the automobile.
> The dam was built by the construction workers.

Active voice is usually the best choice because it is easy to understand and is more powerful. It is easy to understand because the doer of the action is mentioned at the beginning of the sentence before the action. Readers do not have to read the entire sentence before they know who is performing the action. Active voice is more powerful because, at the outset, it identifies the actor as the performer of the action. This focuses attention on the actor and emphasizes the actor's actions.

> **For Example:**
>
> **Active voice:**
> The defendant breached the contract when he failed to deliver the goods on time.

Passive voice:
The contract was breached when the goods were not delivered on time.
  (The actor is not identified.)

b. *Passive Voice*—When passive voice is used, the subject of the sentence is acted upon. The actor is removed from the action or not identified at all. In certain situations, it is appropriate to use passive voice: when the actor is unknown or unimportant or when you do not want to emphasize the actor's conduct. See Chapter 10 for a discussion of the appropriate use of passive voice in court briefs.

For Example:

Actor unknown:
A portion of the transcript was lost.

Actor unimportant:
The bank deposit was found by a passerby.

Actor de-emphasized:
The vase was broken and the plaintiff injured when the vase slipped from the defendant's hand.

8. Action Verbs   Whenever possible, select verbs that are active rather than verbs that show state of being or that are passive.

For Example:

Passive:
Zelda reached the conclusion that Darius was guilty.

Revision:
Zelda concluded that Darius was guilty.

State of being:
The record keeper is Anton Jones.

Revision:
Anton Jones keeps the records.

9. Repeated Prepositions   Avoid repeating a preposition in a sentence. This can be accomplished by rephrasing the sentence to make a compound object.

For Example:

The paralegal had extensive knowledge of domestic relations and of estate planning.
The lawyer informed himself of the contract terms and of the will terms.
The instruction manual may be used to identify the parts, to operate the engine, and to perform maintenance.

> **Revisions:**
> The paralegal had extensive knowledge of domestic relations and estate planning.
> The lawyer informed himself of the terms of the contract and will.
> The instruction manual may be used to identify the parts, operate the engine, and perform maintenance.

10. **Transitions** Transitional words and phrases connect sentences and serve to establish the relationship between the subjects of the sentences. Transitions are important because they guide the reader and make the writing cohesive.

> ◻ *For Example:*
>
> **No transition:**
> The statute requires that fences exceeding five feet in height must be located no closer than ten feet from the property line. Your fence will be six feet high; you must build it ten feet from the property line.
>
> **With transition:**
> The statute requires that fences exceeding five feet in height must be located no closer than ten feet from the property line. *Therefore, since your fence will exceed five feet, you must locate it ten feet from the property line.* (The transition is italicized.)

The following are examples of transitional words and phrases.

above all	even so	instead	specifically
all the same	finally	likewise	still
allegedly	for	meanwhile	subsequently
although	furthermore	more importantly	that is
and	however	moreover	therefore
arguably	in addition	nevertheless	thus
but	in conclusion	nonetheless	to illustrate
clearly	in contrast	on the other hand	undoubtedly
consequently	in other words	simply put	unlike
contrary to	in summary	since	without question
conversely	initially	so	

1.2 PARAGRAPHS

A **paragraph** is a group of sentences that address the same topic. Paragraphs are important because they organize the writing according to topic. They make it easy for the reader to understand the material by separating it into manageable units. A reader may have difficulty understanding the subject matter when it is not divided into paragraphs. Begin a new paragraph when a new idea or topic is addressed and use transitional phrases or sentences to link new paragraphs. A well-drafted paragraph includes all of the information necessary to understand the topic.

A paragraph usually consists of the following elements:

► a topic sentence
► the body
► a closing sentence

All of those elements are not required in every paragraph. A short paragraph, for example, may not have a closing sentence. The following sections discuss the elements of a paragraph and other considerations to keep in mind when writing paragraphs.

1.2 A   TOPIC SENTENCE

The topic sentence identifies the subject of a paragraph. The topic sentence introduces the subject and provides the focus of the paragraph for the reader. The topic sentence is usually placed at the beginning of the paragraph.

> *For Example:*
>
> ► topic sentence of a paragraph that discusses why the exclusionary rule is necessary: The Supreme Court has identified several reasons why the exclusionary rule is necessary.
> ► topic sentence of a paragraph that discusses Mr. Smith's actions: Mr. Smith's actions do not constitute a breach of contract.
> ► topic sentence of a paragraph that addresses required conditions: A warranty of fitness for a particular purpose is created when the following conditions are present.

1.2 B   BODY

The body of a paragraph is composed of a sentence or sentences that support or develop the subject introduced by the topic sentence. The sentence(s) should develop the subject clearly and logically.

> *For Example:*
>
> *In order to support a negligence claim against Mrs. Jacoby, four elements must be proven.* First, we must establish that she had a duty to keep the tree on her property trimmed. Next, we must show that she failed to trim the tree properly. Then it is necessary to prove that as a result of her failure to trim the tree, a branch fell and struck Mr. Paglio. Finally, we must establish that Mr. Paglio's injuries resulted from the branch striking him. (The topic sentence is italicized to separate it from the body.)

Notice in that example that the sentences in the body are presented clearly and logically. Remember, when writing the body of a paragraph, your goal is to draft it clearly, concisely, and logically.

1.2 C   CLOSING SENTENCE

A paragraph should end with a closing sentence. The content of the sentence varies according to the subject matter covered in the paragraph. The closing sentence should summarize the topic addressed in the body or apply the subject discussed to the facts of the case.

> **For Example:**
>
> **Summary:**
> Therefore, to establish a claim for negligence, we must show that Mrs. Jacoby had a duty, the duty was breached, the breach caused the accident, and the accident caused the harm that resulted.
>
> **Application of subject to the facts of the case:**
> The rule of law adopted in the *Craig* case clearly applies in this case because Mr. Stein failed to warn Mr. Zacour that the brakes were defective.

1.2 D   TRANSITION WORDS, PHRASES, AND SENTENCES

Use transitional words and phrases to clarify relationships among the sentences in a paragraph.

> **For Example:**
>
> The corporation president took several steps. His first act was to contact the shareholders by mail. *Next,* he met with the officers that evening. *After meeting with the officers,* he again contacted the shareholders. *Also,* he drafted a letter to the prime contractor. He delivered the letter the following day. *Later the same week* he met with the employees and the main creditors. (The transitional words and phrases are italicized.)

Common transitional words include *also, furthermore, afterward, finally, next, besides, since, similarly, but, however, instead, although, specifically, thus, namely, nevertheless,* and *therefore.*

Transitional words, phrases, or sentences are required to connect the topics discussed in different paragraphs. They serve as a guide for the reader by linking the paragraphs, thereby providing coherence to the overall writing. The topic or closing sentence of a paragraph also may include transitional language. Transitional words, phrases, and sentences are usually placed at the beginning or the end of the paragraph.

> ⬚ *For Example:*
>
> **Transitions at the beginning of a paragraph** (the transitional language is italicized):
> - ▶ If the *above-mentioned* requirements are not met, breach of contract may not be claimed.
> - ▶ There are, *however,* exceptions to this rule.
> - ▶ *In addition to* a cause of action for negligence, Mr. Yee may allege . . . (where the body of the paragraph addresses the other possible causes of action, and the previous paragraph discusses the negligence cause of action)
> - ▶ The *second* element of the statute requires . . . (where separate paragraphs are used to discuss separate elements)
>
> **Transitions at the end of the paragraph** (the transitional language is italicized):
> - ▶ The statute, *however,* does not define "publication"; therefore, case law must be consulted. (where the next paragraph introduces the case law)
> - ▶ *In addition to* this case, there are other cases that discuss the requirements of the statute. (where the following paragraph discusses the other cases)

1.2 E   PARAGRAPH LENGTH

As with sentences, there is no rule that establishes a standard length for paragraphs. Paragraphs are usually three to seven sentences long. Most paragraph topics can be covered in six to seven sentences, although a paragraph may be as short as one sentence or as long as ten sentences. Determine a paragraph's length by keeping in mind the goal of covering the topic of the paragraph clearly and completely. The reader may have difficulty understanding or become confused by extremely long paragraphs. A series of very short paragraphs may lack transition and distract the reader. Therefore, extremely long and short paragraphs are not recommended. The following are examples of short paragraphs.

> ⬚ *For Example:*
>
> The second element of the rule requires that the witness be present at the signing.
>
> Section 2(b) of the statute addresses the requirement of the number and presence of witnesses. It requires that there be a minimum of two witnesses and that both be present at the signing.

Notice that the examples lack transition language or sentences that connect them to the paragraphs that follow.

Exhibit 1-1

Checklist for Sentences and Paragraphs

- ❏ Is each sentence complete? Does each sentence have a subject and verb?
- ❏ Are sentences too long—over 25 words?
- ❏ Is there variety in the sentences—different length and organization?
- ❏ Do sentences have excessive words, phrases, or clauses?
- ❏ Are there run-on sentences or sentence fragments?
- ❏ Are there improper mood shifts?
- ❏ Is there excessive use of passive voice? (Most sentences should be written in active voice.)
- ❏ Does each paragraph have a topic sentence, body, and closing sentence?
- ❏ Are paragraphs too long?
- ❏ Are there transitional sentences connecting the paragraphs?

Chapter 2

Word Selection and Usage, Spelling, Capitalization, Italics, Abbreviations, and Numbers

Contents
2.1 Word Selection and Usage	**2.5** Abbreviations
2.2 Spelling	**2.6** Italics and Underlining
2.3 Numbers	**2.7** Formal Writing Conventions
2.4 Capitalization	

Not only do you need to be skilled in sentence and paragraph construction, you also must be skilled in selecting and using words and in applying the various rules governing the mechanics of writing, such as spelling and capitalization. A proofreading checklist for the topics presented in this chapter is included in Exhibit 7-5.

2.1 WORD SELECTION AND USAGE

This section discusses guidelines on word selection and usage.

2.1 A   NOUN/VERB STRINGS

A noun/verb string is a group of related words used to convey information. It is a form of redundancy that should be avoided when a single descriptive word can accomplish the same end.

> **◻ *For Example:***
>
> The distributor is not responsible for failure to perform due to *riots, floods, earthquakes, and acts of God.*
> A stockholder may not *grant, give, sell, or assign* her interest in the stock without the consent of the other shareholders.
>
> **Revisions:**
> The distributor is not responsible for failure to perform caused by events beyond the distributor's control.
> A stockholder may not transfer her interest in the stock without the consent of the other shareholders.

2.1 B NOMINALIZATIONS

A nominalization is a noun created from a verb.

> **◻ *For Example:***
>
> | **Verb** | **Noun** |
> |---|---|
> | determine | determination |
> | realize | realization |
> | possess | possession |
> | important | importance |

Nominalizations weaken a sentence by taking the action away from the actor. They make the sentence passive and less forceful.

> **◻ *For Example:***
>
> He *came to the realization* that the assignment required more work.
> The *importance of* the opinion is that . . .
> He decided to *make an investment* in the new company.
>
> **Revisions:**
> He *realized* that the assignment required more work.
> The opinion *is important* because . . .
> He decided to *invest* in the new company.

2.1 C LEGALESE

Legalese used here refers to terms of art used in the legal profession that are not generally known outside the profession. The goal of legal writing is to communicate information effectively. *Writing in plain English usually accomplishes that goal, and plain English should be used whenever possible.*

The extent to which you incorporate legal terminology in legal writing is governed by the audience. Legal terms are appropriate when you are communicating with others in the field. When the reader is trained in the law, using legal terms or phrases, such as *res ipsa loquitur,* is much easier than providing a definition or an explanation. When the recipient is a nonlawyer, however, you should avoid the use of legal terms. You *must* define legal terms when communicating with nonlawyers when the meaning of the term is not obvious.

> ■ *For Example:*
>
> The constitution requires *probable cause* before the police can conduct a search of your residence. (Legalese is italicized.)
>
> **Revision:**
> The constitution requires the police to have a valid reason before they can search a house. An example of a valid reason is if a reliable person informed the police that they saw illegal drugs in the house.

2.1 D   ARCHAIC WORDS/EXCESS VERBIAGE

Avoid excess verbiage and archaic terms in legal writing. Archaic terms are words or phrases frequently used in the past that are being phased out of legal writing. Some of these terms are *saith, party of the first part, aforesaid, hereinbefore, hereinafter, henceforth,* and *the said party.*

> ■ *For Example:*
>
> Upon the signing of the Agreement, the *party of the first part* will *hereinafter cease and desist* from attending hearings where the *party of the second part* acts as chairperson.
>
> **Revision:**
> Upon the signing of the Agreement, Mr. Schroman will *not* attend hearings where Ms. Carson acts as chairperson. (Assume the names, Mr. Schroman and Ms. Carson are mentioned earlier in the Agreement. Rather than use the phrase *party of the first part* and *party of the second part,* simply repeat the names of the parties or use a pronoun such as *he* or *she* when it is clear which party is being referred to.)

2.1 E   SEXIST LANGUAGE

In any form of writing, using gender-specific language is prejudicial and not appropriate unless it refers to a specific person and the gender is known. Sexist language has no place in legal writing. The following guidelines will help ensure that you use gender-neutral writing.

1. Words   Change gender-specific terms to gender-neutral terms.

> **For Example:**
>
> | Gender-Specific | Gender-Neutral |
> | --- | --- |
> | chairman | chairperson |
> | wife/husband | spouse |
> | draftsman | drafter |
> | forefathers | forbearers |
> | housewife | homemaker |
> | mankind | people, human beings |
> | workman | worker |
> | anchorman | anchor |
> | congressman | congressperson/representative |

2. **Restructuring Sentences with *He* or *She*** You may use *he* or *she* in place of *he* to render a sentence gender-neutral. The result, however, may be awkward.

> **For Example:**
>
> The rule requires the plaintiff to file his or her response within fifteen days.

There are several alternatives that you may adopt to avoid the use of *his* or *her.*
   a. *Restate the sentence so the antecedent is plural—*

> **For Example:**
>
> The rule requires the plaintiff to file his pleadings . . .
> A paralegal is responsible for the accuracy of his research.
>
> **Revisions:**
> The rule requires plaintiffs to file their pleadings . . .
> Paralegals are responsible for the accuracy of their research.

   b. *Eliminate the use of the pronoun—*

> **For Example:**
>
> The officer is responsible for the actions of his troops.
> A client should aggressively pursue his options.
>
> **Revision:**
> The officer is responsible for the actions of the troops.
> A client should aggressively pursue all options.

   c. *Repeat the noun—*

> **For Example:**
>
> Before the client can liquidate the assets of the company, he must . . .
>
> **Revision:**
> Before the client can liquidate the assets of the company, the client must . . .

d. *Use* **one, you,** *or* **your** *whenever possible—*

> ◼ *For Example:*
>
> Every person has a right to his personal preferences.
>
> **Revisions:**
> Everyone has a right to personal preferences.
> You have a right to your personal preferences.

e. *Rephrase the sentence—*

> ◼ *For Example:*
>
> A legal assistant should not communicate with the litigants he knows we
> do not represent.
>
> **Revision:**
> A legal assistant should not communicate with litigants we do not represent.

3. Appropriate Reference to Gender   Reference to gender is appropriate only when you refer to one sex.

> ◼ *For Example:*
>
> Each member of the women's basketball team had her name printed on the
> back of her uniform.

2.1 F   SPECIFIC WORDS—PROBLEM AREAS

Some words are commonly misused. You can avoid problems of misuse by following these basic rules.

1. Affect/Effect   *Affect* is a verb meaning "to influence." *Effect* can be either a verb or a noun. As a verb, *effect* means "to bring about or cause"; as a noun, it means "result."

> ◼ *For Example:*
>
> His actions will not *affect* (not *effect*) the outcome of the case. The meaning of *affect* is "to influence."
> He tried to *effect* (not *affect*) an agreement. Here the meaning of *effect* is "to bring about."
> The test did not bring about the desired *effect* (not *affect*). The meaning of *effect* is "result."

2. Among/Between   Use *among* when referring to three or more things; use *between* when referring to two.

> ■ *For Example:*
>
> The jury award was divided *among* the six plaintiffs.
> The jury award was divided *between* Julia and Grace.

3. *And/Or* When the word *and* is used in a list of words, all of the items listed are included and required.

> ■ *For Example:*
>
> The case law requires the plaintiff to prove duty, breach of duty, proximate cause, *and* damages. (The use of *and* means that all four elements must be proved. All of the listed items are included in the requirement.)

When *or* is used, all of the items listed are not required to be included. Any one or all of the items are included.

> ■ *For Example:*
>
> The case law requires the corporate president to provide notice orally, by mail, or by facsimile. (All of the listed items are not required. Only one of the items is required. The president has the choice of giving notice by one or all of the means listed.)

The use of *and/or* creates an ambiguity and should be avoided.

> ■ *For Example:*
>
> The statute requires that the notice be given orally, by mail, *and/or* by facsimile. (What does the statute require? Are all of the listed items required? If so, *and* should be used. If only one of the items is required, *or* should be used.)

4. *Bad/Badly* See Chapter 3 Section 3.4 A "Forming Adverbs and Improper Use of Adjectives."

5. Comparisons *than* and *as* See Chapter 3 Section 3.2 E "Pronoun Case."

6. *Council/Counsel* A council is a deliberative or administrative body. A councilor is a member of the body. When used as a verb, *counsel* means "to give advice or guidance." When used as a noun, *counsel* is advice. A counselor (counsel) is a person, such as a lawyer, who gives advice or guidance.

> ■ *For Example:*
>
> She presented the resolution to the city *council*. The city *councilor* received the petition. The school guidance officer provided *counsel* to the new student. The *counselor* informed the shareholders of their legal rights.

7. ***Each Other/One Another***   When referring to two nouns, use *each other.* When referring to more than two nouns, use *one another.*

> **For Example:**
>
> Bob and Misha supported *each other* during the trial.
> The members of the team supported *one another* during the tournament.

8. ***Good/Well***   *Good* is an adjective (adjectives modify nouns and pronouns). *Good* cannot be used as an adverb (adverbs modify verbs, adjectives, and adverbs). *Well* can act as an adverb or an adjective.

> **For Example:**
>
> She worked good.
>
> **Revisions:**
> She worked well. (*Well* is an adverb that modifies the verb *worked.* The use of *good* is inappropriate because *good* is an adjective and should not be used to modify a verb.)
> She did good work. (*Good* is used as an adjective that modifies the noun *work.*)

9. ***Lie/Lay***   *Lie* is an intransitive verb that means "to rest or recline." (An intransitive verb is a verb that does not take a direct object.) Its forms are *lie, lay, lain,* and *lying.*

> **For Example:**
>
> I think I will *lie* (not *lay*) down.
> He was so tired he *lay* (not *laid*) down.
> She has been *lying* (not *laying*) around all day.

Lay is a transitive verb that means "to put or place." (A transitive verb takes a direct object.) Its forms are *lay, laid, laid,* and *laying.*

> **For Example:**
>
> I think I will *lay* (not *lie)* the paper down.
> He *laid* (not *lay*) the paper down.
> He has been *laying* (not *lying*) brick all day.

10. ***Like/As***   *Like* should be used as a preposition; it should be followed by a noun or noun phrase. *As* acts as a conjunction or a preposition in a sentence.

> **For Example:**
>
> In this contract, he used the same technique *as* (not *like)* he did in the other agreement. (The use of *like* would not be appropriate because *as* functions as a conjunction, not a preposition.)

> The legal assistant, *like* all of the other participants, was on time. (The use of *like* is appropriate because it functions as a preposition.)

11. ***Principal/Principle***   When used as a noun, *principal* means "the head of an organization or a school" or "a sum of money"; as an adjective, *principal* means "most important." *Principle* is a noun meaning "a rule of conduct or basic truth."

> ▣ *For Example:*
>
> The *principal* of the loan was subject to adjustment.
> The *principal* reason they adopted the agreement was the deadline clause.
> The parties believed in the *principle* of good faith.

12. ***Shall/May***   The word *shall* is used to impose a duty that is mandatory. The performance of the duty is not optional.

> ▣ *For Example:*
>
> Mr. Ito *shall* terminate all contact with Mrs. Black. (The duty to terminate all communication is mandatory. Mr. Ito has no option.)

The word *may* indicates that the performance of an act is not mandatory. The performance of the act is optional.

> ▣ *For Example:*
>
> Mr. Ito *may* terminate all communication with Mrs. Black. (The act of terminating all communication is optional with Mr. Ito. He can choose whether to terminate the communication.)

13. ***Which, Who, and That***   See Chapter 3 Section 3.1 K "Relative Pronouns—Which, Who, and That—Agreement with Antecedent."
14. ***We or Us before a Noun***   See Chapter 3 Section 3.2 E "Pronoun Case."
15. ***Who/Whom***   See Chapter 3 Section 3.2 E "Pronoun Case."

✦ 2.2   SPELLING

Obviously, all of the words you use must be spelled correctly. If you are in doubt about the spelling of a word, use a dictionary. Legal writing requires that you use both a regular dictionary and a legal dictionary.

If you use the spelling checker on your computer, you still must check for word usage errors. The computer may catch a spelling error, but generally it will not catch the use of the wrong word or typographical errors that result in the use of a wrong word.

> **For Example:**
>
> **Use of a wrong word:**
> You may have used the word *to* when you intended to use *too*. The
> spelling checker on a computer will not catch the use of the wrong
> word.
>
> **Typographical error that results in the use of a wrong word:**
> You may have typed *cast* when you meant to type *case*. *Cast* is a word,
> and the spelling checker would not find this as an error.

2.2 A   BASIC SPELLING RULES

The following is a list of basic spelling rules. If you learn these rules, you will reduce the amount of time you spend looking up words in a dictionary.

1. **ie and ei**   The standard rule is to use *i* before *e* except after *c* or when pro-
nounced as *ay* as in *neighbor* and *weigh*.

> **For Example:**
>
> *i before e:*
> chief, relieve, relief, niece, frieze, believe
>
> *e before i:*
> neighbor, receive, sleigh, eight, deceit
>
> **Exceptions:**
> seize, weird, foreign, counterfeit, either, height, heir, sovereign, weird, neither

2. **Silent e before a Suffix**   When a word ends in a silent *e*, drop the *e* when
adding a suffix that starts with a vowel.

> **For Example:**
>
> desire/desiring   judge/judging   remove/removable
>
> **Exceptions:**
> change/changeable   notice/noticeable

When a word ends in a silent *e*, keep the *e* when adding a suffix that starts with
a consonant.

> **For Example:**
>
> achieve/achievement   hope/hopeful   refine/refinement
>
> **Exceptions:**
> judge/judgment   abridge/abridgment

3. **Doubling Final Consonants**   Double the final consonant of a word before adding a suffix that begins with a vowel (*-ed, -ing*) if (1) the final consonant is preceded by a vowel, and (2) the word is one syllable or the final syllable is accented.

> ⬓ *For Example:*
>
> refer/referred   bet/betting

NOTE: defer/deferment—The final consonant *r* is not doubled because the suffix, *-ment,* does not begin with a vowel.

4. **Suffixes and Words Ending in y**   When a word ends in a *y* preceded by a consonant, the general rule is to change the *y* to an *i* when adding a suffix.

> ⬓ *For Example:*
>
> bury/buried   comedy/comedies
>
> **Exception:**
> dry/dryness

When a word ends in a *y* preceded by a vowel, the *y* is kept.

> ⬓ *For Example:*
>
> joy/joyful   play/played
>
> **Exception:**
> day/daily

The *y* is kept when the suffix is *-ing.*

> ⬓ *For Example:*
>
> bury/burying

5. **Suffixes and *ic* Endings**   When a word ends in *ic,* add *k* before adding a suffix that begins with a vowel.

> ⬓ *For Example:*
>
> traffic/trafficker   mimic/mimicked

6. **Suffixes and *-able* and *-ible***   When the root word is a word by itself, the suffix is usually *-able.*

> ⬓ *For Example:*
>
> manage/manageable   remark/remarkable

When the root word is not a word by itself, the suffix is usually *-ible.*

> **For Example:**
>
> compatible
>
> **Exception:**
> delectable

2.2 B   PLURALS

A challenging area of spelling involves the formation of plurals. There are numerous rules and exceptions. The main rules are presented here.

1. **Basic Rule**   To form the plural of most words, add an *s*.

> **For Example:**
>
> paper/papers   brief/briefs   complaint/complaints   defense/defenses

2. **Words Ending in *s, z, x, sh,* and *ch***   Add *es* to words ending in *s, z, x, sh,* and *ch.*

> **For Example:**
>
> church/churches   box/boxes   rash/rashes

3. **Words Ending in *y***   When the word ends in *y* preceded by a consonant, change the *y* to an *i* and add *es.*

> **For Example:**
>
> baby/babies   jury/juries
>
> **Exception:**
> For proper nouns such as *Kennedy,* just add *s:*   Kennedy/Kennedys.

4. **Words Ending in *o***   The general rule is to add *es* to words ending in *o* preceded by a consonant and *s* to words ending in *o* preceded by a vowel.

> **For Example:**
>
> *o* **preceded by consonant:**
> tomato/tomatoes   hero/heroes
>
> *o* **preceded by vowel:**
> radio/radios   stereo/stereos

Because of the many exceptions to this rule, you should check a dictionary when you have any doubts about forming the correct plural.

> **For Example:**
>
> piano/pianos   memo/memos   solo/solos

5. **Words Ending in *f* and *fe***   Form the plural of some words ending in *f* and *fe* by changing the *f* to a *v* and adding *es* or *s*.

> **For Example:**
>
> self/selves   knife/knives

For other words, add *s*.

> **For Example:**
>
> belief/beliefs   chief/chiefs

6. **Irregular Words**   Irregular words require a different spelling.

> **For Example:**
>
> foot/feet   woman/women   child/children

7. **Foreign Words**   Many words adopted from foreign languages form the plural according to the rules of the foreign language. It is best to check a dictionary when forming the plurals of such words.

> **For Example:**
>
> stimulus/stimuli   memorandum/memorandums   medium/mediums
> radius/radii   alumna/alumnae   criterion/criteria   stigma/stigmata
> bacterium/bacteria

8. **Hyphenated Compound Words**   The general rule is to add *s* to the chief word.

> **For Example:**
>
> brother-in-law/brothers-in-law

Refer to Chapter 4 for general rules governing the use of hyphens.

9. **Compound Nouns**   Pluralize the last word when both words are of approximately equal importance.

> **For Example:**
>
> federal prison/federal prisons

Pluralize the noun when the compound is composed of a noun followed by a modifier.

> **For Example:**
>
> secretary of state/secretaries of state

10. **Words Used as Words** When a word is used as a word, form the plural by italicizing the word and appending an unitalicized *s* or *es*.

> ☐ *For Example:*
>
> There are seven *nine*s in the fourth section of the agreement.

11. **Letters** The plurals of letters are formed with an apostrophe.

> ☐ *For Example:*
>
> How many *e*'s are in the sentence?

12. **Numbers** See Section 2.3 of this chapter.

2.2 C POSSESSIVES

This section discusses many of the rules governing the forming and spelling of possessives. Forming the possessive of numbers is presented in Section 2.3.

1. **Single Nouns** Make singular nouns possessive by adding an apostrophe *s*.

> ☐ *For Example:*
>
> the officer's car
> Mr. Artess's house
> anyone's game

Singular nouns ending in *s* take an apostrophe *s* just like any other singular noun. Note the possessive of *Mr. Artess* in the preceding example.

EXCEPTION: With some words, adding an *s* sounds awkward. It is acceptable to use only an apostrophe in such cases.

> ☐ *For Example:*
>
> Sophocles' dramas

2. **Single Names That Include a Plural Term** Singular names that include a plural term take an apostrophe after the *s*.

> ☐ *For Example:*
>
> the Court of Appeals' opinion
> Delta Airlines' employees

3. **Plural Nouns** Make plural nouns that end in *s* or *es* possessive by adding an apostrophe after the *s*.

> 🔲 *For Example:*
> the players' uniforms
> the workers' organization
> the girls' uniforms
> the Johnsons' cars (where the last name is Johnsons and there is more than
>   one Johnsons family referred to in the sentence)

4. **Plural Nouns That Do Not End in *s* or *z***   Make plural nouns that do not end in *s* or *z* possessive by adding an apostrophe *s*.

> 🔲 *For Example:*
> the children's field

5. **Compound Word or Word Group**   Form the possessive of a compound word or group of words by adding an apostrophe *s* or an apostrophe to the last word.

> 🔲 *For Example:*
> attorney general's office
> someone else's problem
> the mother-in-laws' grandchildren
> the school board's decision

6. **Compound Word or Word Group—Joint Possession**   Use an apostrophe *s* after the last word of a compound word or word group to indicate joint possession.

> 🔲 *For Example:*
> Fred and Hal's car (where Fred and Hal own the same car)

7. **Compound Word or Word Group—Separate Possession**   Use an apostrophe *s* after each word of a compound word or word group to indicate separate possession.

> 🔲 *For Example:*
> Fred's and Hal's cars (where Fred and Hal own separate cars)

8. **Personal Pronouns**   The possessives of personal pronouns do not require an apostrophe.

> 🔲 *For Example:*
> *yours, his, hers, ours, theirs, its* (possessive of *it*), and *whose* (possessive
>   of *who*)

It is easy to confuse contractions and the possessive forms of personal pronouns.

> ☐ *For Example:*
>
> Whose turn is it? (possessive)/Who's going with me? (contraction—Who is going with me?)
> Their tennis rackets need repair. (possessive)/They're going together. (contraction—They are going together.)
> Each engine has its own starter. (possessive)/I'm not responsible if it's not finished. (contraction—I'm not responsible if it is not finished.)

9. **Indefinite Pronouns** Pronouns that do not refer to a definite person or thing are indefinite pronouns (e.g., *anybody, each, either, everyone,* and *someone.*) To form the plural of an indefinite pronoun, add apostrophe *s.*

> ☐ *For Example:*
>
> I found someone's wallet.
> A smile helps everybody's attitude.

2.3   NUMBERS

There are several rules regarding the presentation of numbers. Some of these rules are listed here.

2.3 A   SPELLED-OUT NUMBERS

According to *The Bluebook,* the numbers zero to ninety-nine should be spelled out.

> ☐ *For Example:*
>
> one   twenty-seven   ninety-nine
> The contract has twenty-seven clauses.

Use numerals for numbers that are more than two words long.

> ☐ *For Example:*
>
> 379   1,300   145,378
> The contract has 379 clauses.

EXCEPTION: In a list of numbers, if one of the items should be written with numerals, use numerals for all of the items listed.

> ❑ *For Example:*
>
> The numbers in the code are 16, 44, 397, and 1,001. (*Sixteen* and *forty-four* are not spelled out.)

As a general rule, do not spell out the following numbers: dates, statute numbers, section numbers, volume numbers, exact times and sums of money, addresses, percentages, scores, identification numbers, ratios, statistics decimals and fractions, and measurements with symbols or abbreviations.

> ❑ *For Example:*
>
> **Date:** May 6, 2005
> **Statute:** Title 18 of the code
> **Section:** Section 3212, § 3212
> **Percentage:** 75 percent
> **Score:** The final score was 2 to 1.
> **Exact sum of money:** $34.21
> **Decimal:** 9.38
> **Fraction:** $9\frac{1}{4}$
> **Measurement with symbol:** 9°
> **Exact time:** 5:47 a.m.

NOTE: Times are spelled out when the number is accompanied by *o'clock*.

> ❑ *For Example:*
>
> 11 o'clock
>
> **Revision:**
> eleven o'clock

2.3 B   NUMBERS AT THE BEGINNING OF SENTENCES

Spell out numbers that begin a sentence.

> ❑ *For Example:*
>
> 506 paralegals were present.
>
> **Revision:**
> Five hundred six paralegals were present.

2.3 C   HYPHENATED NUMBERS

Hyphens are used for fractions and numbers from twenty-one to ninety-nine.

> 🔲 *For Example:*
>
> Fifty-six of the stockholders were present.

The thirty-seven shareholders represented three-fourths of the outstanding shares. Do not use *and* when writing whole numbers.

> 🔲 *For Example:*
>
> Two hundred *and* seventy-five dollars was needed to pay the debt.
>
> **Revision:**
> Two hundred seventy-five dollars was needed to pay the debt.

Hyphenate fractions that are spelled out.

> 🔲 *For Example:*
>
> One-fifth of the student body attended the meeting.

2.3 D   PLURAL AND POSSESSIVE NUMBERS

To make a number plural, add *s*.

> 🔲 *For Example:*
>
> 1990s

There were three 190s in the paragraph.
Possessive numbers are not frequently encountered. If you have to form the possessive of a number, add apostrophe *s*.

> 🔲 *For Example:*
>
> The instructor illustrated his point by referring to the 1920's Black Friday.

2.3 E   NUMBERS THAT APPEAR TOGETHER

When two numbers appear together that are not related, the general rule is to spell out the first number.

> 🔲 *For Example:*
>
> There were 190 $50 bills.
>
> **Revision:**
> There were one hundred ninety $50 bills.

2.4   CAPITALIZATION

A summary of the general rules of capitalization is presented in this section. Chapter 5 discusses capitalization and legal citation.

2.4 A   SENTENCES AND QUOTED SENTENCES

Capitalize the first word of a sentence.

> ◻ *For Example:*
>
> *The* jury deliberated for six hours.

Capitalize the first word of a direct question when it is part of a sentence. A direct question stands alone as a sentence.

> ◻ *For Example:*
>
> These events cause one to ponder, *How* can we reach a consensus?

BUT COMPARE: An indirect question is a declaratory statement, and the first word is not capitalized.

> ◻ *For Example:*
>
> The client asked how she should proceed.
> The paralegal wondered how she could prepare the brief on time.

Capitalize the first word of a quotation when it is a complete sentence.

> ◻ *For Example:*
>
> The judge told the defendant, "Do not interrupt the witness."

When the quotation is interrupted, do not capitalize the first word after the interruption.

> ◻ *For Example:*
>
> "Do not submit points and authorities," the judge instructed, "until after the second hearing."

Do not capitalize a quotation that is not a complete sentence or that follows the conjunction *that*.

> ■ *For Example:*
>
> The client claimed "the next door neighbor" removed the boundary marker.
> The manager claimed that "someone else was responsible."

2.4 B   PROPER NOUNS

Capitalize proper nouns. Proper nouns are the names of *specific* persons, places, or things.

> ■ *For Example:*
>
> **Name:** Henry Ford
> **Days/Holidays:** Saturday/Hanukkah/Good Friday **Note:** Do not capitalize
>   seasons such as spring (e.g., the spring term).
> **Events/Documents:** the Battle of the Bulge/the Declaration of Independence
> **Nationalities:** African   American   Japanese
> **Organizations and Businesses:** the American Civil Liberties Union
>   General Electric
> **Institutions and Government Agencies:** the House of Representatives
>   the Social Security Administration the University of California
> **Trademarks/Trade Names:** Coca-Cola®   Post-it®   Coke®   7-Up®
> **Artwork:** the *Mona Lisa*   *The Last Supper*
> **Proper noun phrases:** The Appropriations and Rules committees held a
>   joint session. (*Committees* is a common noun; it is not capitalized when
>   shared by the two proper nouns.) **Compare:** The Appropriations Com-
>   mittee and Rules Committee held a joint session. (*Committee* is capital-
>   ized because it is part of the committee name.)

2.4 C   TITLES

The following is a summary of the rules governing the capitalization of titles.

1. Proper Names   The general rule is that if a title precedes a name, the title is capitalized. When the title follows a name, it is capitalized if it identifies a diplo-matic title, a ruler, a head or an assistant head of government, or a major unit of government.

> ■ *For Example:*
>
> **Title Preceding Name:**
> General Sherman   Judge O'Reilley
> The director of the company is Chairperson Donald Taylor.

> **Title Following Name:**
> George W. Bush, President of the United States
> Maeve Ellis, Ambassador at Large
> Sheldon Tyler, Speaker of the House of Representatives
> Donald Taylor, chairperson
> Donna Sloane, president of Sloane Inc.

Capitalize the title of a person when the title is used as part of a name. A title used by itself is not usually capitalized.

> ☐ *For Example:*
>
> Donald Taylor, Ph.D.   Dr. Donna Sloane
> Judge Mills   The judge was not present. (The title *judge* is not capitalized because it is not used in conjunction with the name.)

2. **Job Titles**   Job titles that are nonprofessional are descriptive; they are not capitalized.

> ☐ *For Example:*
>
> engineering specialist, Carolyn Garcia
> coach of the basketball team, Patrice Monheim   Michael Longo, headwaiter

3. **Titles—Plaintiffs, Defendants, and Court**   When the terms *plaintiff* and *defendant* are preceded by *the*, as a general rule, they are not capitalized. When the terms are used in place of a party's name and are not preceded by *the*, they are capitalized.

> ☐ *For Example:*
>
> After the plaintiff left the boardroom, the defendant called the meeting to order.
> After Plaintiff left the boardroom, Defendant called the meeting to order.

Do not capitalize terms such as *plaintiff, defendant,* and *court* when referring to a court opinion. Note, however, that *court* is capitalized when it is the highest court of the jurisdiction.

> ☐ *For Example:*
>
> The case was removed to the federal court.
> The case was removed to the Supreme Court.
> The court ruled that the defendant was liable.
> The *Court* ruled that the defendant was liable. (where the court is the highest court in the jurisdiction, such as the United States Supreme Court)

4. **Titles of Works**   The major words in the titles and subtitles of works should be capitalized. Minor words, such as articles and prepositions, are not capitalized. Works here include books, magazines, newspapers, articles in legal writing, songs, movies, plays, and paintings.

> ▣ *For Example:*
>
> *The Law of Business Organizations*
> *The Path of the Law*
> *Porgy and Bess*

2.4 D   WORDS FOLLOWING A COLON

The general rule is that the first word following a colon is not capitalized unless it is a proper noun or begins a complete sentence. When the first word begins a complete sentence, capitalization is optional.

> ▣ *For Example:*
>
> The document does not include two rights: referendum and recall.
> The client made a major mistake: he failed to file the annual report.
> The statute requires the following: The will must be witnessed by two witnesses and signed by the testator.

2.4 E   FULL AND SHORT NAMES

When a full name introduced in a writing is followed by a shortened name eleswhere in the text, the shortened name is capitalized.

> ▣ *For Example:*
>
> The Social Security Administration passed new rules with regard to retirement benefits. The *Administration* adopted seven rules that affect our clients.

2.4 F   GEOGRAPHICAL TERMS

Capitalize a term that refers to a specific geographic region or area.

> ▣ *For Example:*
>
> the Sea of Japan   New England

Do not capitalize a geographic term that describes a direction or position unless it is part of a proper name.

> *For Example:*
>
> the *northern* part of the state
> the *South* Pass

Do not capitalize a term that is not considered part of a proper name.

> *For Example:*
>
> the North American *continent*
> the Rocky Mountains (*Mountains* is capitalized because it is part of the name.)

Do not capitalize a political-division term (*state, city,* and *county*) unless it is part of the proper name.

> *For Example:*
>
> southeastern *states*
> the Chester *county* line
> the *State* of New Jersey

2.5   ABBREVIATIONS

Abbreviations should be avoided in formal writing unless they are clearly appropriate, such as when they are part of a title (e.g., Abigail Cartright, M.D.) This section presents a summary of the general rules of abbreviation. See Chapter 5 for the use of abbreviations in legal citations.

2.5 A   TITLES

Abbreviate titles before and after proper names.

> *For Example:*
>
> Andrea Komuro, Ph.D   Kevin Stewart, D.D.S.
> Sen. Jessie Collins   Ms. Megan Edwards   Dr. Isaac Stone   Rep. Stella
>   Matlock

Do not use an abbreviation without the name.

> *For Example:*
>
> The speaker informed the *Dr.* that she had two minutes left.
>
> **Revision:**
> The speaker informed the *doctor* that she had two minutes left.

2.5 B   ORGANIZATIONS, CORPORATIONS, COUNTRIES, AND TECHNICAL TERMS

It is acceptable to use abbreviations for well-known organizations, corporations, countries, and technical terms such as CIA, FBI, NATO, IBM, and UPS.

> *For Example:*
>
> He applied for a position with the FBI.

If the abbreviation is not well known, the first time the name is mentioned, spell it out followed by the abbreviation in parentheses.

> *For Example:*
>
> The National Association of Fiction Writers (NAFW) has members in all fifty states.

2.5 C   TIMES, DATE, AND TEMPERATURES

Capitalize BC ("before Christ") and AD ("anno Domini"). Place BC after the date and AD before the date.

> *For Example:*
>
> 239 BC   AD 45

The abbreviations for time—a.m. and p.m.—are typed in lowercase letters. The abbreviations for temperature—F (Fahrenheit) and C (Celsius)—are capitalized.

> *For Example:*
>
> 6:30 a.m.   9:00 p.m.   190°F   20°C

Use the abbreviations only when they are accompanied by a number.

> *For Example:*
>
> We started in the a.m.
>
> **Revision:**
> We started in the morning.

2.5 D   LATIN ABBREVIATIONS

Latin abbreviations are not considered appropriate in formal writing. The abbreviations should be spelled out. Latin abbreviations are used in legal writing and citation. Refer to *The Bluebook: A Uniform System of Citation* or *ALWD Citation Manual:*

A Professional System of Citation for appropriate use of these abbreviations in legal writing. Also see Chapter 5.

> ☐ *For Example:*
>
> **Formal writing—incorrect:**
> Many of the trial attorneys (e.g., Jack Anderson and Nan Colson) have joined the state trial lawyers association.
>
> **Formal writing—correct:**
> Many of the trial attorneys (for example, Jack Anderson and Nan Colson) have joined the state trial lawyers association.
>
> **Legal Citation:**
> Many additional authorities support this position, *see, e.g., Chandler v. State,* 198 S.E.2d 198, 290 (Ga. 1973).

Some common Latin abbreviations follow.

cf.	*confer*—compare
e.g.	*exempli gratia*—for example
et al.	*et alii*—and others; and elsewhere
i.e.	*id est*—that is
etc.	*et cetera*—and so forth; and so on

2.6   ITALICS AND UNDERLINING

Italics, boldface, and underlining are used in two situations: to emphasize a word or words in the text or to follow prescribed rules. Basic rules concerning the use of italics are discussed here. In some situations in legal citation and writing, rules for the use of italics, boldface, and underling differ from standard rules. Be sure to check *The Bluebook: A Uniform System of Citation* or *ALWD Citation Manual: A Professional System of Citation.* Also see Chapter 5.

2.6 A   TO SHOW EMPHASIS

Use italics to emphasize a word or words in a sentence. The use of italics is preferred over underlining.

> ☐ *For Example:*
>
> You *must* sign the document by noon.
> The client is responsible for both the *time and place* of the meeting.

2.6 B   TITLES AND NAMES

Use italics for the titles of the following: books, magazines, journals, newspapers, Web sites, plays, long poems and musical works, paintings and sculpture, ships, aircraft, spacecraft, trains, radio and television programs, films, comic strips, and software.

> **For Example:**
>
> **Book:** *West's Business Law*
> **Film:** *Titanic*
> **Airplane:** *Sopwith Camel*
> **Play:** *Camelot*
> **Painting:** *The Last Supper*
> **Software:** *Microsoft® Windows XP Home Edition*
> **Television Program:** *60 Minutes*
> **Magazine:** *Newsweek*
> **Pamphlet:** *Common Sense*

Place in quotation marks titles of works such as short stories, short poems and songs, and newspaper and magazine articles. Italicize the names of articles in legal writing. This rule differs from the rule used in standard writing.

2.6 C   WORDS USED AS TERMS

Italicize a letter, word, or phrase used as a term. It is also appropriate to use quotation marks.

> **For Example:**
>
> The letter is either an *s* or a *v.*
> The court adopted several definitions for the term *publication.*

2.6 D   FOREIGN WORDS AND PHRASES

Italicize foreign words and phrases that have not become part of the English language. Check a law dictionary when you are not sure if the word or phrase should be italicized.

> **For Example:**
>
> *modus operandi*   *ipse dixit*

2.7   FORMAL WRITING CONVENTIONS

Most legal writing is considered formal, and formal writing conventions apply, especially to legal briefs and memorandums. Two of these conventions pertain to the use of contractions and personal pronouns.

As is mentioned in Chapter 4 in the discussion of apostrophes, the use of contractions is not considered acceptable in formal writing. Do not use contractions unless instructed to do so.

The general rule is that you should draft legal memorandums or briefs in the third person. Also, unless instructed otherwise, use the third person in correspondence to clients.

> **For Example:**
>
> It is *my* position that the court should grant the motion.
> *We* believe that the contract has been broken.
>
> **Revision:**
> The court should grant the motion. It is Mr. Balim's position that the contract has been broken.

When presenting your position or legal analysis, use present tense.

> **For Example:**
>
> Plaintiff *contends* that the rule requires thirty days' notice.
> It *is* the defendant's position that the contract is void.

When addressing a court opinion that has already been decided, use past tense.

> **For Example:**
>
> In *Smith v. Jones,* the court *held* that the rule does not require thirty days' notice.
> The court *listed* three possible solutions to the problem

When discussing a law or rule still in effect, use present tense.

> **For Example:**
>
> The provisions of section 44-556 *require* a contractor to give thirty days' notice.
> The statute *provides* that the notice must be signed by the owner of the property.

Chapter 3

Grammar

Contents

<table>
<tr><td>3.1 Subject/Verb Agreement</td><td>3.4 Adverbs, Adjectives, and Conjunctions</td></tr>
<tr><td>3.2 Noun/Pronoun Agreement</td><td>3.5 Parallel Construction</td></tr>
<tr><td>3.3 Verb Tense and Superfluous Verbs</td><td>3.6 Modifiers and Infinitives</td></tr>
</table>

The rules of grammar govern the construction of sentences. This chapter introduces some of the basic rules of grammar you should keep in mind when undertaking a writing assignment. A proofreading checklist for the topics presented in this chapter is included in Exhibit 7-5.

3.1 SUBJECT/VERB AGREEMENT

Following are some of the rules governing the relationship between the subject and verb of a sentence.

3.1 A PERSON AND NUMBER

The subject and verb should agree in person and number. This means that singular subjects require singular verbs and plural subjects require plural verbs.

> **■ *For Example:***
>
> The decision in the case *require* the defendant to give notice to the plain-
>   tiff. (This sentence has a singular subject, *decision,* and a plural verb,
>   *require.*)
> A committee, composed of two councilpersons and two citizens selected at
>   large, *are* going to discuss the matter. (The sentence has a singular sub-
>   ject, *committee,* and a plural verb, *are.*)
>
> **Revisions:**
> The decision in the case *requires* the defendant to give notice to the plain-
>   tiff. (The singular subject, *decision,* agrees with the singular verb,
>   *requires.*)
> A committee, composed of two councilpersons and two citizens selected at
>   large, *is* going to discuss the matter. (The singular subject, *committee,*
>   agrees with the singular verb, *is.*)

3.1 B   SUBJECTS JOINED BY *AND*

Two or more subjects joined by *and* usually require a plural verb.

> **■ *For Example:***
>
> Midori and Joan *were* present.

The president, secretary, and treasurer *are* going to the conference.

3.1 C   SUBJECTS JOINED BY *OR* OR *NOR*

Two or more subjects joined by *or* or *nor* require a verb that agrees with the subject closest to the verb.

> **■ *For Example:***
>
> Trevor or his brothers *are* going to attend.
> Either the brothers or Trevor *is* the responsible party.
> Neither Trevor nor his brother *is* going to attend.
> To accept the contract or to draft a new one *is* your option.

3.1 D   COMPOUND SUBJECT WITH SINGULAR MEANING

When a compound subject has a singular meaning, use a singular verb.

> ☐ *For Example:*
>
> The skull and cross bones *was* the pirate's flag.

3.1 E   INDEFINITE PRONOUNS IN GENERAL

A pronoun is a word used in place of a noun. Indefinite pronouns do not refer to a specific person or thing, such as *anyone, everybody, nobody, someone, each, either, neither, no one,* and *something.* Most indefinite pronouns are singular and require singular verbs.

> ☐ *For Example:*
>
> Everybody *is* responsible.
> Each of the members *has* a specific task.
> Neither of the parties *is* required to sign the contract.

3.1 F   INDEFINITE PRONOUNS *ALL, NONE, MOST, SOME,* AND *ANY*

Some indefinite pronouns require a verb that matches the noun to which they refer. Some of these pronouns are *all, none, most, some,* and *any.*

> ☐ *For Example:*
>
> All of the property *is* distributed.
> None of the items *are* missing.

3.1 G   PLURAL INDEFINITE PRONOUNS

Plural indefinite pronouns, such as *both, few, many, several,* and *others,* require a plural verb.

> ☐ *For Example:*
>
> Few *are* selected.
> Although there were multiple presentations, several employees *were* not in attendance.
> The others *are* not required to be present.

3.1 H   COLLECTIVE NOUNS

A noun is the name of a person, place, or thing. A collective noun refers to a group: *jury, family, crowd, majority,* and so on. Collective nouns usually require a singular verb.

> *For Example:*
>
> The jury *was* deadlocked.
> The family *is* present.
> The crowd usually *assembles* after the game.

However, if the action is individual, use a plural verb.

> *For Example:*
>
> The team *perform* their stretching exercises.

In this example, the action is individual, not collective; each member of the team performs the stretching exercises.

3.1 I   PLURAL NOUNS SINGULAR IN MEANING

Nouns plural in form but singular in meaning require a singular verb; for example, *politics, news,* and *tactics.*

> *For Example:*
>
> The news *is* bad.
> The politics of the party *is* corrupt.
> His politics *is* distasteful.

3.1 J   TITLES AND COMPANY NAMES

Titles of literary works and company names take a singular verb.

> *For Example:*
>
> *Military Tactics is* wonderful reading.
> Patterson and Sons *provides* janitorial services.

3.1 K   RELATIVE PRONOUNS—*WHICH, WHO,* AND *THAT*—AGREEMENT WITH ANTECEDENT

A relative pronoun refers to another noun in the sentence. *Which, who,* and *that* are examples of relative pronouns. The noun the relative pronoun refers to is called the antecedent. A relative pronoun requires a verb that agrees with its antecedent.

> ⬛ *For Example:*
>
> Our *client* is one of the persons *who* has been indicted in the case. (*Who* is
>   the relative pronoun, and *client* is the antecedent.)
> If the antecedent is singular, the verb should be singular. If the antecedent
>   is plural, the verb should be plural.
>
> **Singular:**
> Select the form that fits the need. (*Form,* the antecedent of the relative pro-
>   noun *that,* is singular; therefore, *that* takes the singular verb *fits.*)
>
> **Plural:**
> Select the forms that fit the need. (*Forms,* the antecedent of the relative
>   pronoun *that* is plural; therefore, *that* takes the plural verb *fit.*)
>
> **Singular:**
> Our *client, who* was present at the scene, *has* been indicted. (*Client,* the
>   antecedent of the relative pronoun *who,* is singular; therefore, *who*
>   takes the singular verb *has.*)
>
> **Plural:**
> The *clients, who* were present at the scene, *have* been indicted. (*Clients,*
>   the antecedent of the relative pronoun *who,* is plural; therefore, *who*
>   takes the plural verb *have.*)

3.1 L   RELATIVE PRONOUNS—*WHICH, WHO,*
AND *THAT*—PROPER USE

The general rule is to use *who* to refer to people. Use *which* to refer to things,
events, or animals. Use *that* to refer to either people or things, although *who* is the
preferable choice when referring to people.

> ⬛ *For Example:*
>
> The representative *who* wrote the bill received numerous accolades.
> The beaver, *which* lives in the pond, is reeking a lot of havoc.
> Contracts *that* include the restriction clause are preferable.
> It was the house *that* failed to pass the legislation.

It is mandatory to use *that* when reference is to both people and things.

> ⬛ *For Example:*
>
> It was the trial lawyers and their contributions *that* influenced the vote.

NOTE: Use *that* to introduce restrictive clauses and *which* to introduce nonrestric-
    tive clauses. A restrictive clause is necessary to the meaning of the sentence.

> ◻ *For Example:*
>
> You must perform all of the steps *that* are listed in the statute. (The itali-
> cized clause is a restrictive clause. It informs the reader that the re-
> quired steps are the steps listed in the statute. The clause is necessary to
> understand the steps that must be taken.)

A nonrestrictive clause is not necessary to the meaning of the sentence. It can be set off from the rest of the sentence with commas without changing the meaning of the sentence.

> ◻ *For Example:*
>
> I always buy his products, *which* usually are of high quality. (The itali-
> cized clause is a nonrestrictive clause. It is not necessary to the mean-
> ing of the sentence.)

3.1 M   WHERE SUBJECT FOLLOWS VERB

When the subject follows the verb, the verb is plural when the subject is plural and singular when the verb is singular.

> ◻ *For Example:*
>
> Of great significance *are* the second term and third condition.
> Of great significance *is* the third condition.
> Of great significance *are* the conditions.

3.1 N   PLURAL SUBJECT FOLLOWED BY *EACH*

When a plural subject is followed by *each,* use a plural verb. *Each* functions as an adverb.

> ◻ *For Example:*
>
> The members of Congress each will *have* an opportunity to speak.

NOTE: If the subject is composed of compound singular subjects modified by the indefinite pronoun *each* or *every,* use a singular verb. In this situation, the pronouns (*each* or *every*) relate individually to the verb.

> ◻ *For Example:*
>
> Senator Mesa and Senator Kohler each *has* the option to speak.

3.1 O   FORMS OF MEASUREMENT OR AMOUNT

Some forms of measurement or amount, plural in form, take a singular verb.

> ☐ *For Example:*
>
> Fifty dollars *is* the amount of the bill.
> Twenty minutes *is* the time allotted for this section of the test.
> Sixty miles *is* the distance to the next gas station.

3.1 P   SCIENCE OR DISCIPLINE ENDING IN *-ICS*

When the subject of the sentence is a science or discipline ending in *-ics,* the context of the sentence determines whether the verb is singular or plural.

> ☐ *For Example:*
>
> Statistics *is* a critical component of our analysis.
> The statistics *are* clearly not in support of his position.
> Economics *is* a difficult course.
> The economics of the situation *are* clearly going to require further study.

3.2   NOUN/PRONOUN AGREEMENT

Following are some of the rules governing the relationship between pronouns and the nouns to which they refer, their antecedents.

3.2 A   NOUN/PRONOUN AGREEMENT—GENERAL RULE

Pronouns must agree in number (singular/plural), person (first/second/third), and gender (feminine/masculine/neuter) with the nouns to which they refer. Some of the common pronouns are *I, me, mine, my, we, us, our, you, yours, your, he, him, his, she, her, hers, it, its, they, them, their,* and *theirs.*

> ☐ *For Example:*
>
> The *workers* put on *their* helmets when they entered the building. (The pronoun *their* agrees in number [plural] with its antecedent *workers* [plural].)
> *Ereka* was required to wear *her* helmet. The pronoun *her* agrees in number and gender with the antecedent *Ereka.*

3.2 B   INDEFINITE PRONOUNS

As mentioned in the previous section, pronouns that do not refer to a definite person or thing are indefinite pronouns. Examples of indefinite pronouns are *all, anyone, anybody, each, either, everyone, someone, somebody, everything, something, no one* and *none*. Indefinite pronouns are usually singular and take a singular pronoun.

> **■ *For Example:***
>
> *Everyone* has the freedom to select *their* candidate. (The antecedent *everyone* is singular, therefore, the use of *their* [plural] is incorrect.)
>
> **Revisions:**
> *Everyone* has the freedom to select *his* or *her* candidate.
> Individuals have the freedom to select their candidate.

NOTE: Some indefinite pronouns *(both, few many, several,* and *others)* are plural and take a plural pronoun.

> **■ *For Example:***
>
> *Few* know which rules apply to *them.* (Since the antecedent *few* is plural, it takes a plural pronoun, *them.*)

3.2 C   ANTECEDENTS JOINED BY *AND*

Antecedents joined by *and* require a plural pronoun.

> **■ *For Example:***
>
> Joachim and Natalie are separating *their* property.
> Joachim, Jon, and Natalie are going *their* separate ways.

3.2 D   ANTECEDENTS JOINED BY *OR* OR *NOR*

Antecedents joined by *or* or *nor* require a pronoun that agrees in number and gender with the antecedent closest to the pronoun.

> **■ *For Example:***
>
> Jocelyn or the other defendants must conduct *their* investigation.
> The defendants or Jocelyn must conduct *her* investigation.

When the sentence appears awkward, as the second one does, consider rephrasing it.

> **For Example:**
>
> Jocelyn or the defendants must conduct an investigation.

3.2 E   PRONOUN CASE

Pronouns often change form according to their case. A pronoun that functions as a subject or subject complement takes the subjective case. A pronoun that functions as a direct object, an indirect object, or an object of a preposition takes the objective case. A pronoun that functions as a possessive takes the possessive case.

> **For Example:**
>
> I gave the paper to *he*.
> Our teacher asked Tamara and *I* to prepare the presentation.
>
> **Revisions:**
> I gave the paper to *him*. (*Him* is correct because it is the objective case
>   form of *he*, and *him* is in the objective case in the sentence.)
> Our teacher asked Tamara and *me* to prepare the presentation. (*Me* is the
>   object of the verb *asked*. Therefore, the objective case *me* is appropri-
>   ate, not the subjective case *I*.)

A chart of the pronoun case forms is presented below.

SUBJECTIVE CASE	OBJECTIVE CASE	POSSESSIVE CASE
I	me	my, mine
he/she	him/her	his/her/hers
it	it	its
we	us	our
you	you	your
they	them	their/theirs
who	whom	whose

A summary of rules governing pronoun case is presented in this section.

1. **Who and Whom**   The proper case for the pronouns *who* and *whom* depends on their function within the sentence. *Who* is used for the subjective case. *Whom* is used for the objective case.

> **For Example:**
>
> He gives the lecture to *whomever* will listen.
> The senior partner will give the assignments to the junior partners, *who*
>   you will confer with this afternoon.
> *Whom* is responsible for the error?
> *Who* was selected by the board of directors?

Revisions:

He gives the lecture to *whoever* will listen. (*Whoever* functions as the subject of the dependant clause *whoever will listen.*)

The senior partner will give the assignments to the junior partners, *whom* you will confer with this afternoon. (*Whom* is the direct object of the verb *will confer.*)

Who is responsible for the error? (*Who* is the subject of the verb *is responsible.*)

Whom did the board of directors select? (*Whom* is the direct object of the verb *select.*)

2. **Comparisons *Than* and *As***   When a comparison using *than* or *as* ends with a pronoun, look to the pronoun's function in the sentence to determine its case.

For Example:

Consuelo is more careful than me.
Colleen prefers Sebastian more than *I*.

Revisions:

Consuelo is more careful than I. (*I* functions as a subject: Consuelo is more careful than *I am.*)

Colleen prefers Sebastian more than *me*. (*Me* is part of the object in the sentence and takes the object case *me*.)

3. **Pronouns and Compound Constructions**   It often is difficult to choose the correct pronoun when it is part of a compound construction. A simple way to determine which pronoun is correct is to rephrase the sentence with only the pronoun.

For Example:

After the trial was concluded, the attorney, legal assistant, and *me* returned to the law office.

Between you and *I*, I am sure she does not know how to draft the complaint.

Revisions:

After the trial was concluded, the attorney, legal assistant, and *I* returned to the law office. (*I* is part of the subject; therefore, the subjective case *I* is appropriate. The choice is clear when you remove the other nouns from the subject: After the trial was concluded, *I* returned to the law office.)

Between you and *me*, I am sure she does not know how to draft the complaint. (*Me* is the object of the preposition *between*. Therefore, the objective case *me* is appropriate, not the subjective case *I*.)

NOTE: In a compound word group or phrase, the proper form is to place the personal pronoun last.

> ◻ *For Example:*
>
> Between *me* and *you,* I hope he selects you.
> *I,* Thad, and Andrew went to the hearing.
>
> **Revisions:**
> Between *you* and *me,* I hope he selects you.
> Thad, Andrew, and I went to the hearing.

4. **We or Us before a Noun**   When *we* or *us* precedes a noun, use *we* for the subjective case and *us* for the objective case. An easy way to determine which pronoun is appropriate is to omit the noun.

> ◻ *For Example:*
>
> *Us* paralegals would rather not attend the conference.
> The managing partners are mistreating *we* workers.
>
> **Revisions:**
> *We* paralegals would rather not attend the conference. (*Paralegals* is the
>   subject sentence; therefore, the pronoun *we* is appropriate: We would
>   rather not attend the conference. [omitting the noun *paralegals*].)
> The managing partners are mistreating *us* workers. (*Workers* is the direct
>   object of the verb *mistreating;* therefore, the pronoun *us* is appropriate:
>   The managing partners are mistreating *us.* [omitting the noun *workers*].)

5. **Pronoun before a Gerund**   A pronoun that modifies a gerund is in the possessive case. A verb ending in *ing* that functions as a noun is a gerund.

> ◻ *For Example:*
>
> The senior partner was sanctioned for his overcharging the stockholders.
> He disapproved of their taking the case. (not *them taking the case*)

6. **Appositives**   A pronoun in an appositive takes the case of the noun or pronoun it refers to. An appositive is a noun or noun phrase that identifies or names a nearby noun or pronoun. A simple way to determine the correct pronoun is to rephrase the sentence without the word or words the appositive renames.

> ◻ *For Example:*
>
> The lead attorneys, Ms. Talbot and *me,* prepared the brief.
>
> **Revision:**
> The lead attorneys, Ms. Talbot and *I,* prepared the brief. (*Lead attorneys* is
>   the subject of the sentence. Therefore, the pronoun appositive *I* takes
>   the subjective case *I,* not the objective case *me.*)

3.2 F   PRONOUNS AND INFINITIVES

When a pronoun is the subject or object of an infinitive, use the objective case.

> ☐ *For Example:*
>
> The lead attorney instructed Samantha and *I* to take the client and *she* to the court.
> The lead attorney instructed Samantha and *me* to take the client and *her* to the court. *Samantha and me* is the subject and *client and her* is the object of the infinitive.

3.2 G   NUMBER OF A PRONOUN THAT REFERS TO A COLLECTIVE NOUN

A collective noun refers to a group. The number of a pronoun that refers to a collective noun is determined by the function of the collective noun. If the collective noun functions as a unit, the pronoun is singular.

> ☐ *For Example:*
>
> The *committee,* after reviewing the matter, presented *its* conclusion. (The collective noun *committee* functions as a unit; the report is the act of the committee as a whole. Therefore, the pronoun *its* is singular.)

If the collective noun does not function as a unit (that is, the members of the collective noun are acting separately and not as a unit), a plural pronoun is required.

> ☐ *For Example:*
>
> The *team* have stated *their* various positions on the question of whether *they* should wear the new helmets. (The collective noun *team* does not function as a unit; the reference is to the team as individual members. Therefore, the sentence takes the plural pronouns *their* and *they*.)

3.2 H   PRONOUN REFERENCE

The relationship between the pronoun and its antecedent should always be clear.

1. **Ambiguous Reference**   When it is unclear which antecedent a pronoun refers to, replace the pronoun with a noun. This often occurs with the pronouns *this, that, which,* and *it.*

> ### For Example:
>
> The legal assistant retrieved a copy of the case and prepared the rough draft of the brief. When he was finished, he put *it* in the file. (What did he put in the file—a copy of the case or the brief?)
>
> **Revision:**
> The legal assistant retrieved a copy of the case and prepared the rough draft of the brief. When he was finished, he put the *brief* in the file.

2. **Nonexistent Antecedent**   When a pronoun refers to a nonexistent antecedent, replace the pronoun with a noun.

> ### For Example:
>
> The firm decided to purchase new computers. *They* believe that the current computers are too slow. (*They* refers to the attorneys and paralegals, not the firm.)
>
> **Revision:**
> The firm decided to purchase new computers. The attorneys and paralegals believe that the current computers are too slow.

3. **Indefinite References and *They, It,* or *You***   A pronoun should refer to a specific antecedent. Sometimes pronouns such as *they, it,* or *you* refer to antecedents that have not been specifically mentioned. Or the antecedents may be mentioned so remotely in the text that it is difficult for the reader to determine what the pronoun refers to.

> ### For Example:
>
> They clearly did not anticipate the events that followed. (where *they* either are not identified or are referred to earlier in the text and other actors have been mentioned)
>
> **Revision:**
> The partners clearly did not anticipate the events that followed.

Avoid the improper use of *it* in conjunction with phrases that begin with *in.*

> ### For Example:
>
> *In* the criminal law treatise, *it* defines first degree murder.
>
> **Revision:**
> The criminal law treatise defines first degree murder.

Use the pronoun *you* to address the writer directly. In formal writing, it is not appropriate to use *you* to indicate anyone in general.

> **For Example:**
>
> The law office guidelines provide that *you* should not take files home.
>
> **Revision:**
> The law office guidelines provide that *employees* should not take files home.

3.2 I   GENERIC NOUNS

A generic noun represents a member of a group. Generic nouns are singular.

> **For Example:**
>
> A *legal assistant* must take continuing education courses if *they* want to stay current.
>
> **Revision:**
> A *legal assistant* must take continuing education courses if *he or she* wants to stay current. (Another way to correct the sentence is by changing the generic noun: *Legal assistants* must take continuing education courses if *they* want to stay current.)

3.2 K   FORMAL WRITING AND PLACEMENT OF A PRONOUN

Do not use a pronoun before its antecedent in formal writing.

> **For Example:**
>
> Since *she* was uncertain of the outcome of the case, *Danielle* was willing to accept the settlement offer.
>
> **Revision:**
> Since *Danielle* was uncertain of the outcome of the case, *she* was willing to accept the settlement offer.

3.3   VERB TENSE AND SUPERFLUOUS VERBS

Following is a summary of the rules governing verb tense and superfluous verbs.

3.3 A   VERB TENSE IN GENERAL

Verb tense is the time in which a verb's action occurs. Events happening in the present use the present tense, events that occurred in the past use the past tense, and events that will take place in the future use the future tense.

1. **General Rule**   Sentences and paragraphs are usually written in the same tense. You should ensure that your writing does not have inappropriate changes in verb tense.

> **For Example:**
>
> The complaint *was* filed on January 1, 2003. The defendants *move* to dismiss the complaint. The motion *was* denied. (The verb tense in this sentence moves from past (*was*), to present (*move*), then back to past tense (*was*).)
>
> **Revision:**
> The complaint *was* filed on January 1, 2003. The defendants *moved* to dismiss the complaint. The motion *was* denied. (All of the verbs are in the past tense.)

2. **Presenting a Legal Position or Legal Analysis**   When presenting your position or legal analysis, use present tense.

> **For Example:**
> Plaintiff contends that the rule requires thirty days' notice.
> It is the defendant's position that the contract is void.

3. **Discussing a Court Opinion**   When addressing a court opinion that has already been decided, use past tense.

> **For Example:**
> In *Smith v. Jones,* the court *held* that the rule does not require thirty days' notice.
> The court *listed* three possible solutions to the problem

4. **Discussing a Law or Rule Still in Effect**   When discussing a law or rule that is still in effect, use present tense.

> **For Example:**
> The provisions of section 44-556 *require* a contractor to give thirty days' notice.
> The statute *provides* that the notice must be signed by the owner of the property.

3.3 B   SUPERFLUOUS VERBS

Avoid the use of verb constructions that are unnecessarily wordy. (Superfluous verbs are italicized.)

> **For Example:**
> - He decided to *perform an investigation* into the matter.
> - The arbitrator decided to *give consideration* to the argument.
> - The judge *reached a decision* on the question.
> - The contractor *made an attempt* to complete the contract on time.
>
> **Revisions without superfluous verbs:**
> - He decided to *investigate* the matter.
> - The arbitrator *considered* the argument.
> - The judge *decided* the question.
> - The contractor *attempted* to complete the contract on time.

3.4   ADVERBS, ADJECTIVES, AND CONJUNCTIONS

An adjective is a word used to modify a noun or pronoun.

> **For Example:**
> She wore a *red* dress to the party.
> The *race* car had *vinyl* seats.

An adverb is a word used to modify a verb, an adjective, or another adverb.

> **For Example:**
> Antonio ran *quickly* into the house

A conjunction is a word that connects words, phrases, clauses, or sentences.

> **For Example:**
> We can select the first clause *or* the entire second paragraph.
> All of the participants had heard of the agreement, *but* none had seen it.

3.4 A   FORMING ADVERBS AND IMPROPER USE OF ADJECTIVES

Many but not all adverbs are formed by adding *ly* to a word. A common problem
occurs when an adjective is used incorrectly to modify a verb.

> **For Example:**
> The plant supervisor must see that the factory machinery runs *efficient*.
> Desmond behaves *conservative* around his parents.

Revisions:
The plant supervisor must see that the factory machinery runs *efficiently*.
Desmond behaves *conservatively* around his parents. (In this sentence,
 conservatively is an adverb; it modifies the verb *behaves*).
Desmond's *conservative* behavior pleases his parents. (In this sentence,
 conservative is an adjective; it modifies the noun *behavior*).

3.4 B   ADJECTIVES, ADVERBS, AND LINKING VERBS

In some situations, it is difficult to determine whether you should use an adjective
or an adverb. This often occurs with words that follow linking verbs, such as *feel,
look, believe, become, grow, smell, taste,* and *appear.* A linking verb does not show
physical or emotional action; rather, it suggests a state of being. Use an adjective
when the word following the verb describes the subject of the sentence; use an adverb when the word refers to the verb.

For Example:

The inspector felt *careful.* (The adjective *careful* is used because it describes the inspector [the subject].)
The inspector felt *carefully* when he searched the table. (The adverb *carefully* is used because it shows action—how the inspector searched the
 table [he felt *carefully*]; it modifies the verb *felt.*)
Cole looked *sad.* (*Looked* describes Cole. *Looked* is a linking verb because
 it does not show action. The adjective *sad* is used because it modifies
 the noun *Cole.*)
Cole looked *quickly* around the room. (The verb *looked* shows action and,
 therefore, is not a linking verb. The adverb *quickly* is used because it
 modifies [describes] the verb *looked.*)

3.4 C   COMPARATIVES AND SUPERLATIVES

Use a comparative to indicate a comparison between two things (e.g., *better, older,
easier, faster,* and *worse*). Use a superlative to indicate a comparison between three
or more things (e.g., *best, oldest, easiest, fastest,* and *worst*).

For Example:

He is the *best* of the two applicants.
Rosa is the *fastest* of the two runners.

Revisions:
He is the *better* of the two applicants.
Rosa is the *faster* of the two runners.

> The comparatives *better* and *faster* are used because two things are being
> compared.

> ■ *For Example:*
> He is the *better* of the three applicants.
> Rosa is the *faster* of all of the runners.
>
> **Revisions:**
> He is the *best* of the three applicants.
> Rosa is the *fastest* of all of the runners.
>
> The comparatives *best* and *fastest* are used because more than two things
> are being compared.

To form the comparative and superlative of most one- and two-syllable adjectives, add *er* or *est: big, bigger, biggest; old, older, oldest; funny, funnier, funniest.*

For some two-syllable adjectives and long adjectives, form the comparative by
using *more* and the superlative by using *most: more outrageous, most outrageous;
more entertaining, most entertaining.*

To form the comparative and superlative of some one-syllable adverbs, use *er*
and *est: faster, fastest; sooner, soonest.* To form the comparative and superlative of
longer adverbs and those ending in *-ly,* use *more/less* for the comparative and
most/least for the superlative: *more slowly, most slowly; more likely, most likely.*

Comparatives are not used with concepts that are absolute, such as *perfect,
unique, empty, impossible,* and *excellent.*

> ■ *For Example:*
> It was a most perfect story.
>
> **Revision:**
> It was a perfect story.

3.4 D　ADVERBS USED FOR EMPHASIS

Place adverbs used for emphasis immediately before the word or phrase they modify. Examples of words of emphasis are *only, so, very,* and *quite.*

> ■ *For Example:*
> D.J. intended only to influence the outcome of the meeting. (*Only* modifies
> the phrase that follows: to influence the outcome of the meeting.)

3.4 E　COORDINATING CONJUNCTIONS

Use a coordinating conjunction when joining clauses and words of equal rank.
Some coordinating conjunctions are *and, or, but, for, so, yet,* and *nor.*

> ◘ *For Example:*
>
> We have three selections available: section a, section b, *or* section c.
>   (*Or* joins equal words.)
> The landlord had the option to seek restitution, *but* he did not choose that
>   option. (*But* joins equal clauses.)

3.4 F   CORRELATIVE CONJUNCTIONS

Correlative conjunctions are also used to link items of equal rank. Correlative conjunctions are used in pairs. Some correlative conjunctions are *either/or, neither/ nor, if/then, both/and,* and *since/therefore.*

> ◘ *For Example:*
>
> *Either* they will sign the agreement, *or* we will select another vendor.
> *If* we are forced to pursue that option, *then* we will require additional
>   funds.
> *Both* Reynolds *and* Haynes are present.

Grammar

◆ 3.5   PARALLEL CONSTRUCTION

Parallel construction means that all items listed are similar in grammatical structure. It means that in sentences that include a list, a group of activities, and so on, each of the items must use the same grammatical form; that is, all of the items or members of the group should agree in verb tense, number, and so on.

> ◘ *For Example:*
>
> **Lack parallel construction:**
> ► The defendant is a trained officer with fifteen years' experience who
>   has won several service medals.
> ► The goals of the association are as follows:
>   a. educating the public about crime
>   b. to provide support for the police
>   c. improvement of local neighborhood watch groups
> ► Most states have passed uniform laws for corporations, partnerships,
>   and that allow limited liability companies.
> ► The client gave consideration not only to the exclusion term but also
>   the waiver clause.
>
> **Revisions with parallel construction:**
> ► The defendant is a trained officer *who has* fifteen years' experience and
>   *who has* won several service medals.

> ▶ The goals of the association are as follows:
>   a. *to educate* the public about crime
>   b. *to provide* support for the police
>   c. *to improve* local neighborhood watch groups
> ▶ Most states have passed uniform laws for corporations, partnerships, and limited liability companies.
> ▶ The client gave consideration not only *to the* exclusion term but also *to the* waiver clause.

✦ 3.6 MODIFIERS AND INFINITIVES

Modifiers are words or phrases that provide descriptions of the subject, verb, or object in a sentence. Four types of common errors involving modifiers are the following.

3.6 A MISPLACED MODIFIERS

A misplaced modifier is a word or phrase that is placed in the wrong location in a sentence. Because of its placement, it appears to modify one word or phrase when it is intended to modify another. You may create an ambiguity or cause a loss of clarity by misplacing a modifier. The solution is to rephrase the sentence or move the modifier. Usually, this means placing the modifier before or after the word or phrase it modifies.

> ◨ *For Example:*
> ▶ If we contend that the contract applies, it will be attacked by the defense. (What will be attacked—our contention or the contract?)
> ▶ Present the client's counterargument only in the third section of the brief. (Does this mean the counterargument should be presented in the third section and no other section, or does it mean that the third section should consist only of the counterargument?)
> ▶ He was listed as older, with gray hair approximately six feet tall. (As the sentence reads, the hair is approximately six feet tall.)
>
> **Revision—sentence rephrased:**
> ▶ If we contend that the contract applies, the contention will be attacked by the defense.
>
> **Revision—modifier moved:**
> ▶ In the third section of the brief, present only the client's counterargument.
> ▶ He was listed as older, approximately six feet tall, with gray hair.

3.6 B   DANGLING MODIFIERS

Modifiers that do not modify any other part of a sentence are dangling modifiers.

> ◘ *For Example:*
>
> *To determine whether it was breached,* the provisions of the statute
>   must be referred to. (The italicized modifier does not refer to or modify
>   any part of the sentence. It refers to a contract mentioned in another
>   sentence.)
> *While working on the project,* two clients entered the room. (The two
>   clients were not working on the project when they entered the room.
>   The dangling modifier refers to another actor.)

The problem may be corrected by rewriting the sentence to make sure modifiers
refer to a noun or nouns in the sentence.

> ◘ *For Example:*
>
> **Dangling modifier eliminated:**
> To determine whether the terms of the contract violate the statute, the
>   statutory provisions must be referred to.
> While he was working on the project, two clients entered the room.

3.6 C   SQUINTING MODIFIERS

A squinting modifier is located in a sentence such that it is unclear whether the
modifier refers to the word that precedes it or the word that follows it. Avoid squinting modifiers when you edit your writing. (The squinting modifier is italicized.)

> ◘ *For Example:*
>
> The report that was prepared *routinely* indicated that the structure was un-
>   safe. (Was the report prepared routinely, or did the report routinely in-
>   dicate the structure was unsafe?)
>
> **Revision:**
> The report that was routinely prepared indicated that the structure was unsafe.

   Limiting modifiers, such as *only, even, almost, nearly,* and *just,* are often misplaced. Those modifiers should be placed in front of the word they modify.

> ◘ *For Example:*
>
> The lawyer only prepared the document. (As the sentence reads, the lawyer
>   prepared the document and nothing else. If the sentence is intended to
>   mean that the lawyer and no one else prepared the document, *only*

> is misplaced. The correction reads as follows: Only the lawyer prepared
> the document.)

3.6 D   SPLIT INFINITIVES

An infinitive is a verb form that functions as a noun or as an auxiliary verb, such as *to argue, to understand,* and *to consider.* The general rule is that infinitives should not be split; that is, an adverb should not be placed after the *to* and before the verb.

> ◻ *For Example:*
>
> to completely understand
> to rapidly climb
> to thoroughly test
> (An adverb is placed between the *to* and the verb.)
>
> **Revisions:**
> to understand completely
> to climb rapidly
> to test thoroughly

Punctuation

Contents

Punctuation is designed to make writing clear and easy to understand. Poor punctuation may cause the reader to misunderstand the context or be distracted by the errors and not focus on the context. Poor punctuation usually causes the reader to question the competency of the author. A comprehensive discussion of all of the rules governing punctuation would require an entire text. This chapter discusses the major elements of punctuation and summarizes common punctuation rules.

4.1 COMMA (,)

The function of a comma is to separate the parts of a sentence so that the meaning is clear. It is the most frequently used punctuation mark. Following are some basic rules that apply to commas.

1. **Use a comma before a coordinating conjunction that joins two main, or independent, clauses** (*and, but, or, nor, for, yet,* and *so*). An independent clause is a clause that could stand alone as a complete sentence.

> ❏ *For Example:*
>
> The statute provides that the contract must be witnessed, but it does not require that the contract be in writing. (Note that each clause of the sentence could be a complete sentence: The statute provides that the contract must be witnessed. It does not require that the contract be in writing.)

2. Set off introductory words, phrases, or clauses with a comma.

> ❏ *For Example:*
>
> *Clearly,* Santana had more to say on the subject. (The introductory word is italicized.)
> *After the prosecutor's opening statement,* the court declared a recess. (The introductory phrase is italicized.)
> *If the parties can come to terms on the first issue,* then the negotiations can continue. (The introductory clause is italicized.)

NOTE: If the introductory clause or phrase is short (usually three words or less) and the meaning of the sentence is clear, the comma may be omitted.

> ❏ *For Example:*
>
> After the test I'm going to sleep.
> In every situation you should read the contract.

3. Use a comma after each item in a series of three or more items and place a comma before *and* or *or* at the end of the series.

> ❏ *For Example:*
>
> The defendant had no identification, money, or other possessions.
> Bicycles, tricycles, unicycles, and other nonmotorized vehicles are covered by the statute.
> His duties included interviewing witnesses, performing research, and drafting memos.

A comma is not required when the items are joined by conjunctions.

> ❏ *For Example:*
>
> He was angry and tired and exasperated.

4. Use a comma to avoid a misreading of the subject.

> ❏ *For Example:*
>
> Instead of rule A, rule B applies in this situation.

5. **Separate coordinate adjectives and adverbs with a comma.** Coordinate adjectives and adverbs independently modify the same word. To determine if the modifiers are coordinate, reverse their order or insert *and* between them. If the meaning does not change, they are coordinate.

> ■ *For Example:*
>
> The *correct, concise* interpretation is that . . . The *concise, correct* interpretation is that . . . (The coordinating adjectives are italicized.)
> The killer *calmly, quietly* murdered the victim. The killer calmly and quietly murdered the victim. (The coordinating adverbs are italicized.)

6. **Set off transitional or interpretive words or phrases with a comma.** These are words or phrases that provide qualification or clarification but are not essential to the meaning of a sentence.

> ■ *For Example:*
>
> The plaintiffs, however, have failed to comply.
> The correct course, therefore, is to settle the case.
> The harvester, for example, is one type of equipment that applies this technology.

7. **Set off nonrestrictive phrases or clauses with a comma.** A nonrestrictive phrase or clause is not necessary to the meaning of the sentence. (Nonrestrictive clauses are italicized.)

> ■ *For Example:*
>
> The court of appeals denied the appeal, *finding that the evidence was properly admitted.*
> Penny Blais, *who recently graduated from law school,* is employed at the Tate law firm.

8. **Use a comma to set off appositives.** An appositive is a noun or noun phrase that further identifies another noun or noun phrase. (Appositives are italicized.)

> ■ *For Example:*
>
> The client, *Ms. Mendoza,* was elected to the position.
> The plaintiffs, *Mr. Evans and Ms. Able,* were present at the hearing.

9. **Set off contrasting phrases with a comma or commas.**

> ■ *For Example:*
>
> Mr., *not Ms.,* was the guilty party. (The contrasting phrase is italicized.)

10. Set off miscellaneous nonessential words or phrases with a comma.

> *For Example:*
>
> Well, you should have been here earlier.
> You could help me with this, couldn't you?

11. Use commas when required to set off quotations. Place the comma between the quotation and the attribution.

> *For Example:*
>
> He said, "I did not do it."
> "I want you to know," Carl said, "that you are always welcome here."

12. Do not use commas to set off a partial quotation that is part of the sentence.

> *For Example:*
>
> Bennett stated that he "did not plan to commit a murder."

13. Place a comma inside the closing quotation mark, not outside the quotation mark.

> *For Example:*
>
> "Witnessing is not required," he said.

14. Place a comma before and after descriptive titles such as *M.D., Ph.D.,* and *Esq.*

> *For Example:*
>
> The doctor in this case is Evelyn Place, M.D., who attended medical
>   school at Yale.

NOTE: Do not use a comma before *Jr., II,* and so on, after a personal name.

> *For Example:*
>
> Mr. Juan Rojas Jr. and Arthur Cleaver II delivered the closing address.

15. Do not use a comma before parentheses (see Section 4.11 "Parentheses").

> *For Example:*
>
> All employees (executives and assistants) shall arrive at work at 8:00 a.m.

16. Place a comma between the day and year when the full date is written.

> **For Example:**
>
> The hearing was held on November 16, 2004.

When only the month and year are written, no comma is used.

> **For Example:**
>
> There were no hearings during November 2004.

17. Use a comma when a word or group of words is omitted but the meaning of the sentence is clear.

> **For Example:**
>
> Amanda represents the northern and eastern districts; Morley, the southern district.
> Elizabeth prepared the opening and analysis; Jane, the closing.

18. See Chapter 2 for the use of commas in numbers.

4.2   SEMICOLON (;)

A semicolon is used primarily in two situations:

- ▶ to separate major elements of complex sentences
- ▶ to separate items in a series when the items are long or when one of the items has internal commas

With regard to these situations, note the following rules:

1. Use a semicolon to separate main, or independent, clauses that are *not* joined by a coordinating conjunction. Main, or independent, clauses contain a subject and a verb. Each clause could be a separate sentence. A conjunction is a word that is used to connect words and phrases. A coordinating conjunction such as *and, but,* or *or* connects like elements.

> **For Example:**
>
> The shareholders held their meeting at noon, the board of directors met immediately thereafter. (The use of the comma is incorrect because there is no coordinating conjunction such as *and* connecting the two clauses.)

> **Revision—coordinating conjunction used:**
> The shareholders held their meeting at noon, *and* the board of directors met immediately thereafter. (The coordinating conjunction is italicized.)
>
> **Revision—semicolon used:**
> The shareholders held their meeting at noon; the board of directors met immediately thereafter.

2. **Use a semicolon when independent clauses are joined by a conjunctive adverb.** Examples of conjunctive adverbs include *therefore, however, further, furthermore, now, still, then, therefore, consequently, likewise,* and *nevertheless.*

> ▣ *For Example:*
>
> The rule requires that the will must be witnessed in writing; *however,* there are three exceptions.
> Our client took all of the steps he believed were necessary; *still,* there are additional steps that must be taken.

3. **At the end of a sentence, use a semicolon to separate an appositive introduced by terms such as *that is* and *for example*.**

> ▣ *For Example:*
>
> For the instrument to be validly executed, there are three requirements; namely, the signature of the maker, the signature of two witnesses, and notarization.

4. **When a series of items is long or commas are already used in some of the items in the series, use a semicolon to separate the items.** The role of the semicolon in this context is to provide clarity.

> ▣ *For Example:*
>
> **Long items:**
> The plaintiffs must prove the following to establish that the will was validly witnessed:
>   a. there were two witnesses to the will;
>   b. the witnesses were present in the room when the will was signed;
>   c. the witnesses were not related to the testator or were not bequeathed anything in the will
>
> **List of items with internal commas:**
> The stockholders present were Jillian Hart, the president; Clyde Grayson, the secretary; and Monica Murton, the treasurer.
> The executive officer will visit Denver, Colorado; Houston, Texas; Bakersfield, California; and Boise, Idaho.

4.3   COLON (:)

Use a colon when you want to introduce or call attention to information that follows, such as lists, conclusions, explanations, and quotations. The function of a colon is to introduce what follows.

1. **A colon is used to introduce a list or series.** When a colon introduces a list or series, it must be preceded by a main clause that is grammatically complete; that is, a complete sentence.

□ *For Example:*

The statutory requirements are: the will must be witnessed by two witnesses, the witnesses must be present when the testator signs the will, and the witnesses must sign the will. (The sentence is incorrect because the use of the colon is not preceded by a main clause that is grammatically complete; the clause lacks an object.)

Revision:
The statutory requirements are the following: the will must be witnessed by two witnesses, . . .

□ *For Example:*

The statute provides that three steps must be performed before the water right is established: (1) a permit must be obtained from the state engineer, (2) the water must be applied to a beneficial use, and (3) the beneficial use must be continuous for a period of three years.

2. **A colon may be used to introduce quotations.** A colon may be used to introduce a short quotation introduced by an independent clause.

□ *For Example:*

Standing in open court, Franklin loudly entered his plea: "I am not guilty."

A colon may be used to emphasize a quotation.

□ *For Example:*

The senator concluded his remarks with the following statement: "I do not choose to run for reelection."

A colon is usually used to introduce block quotations, transcripts, and statutes.

□ *For Example:*

After reviewing the matter at length, the court adopted the following rule: (Block Quotation)

3. **A colon may be used to join two separate but related clauses.** In this instance, the colon is used to emphasize the information that follows.

> ◻ *For Example:*
>
> The client made a major mistake: he failed to file the annual report.

◆ 4.4 APOSTROPHE (')

An apostrophe serves to indicate possession, to form a contraction, and to form the plural of some words. The rules governing the use of an apostrophe to indicate possession are presented in Chapter 2 Section 2.2 C "Possessives." The rules governing the use of an apostrophe in conjunction with numbers are discussed in Chapter 2 Section 2.3 D "Plural and Possessive Numbers." The use of apostrophes to form contractions are covered here.

Contractions are considered inappropriate for use in legal writing and generally are not used in formal writing. Contracted abbreviations, however, are frequently used in case names (see Chapter 5 "Legal Citation"). To make a contraction, use an apostrophe in place of the omitted letter or letters.

> ◻ *For Example:*
>
> they're (they are); can't (cannot); don't (do not); who's (who is) (*whose* is the possessive form); it's (it is); I'm (I am); isn't (is not)

Note the difference between *it's* and *its*. *It's* is the contraction for *it is*. *Its* is the possessive pronoun form of *it*.

In *informal* writing, an apostrophe may be used to indicate the omission of the century.

> ◻ *For Example:*
>
> This was the popular music of the '70s. (The apostrophe replaces 19 in 1970.)

◆ 4.5 QUOTATION MARKS (" ")

Use quotation marks to identify and set off quoted material, titles, and words used in a special way. Note the following guidelines when quoting material.

1. **Long quotations are not set off by quotation marks.** Instead, they are set off from the rest of the text by a 0.5 inch indentation from the left and right margins.

They are also single-spaced. These quotations are called block quotations and, according to *The Bluebook* and *ALWD* should be used for quotations of 50 words or more (see Chapter 5).

> ▣ *For Example:*
>
> The court made the following statements with regard to the requirement of the presence of the witness:
>
> The statute requires the witnesses to be present when the testator signs the will. The witnesses must be in the same room with the testator, not in a separate room from which they can see the testator. The witnesses also must actually see the testator sign the will. Their presence in the room is not sufficient if they do not actually see the testator sign the will.

As readers tend to skip over or skim long quotations, use long quotations sparingly and only when the entire language, verbatim, is essential.

2. Periods and commas are placed inside the quotation marks.

> ▣ *For Example:*
>
> "He is a dangerous individual," the police officer warned.
> He was described as "a dangerous individual."
> "Watch out," Justin exclaimed. "He is coming your way."
> "We may never know," Consuelo said, "what the defendant intended."

Other punctuation, such as semicolons, colons, question marks, and exclamation marks, are placed outside the quotation marks unless they are a part of the quotation.

> ▣ *For Example:*
>
> The court defined publication as "communication to a third party";
>   therefore . . .
> The victim then shouted, "I've been hit!" (The exclamation mark is part of the quotation; therefore, it belongs inside the quotation marks.)

3. Quotation marks may be used to indicate that a word is used in a special way or is a special term.

> ▣ *For Example:*
>
> The attorney acted as a "hired gun" in the case.
> He is a member of the "special" generation.
> The term "oppressive conduct" has a special meaning in corporation law.

Punctuation

4. With a quote within a quote, single quotation marks are used.

> ◻ *For Example:*
>
> The court held that "the term 'oppressive conduct' requires that the share-
> holder engage in some wrongful conduct."
> The court characterized the corporate director as "an individual who regu-
> larly engaged in 'oppressive conduct.'"

When the quote within a quote is part of a block quotation, use double quotation marks to set off the quote.

> ◻ *For Example:*
>
> The court made the following statements with regard to the requirement of
> the presence of the witness:
>
> The statute requires the witnesses to be present when the testator signs
> the will. The witnesses must be in the same room with the testator, not
> in a separate room from which they can see the testator. The witnesses
> also must "actually see" the testator sign the will. Their presence in the
> room is not sufficient if they do not actually see the testator sign the
> will.

5. Quotation marks may also be used to indicate that a term is informal or questionable.

> ◻ *For Example:*
>
> William "Wild Bill" James
> The only "injury" sustained in this lawsuit was the cost of the litigation.

4.6 PERIOD (.)

The period is one of the most commonly used punctuation marks. It is used as a mark at the end of a sentence, in abbreviations, as a decimal point in numbers, and after letters and numbers in an outline or list.

1. Use a period to indicate the end of a sentence that is not a question or an exclamation.

> ◻ *For Example:*
>
> It is clear that the client is not telling the entire story.
> Please tell us what you want.

2. Use a period with letters and numbers in an outline or a list.

For Example:

Outline:
  I. Introduction
      A. Introduction
      B. Body
          1. Introductory Sentence
          2. Body

Lists:
In a list, the number or letter is placed in parentheses or is followed by a
    period, but not both parentheses and a period.
(1.) Creditors
(2.) Investors
(3.) Debtors

Revisions:
(1) Creditors   1. Creditors
(2) Investors   2. Investors
(3) Debtors   3. Debtors

**3. Use a period after a heading when the heading is a complete sentence or
runs in with the text.**

For Example:

Complete sentence:
  I. The position relied on no longer represents sound public policy and
      should not be relied on.

Heading runs in with text:
  1. The prewriting stage. The prewriting stage begins with a review of the
      assignment.

4. Use a period in most abbreviations.

For Example:

Mr. for *Mister, Sept.* for *September, Co.* for *company.*

Do not add an additional period when a period in an abbreviation ends a sentence.

For Example:

The meeting will begin promptly at 8 a.m.

Abbreviations of corporations, government agencies, and scientific and technical
terms or abbreviations composed of all capital letters do not use periods unless the
initials stand for a person's name or a different style is specified.

Punctuation

> *For Example:*
>
> NASA,   DNA,   FBI,   CD-ROM,   J. R. Cavanaugh (a person's name;
> periods are used)

NOTE: For the rules governing abbreviations in conjunction with legal citation, see
Chapter 5.

4.7   QUESTION MARK (?)

A question mark is used at the end of a sentence that asks a direct question.

> *For Example:*
>
> Has the client made a follow-up appointment?
> You filed the deed even when we told you not to, didn't you?

With regard to the use of question marks, note the following guidelines:

**1. In a compound sentence, use a question mark when the ending clause is a
question.**

> *For Example:*
>
> Although we have discussed this several times, do you still maintain your
> innocence?

**2. When there are multiple endings to a question, use a question mark after
each ending word or phrase.**

> *For Example:*
>
> Is the person responsible for this the president? the secretary? the
> treasurer?

NOTE: The first word of the ending phrases (*the*) is not capitalized.

**3. Place a question mark in parentheses following a term (usually a number
or date) to indicate uncertainty.**

> *For Example:*
>
> Mr. Hanmond left his hometown in 1988 (?) and moved to New Orleans.
> It appears that only one state, Mississippi (?), has adopted this position.

⬥ 4.8 EXCLAMATION POINT (!)

An exclamation point is used to indicate the end of a sentence that expresses emotion or that deserves special emphasis.

NOTE: Exclamation points are rarely used in legal writing unless they are part of a quote. Keep in mind the following when using exclamation marks.

1. Use an exclamation point to express a demand or to show surprise, or emotion.

> ◻ *For Example:*
>
> Hurry up! He's coming!
> Come here right now!
> You must pay me immediately!

2. Use an exclamation point to emphasize an interjection or a command.

> ◻ *For Example:*
>
> No! Don't touch that!
> Oh my goodness! How could I have done that?

⬥ 4.9 ELLIPSES (. . .)

The function of an ellipsis (three spaced dots) is to indicate the omission of part of a quotation.

> ◻ *For Example:*
>
> The statute provides that skiers are "responsible for . . . snow and ice
>   conditions . . . ."

Note the following rules with regard to the use of ellipses:

1. When the omission occurs inside a quotation, use three ellipsis dots. Use a hard space after the last quoted word, between each ellipsis dot, and before the next quoted word.

> ◻ *For Example:*
>
> When I went on my trip, I first went to the tower . . . and saw the mountains
>   on the horizon.

Retain any punctuation that appears before or after the omitted material when it is grammatically necessary for the restructured sentence.

> ◘ *For Example:*
>
> When I went on the tour of the villa, . . . we also visited the famous gardens.

2. **When the end of a quoted sentence is omitted, add a period for the punctuation to end the sentence.** Follow the last word with a space, the three ellipsis dots, and a period. Place a hard space between each dot and the period.

> ◘ *For Example:*
>
> The statute requires that "the majority shareholder must refrain from engaging in oppressive conduct . . . ."

3. **When the omission is at the beginning of a quote, do not use an ellipsis.** In legal writing the bracketed first letter signals that the beginning of the quote has been left out.

> ◘ *For Example:*
>
> In this case, the court stated that ". . . the act does not require specific intent."
>
> **Revision:**
> In this case, the court stated that "[t]he act does not require specific intent."

4. **When the quote is a phrase or clause, do not use an ellipsis.**

> ◘ *For Example:*
>
> The state must establish ". . . specific intent."
>
> **Revision:**
> The state must establish "specific intent."

4.10   BRACKETS ([ ])

Brackets usually perform two separate functions:

▶ to show changes in, to comment on, or to add information to quotations, usually for the purpose of providing clarification to the quotation
▶ to indicate an error in the original quotation

To show changes in a quotation:
"The privilege [against self-incrimination] allows an individual to remain silent."

To show omissions or substitutions of characters in words:
The charter allows "the shareholder[s] to take action against the director."

To add an editorial comment:
"The charter authorizes [it does not require] the director to seek additional contributions from the shareholders."

To indicate an error in the original quoted material:
"The bord [sic] of directors voted against the proposal."

NOTE: Place *sic* in brackets following the error to indicate an error in the original quote.

In legal writing, do not use brackets to indicate parentheses that fall within parentheses.

■ *For Example:*

(When the annual meeting was held [June of 2004], it was decided to call for a vote of the members.)

Revision:
(When the annual meeting was held (June of 2004), it was decided to call for a vote of the members.)

4.11   PARENTHESES ( )

Use parentheses to add additional information to a sentence that is outside the main idea of the sentence or that is of lesser importance. The use of parentheses in legal citations is discussed in Chapter 5.

1. Set off nonessential material, such as a reference or comment, with parentheses.

■ *For Example:*

The cost of the paper (only $2) was not included in the invoice.
He purchased the bottle (the last one on the shelf) from the display next to the dairy case.

2. Set off letters and numbers that are part of a list.

> **□ *For Example:***
>
> The clerk noted that the following steps must be taken: (1) a filing fee must be paid, (2) three copies must be submitted for filing, and (3) an affidavit of the petitioner must accompany the original.
> The clerk noted that the following steps must be taken:
>
> (1) A filing fee must be paid,
> (2) Three copies must be submitted for filing, and
> (3) An affidavit of the petitioner must accompany the original.

3. Use parentheses to identify a quick reference to a longer name.

> **□ *For Example:***
>
> The Jason, Thurman, and Bailey Co. (the Company) is a party to the litigation.
> The Denton Gardner Reflex Test (DGR) is commonly accepted in the scientific community.

4. Use parentheses when referring the reader to other cases, attached material, or an appendix or when providing summary information following a case citation.

> **□ *For Example:***
>
> **Reference to an appendix:**
> (See Appendix A.)
>
> **Reference to other cases:**
> See also *Smith v. Jones,* 981 N.E.2d 441 (N. Wash. 1993) (where the court required specific intent in a similar situation).

5. When the parentheses is at the end of the sentence, place the punctuation outside the closing parenthesis unless the entire sentence is in parentheses.

> **□ *For Example:***
>
> The meeting was held on Tuesday morning (as scheduled).
> The chairman of the board has been with the company for five years. (He was elected in 2000.)

4.12   HYPHEN (-)

A hyphen is used to form compound modifiers and compound nouns. Consult a recently published dictionary when in doubt about whether a word should be hyphenated because this is an area of the English language that frequently changes.

Hyphens are also used to divide a word at the end of a line. Following are some guidelines for the use of hyphens.

1. **Use a hyphen when a compound adjective comes before the noun it modifies.** A compound adjective is two or more words that function as an adjective.

> ■ *For Example:*
>
> The first-year student was the one we employed.
> The government-sponsored programs were being eliminated.
> He is a well-known personality.

When the compound adjective follows the noun it modifies, do not hyphenate it unless it is a standard phrase that is usually hyphenated, such as *drug-free*.

> ■ *For Example:*
>
> The programs being eliminated were those that were government sponsored.
> He is a person who is well known in the community.

Do not hyphenate a compound adjective formed with an adverb that ends in *-ly*.

> ■ *For Example:*
>
> A badly managed company will not survive in this environment.

2. **When a proper noun is used as an adjective, do not use a hyphen.**

> ■ *For Example:*
>
> He is a Nobel Prize winning author. (*Nobel Prize* is not hyphenated.)

3. **Use a hyphen between a prefix of a proper noun or an adjective.**

> ■ *For Example:*
>
> pre-Columbian; anti-American; mid-April

4. **A hyphen is usually required after the following prefixes:** *all-, ex-, half-, self-, quasi-, quarter-.*

> ■ *For Example:*
>
> ex-president; quasi-contract; self-executing

5. **When it is necessary to break a word at the end of a line, place the hyphen between two syllables of the word.** Consult a dictionary if necessary. Never divide a word at the end of a page.

> 🔲 *For Example:*
>
> The partners determined that they did not have a sufficient num-
> ber of claimants to form a class action.

6. Refer to Chapter 2 for using hyphens with numbers and for forming the plural of hyphenated words.

4.13   DASH (—)

A dash is often referred to as an em dash or a long dash. Use a dash in the following situations:

- ▶ to emphasize something
- ▶ to set off lists or to briefly summarize material containing commas
- ▶ to show an abrupt change of thought or direction

> 🔲 *For Example:*
>
> **To emphasize:**
> The child—only eight years old—was clearly not capable of understanding what he was doing.
>
> **To set off a list:**
> The items located at the scene—the knife, the drugs, and the scarf—have disappeared from the evidence room.
>
> **To show a sudden break:**
> Basel Corporation—primarily known for its herbs—is involved in the manufacture of glassware.

4.14   SLASH (/)

A slash is not frequently used in legal writing. Note the following when using slashes.

1. Use a slash to separate one option from another or to indicate alternatives.

> 🔲 *For Example:*
>
> The either/or option is not acceptable.
> The course was offered on a pass/fail basis.
> Ms. Darling was the writer/producer.

2. Use a slash when writing dates informally.

3. Use a slash to separate line breaks in poetry.

4. Refer to Chapter 2 for the use of a slash with numbers.

Chapter 5

Legal Citation

Contents

5.1 INTRODUCTION

5.1 A   IN GENERAL

Whenever a reference is made in legal writing to the law (primary authority) or to a non-law source a court may rely on (secondary authority), the source of the reference should be identified. The writer cannot simply say, "This is what the law provides" without referencing the legal authority that supports the statement. Thus, when an argument is made that a certain legal principle governs a particular set of facts or a legal question, a reference must be made to the source of the principle. That reference is called a citation.

A **citation** provides the information necessary for the reader to locate the reference (i.e., the specific statute, court opinion, law review, encyclopedia, and so on), thus allowing the reader to check the content of the reference. Citations are usually required in case citations, office legal memorandums, court briefs, and scholarly writings such as law review articles. They also may be included in general legal correspondence or other documents when there is reference to legal authority.

The information included in a citation must be correct. It is useless to refer a reader to a source of information and incorrectly identify the location of the source.

The writer's research and analysis skills may become suspect when research sources are not properly presented. One's professional reputation is often determined by the quality of his or her work product.

5.1 B   THE *BLUEBOOK* AND THE *ALWD CITATION MANUAL*

Unfortunately, there is no single standard set of rules governing citation form adopted by the jurisdictions in the United States. The main guide and source of authority on legal citations for the past 75 years is *The Bluebook: A Uniform System of Citation (Bluebook)* published by the Harvard Law Review Association. It presents the rules and proper format for citing constitutions; statutes; regulations; rules; cases; and other legal sources, such as legal encyclopedias, law reviews, and so on. Some states have adopted the *Bluebook* in whole or in part as the official citation reference for pleadings and papers filed in the state courts. Many states have adopted at least some citation rules that differ from the *Bluebook,* especially in the area of citation to state court opinions and statutes. *Therefore, it is necessary to check the state rules whenever preparing a document to be submitted to a court or for an in-state legal publication.*

As an alternative to the *Bluebook,* the Association of Legal Writing Directors created the *ALWD Citation Manual: A Professional System of Citation (ALWD).* The Association's members are professors from almost all of the American law schools. The *ALWD* manual was drafted by an authority on American legal citation, Professor and Associate Dean Darby Dickerson of the Stetson University College of Law. Aspen Publishers published the first edition in 2000. The manual is designed to be easy to understand and to use because it provides a single set of rules for all forms of legal writing.

Inasmuch as the *Bluebook* is composed of 392 pages and the *ALWD,* second edition, 491 pages, a detailed discussion of the citation rules of either text is beyond the scope of this chapter. The following discussion presents a brief review of the main rules of citation with references to both the *ALWD* and the *Bluebook.* The goal of the chapter is to provide you with quick access to the main rules of citation in both authorities. The discussion and examples are based on *The Bluebook: A Uniform System of Citation* (17th ed. © 2000) and the *ALWD Citation Manual: A Professional System of Citation,* (2nd ed. © 2003). The format of both texts begins with an introduction followed by the general/basic rules of citation, then citation to primary sources (cases, constitutions, and statutes) and secondary sources. Since most researchers are concerned with the citation rules for primary and secondary authority, the chapter presents those rules first, followed by the general rules of citation.

In the *Bluebook,* there are some differences between the citation format used when citing authorities in court documents and legal memorandums and the citation format used in scholarly pieces such as law review articles. Most of the differences involve the use of typefaces. In the *ALWD,* the same format is used for all types of documents. The type of formal legal writing usually engaged in by practitioners, law students, and paralegals involves court documents and legal memorandums, rather than law review articles. Therefore, this chapter focuses on the citation format used in court documents and legal memorandums and the examples are to citation forms used in those types of legal writing.

Most of the examples provided in the white pages of the *Bluebook* are for citation when writing a law review. The first section of light blue pages in the *Bluebook,* called "Practitioner's Notes," provide guidance on how to adapt the examples found throughout the body of the *Bluebook* to the drafting of legal memorandums and court documents. There are cross-references to the Practitioner's Notes in the margins of the *Bluebook* rules and tables. Also at the end of the *Bluebook* is a "Quick Reference" section that provides examples of citation forms commonly used in court documents and legal memorandums.

5.2 PRIMARY AUTHORITY

This section presents an overview of rules of citation to be used when citing primary authority; that is case, constitutional, and enacted (statutory) law. The citation format for rules such as procedural and evidentiary rules are also included in this section. The examples are to citation forms used in court documents and legal memorandums rather than law review articles. See Exhibit 5-1 for a chart listing the primary authority sources and the citation rule references.

The rules discussed in this section and the following sections are referenced as follows: references to *The Bluebook: A Uniform System of Citation* are Bluebook R ___ (Rule Number) or Bluebook P___ (Practitioner's Notes Number); references to the *ALWD Citation Manual: A Professional System of Citation* are ALWD-___(Rule Number).

> **For Example:**
>
> Bluebook R-2 refers to Rule 2 of the *Bluebook*. Bluebook P1 refers to number 1 of the *Bluebook*'s Practitioner's Notes. ALWD 1 refers to rule 1 of the *ALWD Citation Manual: A Professional System of Citation.*

The general rules governing each type of primary authority are listed following the section/subsection title. A detailed discussion of each rule is beyond the scope of this text.

Note that although most of the citation conventions are the same in both manuals, there are differences between the Bluebook *and the* ALWD. *Do not assume that you can substitute one for the other. Always check the rules when preparing these citations.*

When the citation rules of the jurisdiction where you are filing a brief or another court document require the use of the *Bluebook,* you must cite according to the *Bluebook* rules. Do not substitute the *ALWD* format if it differs from that of the *Bluebook.*

5.2 A   CASE LAW—BLUEBOOK R-10 & P1; ALWD-12

The following is a list of the components of case citations with examples and a summary of the applicable rules. Citations to federal and state cases are similar in form.

1. Citation Components—BLUEBOOK R-10.1; ALWD-12.1   The components of a case citation are as follows:

1. the case name
2. the reporter in which the case is published (the volume number, abbreviation of the reporter, and page number where the case begins)
3. pinpoint page when the citation is to a specific page
4. the parallel (unofficial) publication, if any (the volume number, abbreviation of the publication, and page number where the case begins)
5. the abbreviation for the court issuing the opinion, unless the issuing court is included in the reporter abbreviation
6. the year of the decision in parenthesis
7. subsequent history of the case, if any.

Some examples are presented first with a ^ symbol indicating where spaces are placed, followed by the example without the space symbol.

📖 *For Example:*

Federal Court Decisions

United States Supreme Court
United ^ States ^ v.^ Matlock, ^ 415 ^ U.S.^ 164 ^ (1974)
United States v. Matlock, 415 U.S. 164 (1974)

1. *United States v. Matlock*—case name
2. **415 U.S. 164**—the reporter in which the case is published: 415 is the volume number, 164 is the page number, and *U.S.* is the abbreviation of the case reporter.
3. No parallel publication is included in this citation.
4. The court issuing the opinion is not identified because it is apparent from the citation. U.S. Reports contains the opinions of the United States Supreme Court. Notice that in the next two examples, the identity of the court issuing the opinion is included—9th Cir. and N.D. Ill.
5. **1974**—the year of the decision

United States Court of Appeals
United ^ States ^ v. ^ Martinez-Jiminez, ^ 864 ^ F.2d ^ 664 ^ (9th Cir.^1989)
United States v. Martinez-Jiminez, 864 F.2d 664 (9th Cir. 1989)

United States District Court
*United ^ States ^ v.^ Central ^ R.R.,^ 436^ F.^ Supp.^ 739 ^ (N.D.^
   Ill.^1990)*
United States v. Central R.R., 436 F. Supp. 739 (N.D. Ill. 1990)

State Court Decisions
Britton ^ v.^ Britton, ^ 100 ^ N.M.^ 424,^ 671^ P.2d ^1135 ^ (1983)
Britton v. Britton, 100 N.M. 424, 671 P.2d 1135 (1983)
Burnon^ v.^ State,^ 55 ^S.W.3d ^752^ (Tex.^ Crim.^ App.^ 2001)
Burnon v. State, 55 S.W.3d 752 (Tex. Crim. App. 2001)

1. ***Britton v. Britton*** and ***Burnon v. State***—case names
2. **100 N.M. 424**—the state reporter in which the case is published: 100 is
   the volume number, 424 is the page number, and N.M. is the abbreviation
   of the case reporter; **55 S.W.3d 752**—the regional reporter where the
   Texas cases are published. Texas does not have a state reporter; therefore;
   there is no parallel citation.
3. **671 P.2d 1135**—the parallel (unofficial) publication: 671 is the volume
   number, 1135 is the page number, and P.2d is the abbreviation of the
   parallel publication.
4. The New Mexico court issuing the opinion is not identified because it is
   apparent from the citation. The decision was rendered by the New
   Mexico Supreme Court. If a court other than the New Mexico Supreme
   Court issued the decision, the initials of the court would be included
   with the year of the opinion; i.e., (Ct. App. 1983); **Tex. Crim. App.**—
   the Texas court that rendered the decision.
5. **1983 and 2001**—the year of the decisions

2. **Case Names—BLUEBOOK R-10.2; ALWD-12.2**   The *Bluebook* rules for ab-
   breviating case names have many more exceptions than the *ALWD* does.
   But both books have numerous detailed rules governing case names. Always check the rules when preparing case citations. Following is a summary of the rules on case names. The case names may be italicized or underlined. The names are italicized in most of the examples in this chapter.
   (The *ALWD* provides that case names be printed the same in court and other
   documents).
   a. *Individual Names*—Cite the last names of the individuals, not the first names.

For Example:

Correct:
Clothier v. Guillez
Clothier v. Guillez

Incorrect:
Daniel J. Clothier v. Mary Guillez

b. *Organization and Business Names*—Include an organization's full name. When a business has more than one legal designation (e.g., *Co., Ltd. Corp., Inc.*), use the first designation and omit the others.

> **For Example:**
>
> **Correct:**
> *Clothier v. David Johnson Packing Co.*
>
> **Incorrect:**
> *Clothier v. Johnson*
>
> **Correct:**
> *Davis v. Sally Smits Co.*
>
> **Incorrect:**
> *Davis v. Sally Smits Co., Inc.*

When an organization or a business is commonly known by its initials, you may substitute the initials for the name. Do not use periods with the initials.

> **For Example:**
>
> **Correct:**
> *ACLU v. Houseman*
>
> **Incorrect:**
> *A.C.L.U. v. Houseman*

c. *Abbreviations*—The abbreviations to be used in party names are presented in Table T.6 of the *Bluebook* and in Appendix 3 of the *ALWD*. Do not abbreviate names that are not listed.

> **For Example:**
>
> Corporation—Corp.; Market—Mkt.

d. *Multiple Parties*—When there are multiple plaintiffs or defendants, include only the first party on each side of the case. Do not use *et al.* or *et ux.* to indicate additional parties.

> **For Example:**
>
> **Correct:**
> *Pugh v. Holmes*
>
> **Incorrect:**
> *Pugh, Smith, Reasoner v. Holmes, Taylor, Johnson*
>
> **Incorrect:**
> *Pugh, et al. v. Holmes, et al.*

e. *Consolidated Cases*—When the case consists of more than one case consolidated together, list only the first case.

For Example:

Correct:
Davis v. Outland

Incorrect:
Davis v. Outland, McCray v. Whensal

f. *United States*—When the United States is a party, both the *Bluebook* and the *ALWD* provide that *America* be omitted. The *Bluebook* requires that *United States* be spelled out. The *ALWD* provides that it be abbreviated.

For Example:

Bluebook: United States v. Leon
ALWD: U.S. v Leon

g. *State or Commonwealth*—When citing a decision of a court of your state where the state or commonwealth is a party, refer only to the state, commonwealth, or people. Do not refer to the state, for example, as "State of Colorado" or "Commonwealth of Massachusetts."

For Example:

Correct:
State v. Benner

Incorrect:
State of Maine v. Benner

Correct:
Commonwealth v. Shae

Incorrect:
Commonwealth of Massachusetts v. Shae

If you are referring to the decision of another state where the state or commonwealth is a party, refer to the party by state name and do not include *State of* or *Commonwealth of.*

For Example:

Correct:
Maine v. Benner

Incorrect:
State v. Benner

> **Correct:**
> *Massachusetts v. Shae*
>
> **Incorrect:**
> *Commonwealth of Massachusetts v. Shae*

   h. *Geographical Terms*—Include in the citation only the first geographical location in a party's name.

> ▢ *For Example:*
> **Correct:**
> *Smith v. City of Boston*
>
> **Incorrect:**
> *Smith v. City of Boston, Massachusetts*
>
> **Correct:**
> *Smith v. County Commission*
>
> **Incorrect:**
> *Smith v. County Commission of Johnson County*

   i. *Procedural Phrases—In Re, Ex Parte, and Ex Rel.*—*In re* refers to an action that does not involve adversarial parties but something such as an estate. *Ex parte* refers to an action on behalf of one party without contest by the other side, such as a divorce where one party does not participate. *Ex rel.* refers to an action by one person on behalf of another, such as a parent on behalf of a child. When using *ex rel.,* include the names of both parties. These phrases are included when they appear in case names.

> ▢ *For Example:*
> *In re Estate of Jones; Ex Parte Turner; New York ex rel. Smith v. Hardworth; Johnson ex rel. Casey v. Carrington.*

   j. *The*—Do not include *The* in a citation when it is the first word of a party name.

> ▢ *For Example:*
> **Correct:**
> *Los Angeles Times v. Jones*
>
> **Incorrect:**
> *The Los Angeles Times v. Jones*

   k. *Property*—When property is a party, such as when the government is seizing property, include only the first listed piece of property.

> **For Example:**
>
> **Correct:**
> *Maine v. One 1998 Cadillac Seville*
>
> **Incorrect:**
> *Maine v. One 1998 Cadillac Seville, Serial No. 134998 and One 2001 Toyota Corolla, Serial No. 77564432.*

    l. *Punctuation*—The case name is followed by a comma (then the reporter information); the comma is not italicized or underlined.

> **For Example:**
>
> **Correct:**
> *Smith v. Jones,* or <u>Smith v. Jones,</u>
>
> **Incorrect:**
> *Smith v. Jones,* or <u>Smith v. Jones,</u>

    m. *Citations as Part of a Sentence*—See "Authorities Included in the Text of a Sentence" in Subsection 5.4 D.2.

3. Volume, Reporter, and Page—BLUEBOOK R-10.3; ALWD-12.3 to 12.5 Following the case name in a citation is the reference to the reporter where the case is printed. This reference includes the volume number of the reporter and the page where the case begins. The volume number precedes the abbreviation for the reporter, which is followed by the page of the case. The following is a summary of the rules governing citation to reporters. Note that local court rules may require differences in citation; therefore, always check the rules.

    a. *Abbreviations*—Do not assume you know the abbreviations for the various reporters. Consult either *Bluebook* Table T.1 or the *ALWD* Chart 12.1 and Appendix 2. Also, refer to the general rules governing abbreviations presented in Section 5.4 D.

    b. *Spacing*—Refer to the general rules governing spacing presented in Subsection 5.4 D.2 "Spacing."

    c. *United States Supreme Court*—Unless required by local rule, citation to decisions of the United States Supreme Court should be to the official reporter only, the *United States Reports.* A parallel citation to another reporter, such as the *Supreme Court Reporter* or the *United States Supreme Court Reports, Lawyers' Edition,* should not be included.

> **For Example:**
>
> **Correct:**
> *United States v. Matlock,* 415 U.S. 164 (1974).

> **Incorrect:**
> *United States v. Matlock,* 415 U.S. 164, 94 S. Ct. 988, 39 L. Ed. 2d 242
>   (1974). (Note that this citation would be correct if the court rule re-
>   quired or allowed parallel citations.)

If the *United States Reports* citation is not available, you may site to another reporter, such as the *Supreme Court Reporter* (S. Ct.). The order of preference is to cite to the *Supreme Court Reporter* and if it is not available, then to the *United States Supreme Court Reports, Lawyers' Edition.*

> ■ *For Example:*
>
> If the opinion in the previous example was not yet available in the *United States Reports,* a proper citation would be *United States v. Matlock,* __U.S.__, 94 S. Ct. 988, (1974).

    d. *United States Court of Appeals*—Decisions to the United States Court of Appeals are cited to the *Federal Reporter.* Note that the circuit that rendered the decision is included in the citation in parentheses.

> ■ *For Example:*
>
> *United States v. Martinez-Jiminez,* 864 F.2d 664 (9th Cir. 1989).

    e. *United States District Courts*—Decisions to the United States district courts are cited to the *Federal Supplement.* Note that the district that rendered the decision is included in the citation in parentheses.

> ■ *For Example:*
>
> *United States v. Central R.R.,* 436 F. Supp. 739 (N.D. Ill. 1990).

    f. *State Court and Parallel Citations*—The format and abbreviations for citing state court decisions are presented in Table T.1 in the *Bluebook* and Appendix 1 in the *ALWD.* Again, be sure to check local rules. The general rule for state court decisions is to cite to the relevant regional reporter.

> ■ *For Example:*
>
> *Guilbear v. Guilbear,* 326 So.2d 654 (La. App. 1976).

Many state court decisions are published in a regional reporter and a state reporter. When a citation includes a reference to more than one reporter, it is called a parallel citation. Generally, a parallel citation is used only when it involves a citation to a state court case in a document submitted to a court in that state. Check the state court citation rules to determine when parallel citations are required.

When a parallel citation is required, cite the official reporter before the unofficial reporter and separate each citation with a comma and one space.

For Example:

Race Fork Coal v. Turner, 5 Va. App. 350, 363 S.E.2d 423 (1985).

g. *Page Numbers*—The page number on which the case begins follows the reporter abbreviation. When the reference is to a specific page within the case, the reference to the specific page (pinpoint citations) follows the initial page reference. See Section 5.4 G "Page Numbers (Pinpoint Citations)."

For Example:

Guilbear v. Guilbear, 326 So.2d 654, 658 (La. App. 1976).
Race Fork Coal v. Turner, 5 Va. App. 350, 352, 363 S.E.2d 423, 425
    (1985). (Note that in the second example, the pinpoint citation is
    included with both the state and the parallel regional reporter citations.)

Some of the West reporters, such as the *Supreme Court Reports,* include throughout the text of reported cases cross-references to the pages in the official reporter. This cross-reference system is called **star paging.** It saves you the time of looking up a case in more than one reporter when citing page numbers in parallel citations. The cross-reference appears as an upside-down T with the page number ($\perp$234) and is inserted in the text to indicate the beginning of a page in an official reporter.

For Example:

Thus, the tolling provision does $\perp$234 not apply, and count two is subject to
    the two-year statute of limitations and was properly dismissed. (Page
    234 of the official reporter begins with *not apply.*)

h. *Cases Not Yet Reported–Slip Opinions*—A case may be unreported or not yet published in a reporter and may be available only as a separate slip opinion or in looseleaf form. In this situation, the citation should include the case name, docket number, court abbreviation, and date of disposition.

For Example:

Jason v. Kelly, No. 22-231 (Colo. App. Aug. 15, 2002).

4. **Date and Court Abbreviation—BLUEBOOK R-10.4 & R-10.5; ALWD-12.5 & 12.6** In parentheses following the reporter and page citation are the court abbreviation (if necessary) and the date on which the case was decided. If the decision is by the United States Supreme Court or highest court of a state, you do not have to insert the court abbreviation. The date appears alone in parentheses. The fact that only the date appears in parentheses tells the reader it is the highest court. The information in parentheses is separated from the reporter page by a space. There is no comma.

> **□ *For Example:***
>
> *United States v. Matlock,* 415 U.S. 164 (1974);
> *Kline v. Angle,* 216 Kan. 328, 532 P.2d 1093 (1975).

For any other court decision, include the court abbreviation. The abbreviations are in Tables T.1, T.7, and T.11 in the *Bluebook* and in Appendices 1 and 4 in the *ALWD.*

> **□ *For Example:***
>
> *United States v. Central R.R.,* 436 F. Supp. 739 (N.D. Ill. 1990);
> *Burnon v. State,* 55 S.W.3d 752 (Tex. Crim. App. 2001).

The court abbreviation is not required when the court that decided the case is apparent from the name of the reporter.

> **□ *For Example:***
>
> *Race Fork Coal v. Turner,* 5 Va. App. 350, 353, 363 S.E.2d 423, 425
> (1985). (It is apparent from the citation (Va. App.) that the court is the
> Virginia Court of Appeals.)

5. **Subsequent History—BLUEBOOK R-10.7; ALWD-12.8**   The *Bluebook* and the *ALWD* provide that the subsequent history should be included in the citation unless it refers to the history on remand, a denial of rehearing, or a denial of certiorari or similar discretionary appeals (where the cited case is more than two years old). The *ALWD* Rule 12.8(a) includes an exhaustive list of subsequent history actions that should be included. The subsequent history is placed after the full citation. Place a comma after the court and date parenthetical, and the italicized history designation, followed by the citation.

> **□ *For Example:***
>
> *Jackson v. State,* 225 Ga. 790, 167 S.E.2d 628 (1969), *rev'd, Furman v.*
> *Georgia,* 408 U.S. 238 (1972).

6. **Prior History—BLUEBOOK R-10.7; ALWD-12.9**   The prior history of a case is not required and should be included in a citation only when it is significant to a point presented in your writing. Place the prior history after the full citation.

> **□ *For Example:***
>
> *Furman v. Georgia,* 408 U.S. 238 (1972), *rev'g, Jackson v. State,* 225 Ga.
> 790, 167 S.E.2d 628 (1969).

7. **Parenthetical Information—Concurring, Dissenting, and Plurality Opinion—BLUEBOOK R-10.6; ALWD-12.11**   When the reference in your writing is to a part of an opinion other than the majority opinion, you must indicate this fact

in a parenthetical following the full citation. You may also include parenthetically information about the weight of the case, such as the size of the majority. Insert one space, without a comma, between the court and date parenthetical of the full citation and the parenthetical containing the additional information. When the information in the parenthetical is not a full sentence, do not include final punctuation, such as a period in the parenthetical.

> ◘ *For Example:*
>
> *United States v. Leon,* 468 U.S. 897 (1984) (Powell, J., dissenting); *United States v. Leon,* 468 U.S. 897 (1984) (5-4 decision).

8. **Short Citation Format—BLUEBOOK P4; ALWD-12.21**   Once a case has been cited in full, several short citation formats may be used depending on the situation. Do not include subsequent or prior history with a short citation. When the use of *id.* is appropriate (see "*Id.* as a Short Citation" in Section 5.4 I), it is the preferred short citation format.

> ◘ *For Example:*
>
> *Id.* at 755.

   When *id.* cannot be used and the case name or part of the case name is *not* included in the sentence, use one party's name, the volume number, reporter, and page reference. Use the first party's name unless it would be confusing.

> ◘ *For Example:*
>
> **Full Citation:**
> *Burnon v. State,* 55 S.W.3d 752 (Tex. Crim. App. 2001).
>
> **Short Citation:**
> *Burnon,* 55 S.W.3d at 755.

   When making a reference to the case in general rather than to a specific page, do not use *at.*

> ◘ *For Example:*
>
> **Full Citation:**
> *Burnon v. State,* 55 S.W.3d 752 (Tex. Crim. App. 2001).
>
> **Short Citation:**
> *Burnon,* 55 S.W.3d 752.

   When the case name or part of the case name *is* included in the sentence, use only the volume number, reporter, and page reference.

> ▫ *For Example:*
>
> In *Burnon,* the court held that the defendant had the required intent. 55 S.W.3d at 755 (or 55 S.W.3d 752 if the reference is to the case in general).

If the case has a parallel citation, the short citation includes the parallel citations.

> ▫ *For Example:*
>
> **Full Citation:**
> *Race Fork Coal v. Turner,* 5 Va. App. 350, 363 S.E.2d 423 (1985).
>
> **Short Citation:**
> *Race Fork Coal,* 5 Va. App. at 355, 363 S.E.2d at 427. The *ALWD* also allows reference to the regional reporter only—*Race Fork Coal,* 363 S.E.2d at 427.

The *Bluebook* Practitioner's Notes P.4 allows the use of *id.* as a short form with parallel citations. The *ALWD* Rule 12.21(f) states that the use of *id.* is not appropriate with parallel citations.

> ▫ *For Example:*
>
> **Full Citation:**
> *Race Fork Coal v. Turner,* 5 Va. App. 350, 363 S.E.2d 423 (1985).
>
> **Short Citation:**
> *Bluebook: Id.* at 355, 363 S.E.2d at 427.

9. **Neutral/Public Domain Citations—BLUEBOOK R-10.3.3; ALWD-12.16**   More court decisions are now available through court Web sites or other sources as public domain citations (also referred to as neutral or vendor neutral citations). These citations do not refer to a particular vendor source, such as a West Group reporter. When such citations are available in a jurisdiction, you must check the local rule to determine what the citation format is and whether the neutral citation is required. See Table T.1 in the *Bluebook* and Appendix 2 in the *ALWD.* The standard neutral citation includes the case name, year of the decision, court abbreviation, case number, and citation to a reporter or an online source.

> ▫ *For Example:*
>
> *State v. Foster,* 1998-NMCA-163, 976 P.2d 852. (The year published is 1998. NMCA is the court—the New Mexico Court of Appeals. The last number, 163, is the case number. The reporter citation is 976 P.2d 852.)

10. **Cases—Electronic Sources**   See Section 5.4 M "Electronic Sources" for citations to electronic sources.

5.2 B   CONSTITUTIONS—BLUEBOOK R-11; ALWD-13

Constitutions are usually composed of articles and amendments. According to the *Bluebook,* the citation form for a constitution consists of the abbreviated name of the constitution, the article or amendment number, and the section number. The *ALWD* requires the abbreviated name of the constitution and a pinpoint reference. (The pinpoint reference is the article or amendment number and the section number.) Regardless of these descriptive differences, the citation format is the same in both the *Bluebook* and the *ALWD*. The *Bluebook* provides that constitutional subdivisions be abbreviated according to Table T.17; the *ALWD* provides that the jurisdictional and subdivision abbreviations in Appendix 3 be used. Each example is presented first with a ^ symbol indicating where spaces are placed, followed by the example without the space symbol.

> **For Example:**
>
> U.S.^ Const.^ art. ^ IV, ^ § ^ 3
> U.S. Const. art. IV, § 3
> Conn.^ Const. ^ art. ^ XII,^ § ^ 1
> Conn. Const. art. XII, § 1
>
> In these examples, the elements of the citation are as follows:
>
> 1. **U.S. Const.—Conn. Const.** the abbreviated name
> 2. **art. IV—art. XII** the article number
> 3. **§ 3—§ 1** the section number (pinpoint reference)

Include in parentheses information about an article or amendment when the provision has been repealed or superceded.

> **For Example:**
>
> U.S. Const. amend XVIII (repealed 1933 by U.S. Const. amend. XXI).

The only short-form citation appropriate for use with constitutional citations is *id.* When the use of *id.* is not appropriate (see "*Id.* as a Short Citation" in Section 5.4 I), the full citation must be given.

5.2 C   STATUTORY LAW—BLUEBOOK R-12 & P5; ALWD-14

Statutes may be cited to the official or unofficial code, session law, or secondary sources. The preference is to cite to the official code and then the unofficial code when the citation is not available in the official code and when the citation is not available in the official or unofficial codes, then to the session law. The abbreviations and formats for codes and session laws are presented in Table T.1 in the *Bluebook* and in Appendix 1 in the *ALWD*.

1. **General Rules When Citing Statutes**   The following rules apply when citing both federal and state statutes
   a. *Main Text and Supplements*—When the cited material is taken from the main text, the year of the volume of the text is placed in parentheses at the end of the citation (the year the volume was published, usually appearing on the spine of the volume). When the cited material appears only in the supplement, you must indicate that fact in parentheses with the date. When the cited material is taken from the main text and the supplement, indicate the date.

> *For Example:*
>
> **Citation from main text:**
> 15 U.S.C. § 7 (1988).
>
> **Citation from supplement only:**
> 15 U.S.C. § 7 (Supp. 2002).
>
> **Citation from main text and supplement:**
> 15 U.S.C. § 7 (1988 & Supp. 2002).
>
> **Citation from main text and supplement, unofficial commercial publisher:**
> 15 U.S.C.A. § 7 (West 1984 & Supp. 2002).

   b. *Section Symbol (§) and Multiple Sections*—The section symbol (§) is used to indicate a section of a statute. Note, however, that you may not use the symbol to start a sentence. In such cases, the word *section* is used.

> *For Example:*
>
> **Correct:**
> Section 2253 of the Act provides . . .
>
> **Incorrect:**
> § 2253 of the Act provides . . .

   Refer to Section 5.4 L "Sections and Paragraphs" for the rules on citing multiple sections.
   c. *Name of Act*—Although it is not required, the name of the act may be included in the citation. In the examples in the *Bluebook,* the name of the act is in regular print. In the *ALWD,* Rule 14.2(g) provides that the name be in italics.

> *For Example:*
>
> *Bluebook:*
> Robinson-Patman Act, 15 U.S.C. § 7 (1988).
>
> *ALWD:*
> *Robinson-Patman Act, 15 U.S.C. § 7 (1988).*

2. Federal Statutes—BLUEBOOK R-12; ALWD-14.2   The federal statutes of general public interest are printed in three separate publications:
- ▶ United States Code (U.S.C.)—the official code
- ▶ United States Code Annotated (U.S.C.A.)—West Group
- ▶ United States Code Service (U.S.C.S.)—LexisNexis®

The citation format for federal statutes is composed of the following elements:

1. title number
2. code abbreviation
3. section symbol (§)
4. section number
5. publisher if it is a commercial publication—in parentheses
6. year of the publication or supplement (year the volume was published, usually appearing on the spine of the volume)—in parentheses

For Example:

Official code:
15 ^ U.S.C.^ § ^ 7 ^ (1988).
15 U.S.C. § 7 (1988).

Unofficial codes:
15 U.S.C.A. § 7 (West 1984).
15 U.S.C.S. § 7 (LexisNexis 1984).

1. **15**—title number
2. **U.S.C., U.S.C.A, and U.S.C.S.**—abbreviated name of the codes
3. **§ 7**—Section symbol and number
4. **(1988) (West 1984) (LexisNexis 1984)**—year of the publication and publisher for unofficial codes

When citing to the Internal Revenue Code, substitute I.R.C. for U.S.C. and omit the title number.

For Example:

Correct:
I.R.C. § 100 (1994).

Incorrect:
26 U.S.C. § 100 (1994).

Short Citation Format State and Federal Statutes—BLUEBOOK R-12.9; ALWD-14.5. When the use of *id.* is appropriate (see "*Id.* as a Short Citation" in Section 5.4 I), it is the preferred short citation format. Otherwise, the short citation is the full citation format without the parenthetical information.

> **For Example:**
>
> **Full Citation:**
> 15 U.S.C. § 7 (1988 & Supp. 2002); Minn. Stat. § 519 (1990).
>
> **Short Citations:**
> 15 U.S.C. § 7; *Id.* § 7; Minn. Stat. § 519; *Id.* § 519.

3. State Statutes—BLUEBOOK R-12; ALWD-14.4   The citation form for state statutes varies from state to state. The abbreviations and formats for state statutes are presented in Table T.1 in the *Bluebook* and in Appendix 1 in the *ALWD*. Also, note that some states have local citation rules that require a citation format different from that presented in the *Bluebook* and the *ALWD*. The local court rules should be consulted for the proper citation format. The local rules are included in Appendix 2 in the *ALWD*.

The citation format for state statutes usually includes the following elements:

1. name of the code
2. section symbol (§)
3 chapter/title/section number
4. publisher if it is a commercial publication—in parentheses
5. year of the publication or supplement (year the volume was published, usually appearing on the spine of the volume)—in parentheses

> **For Example:**
>
> **Official Code:**
> Minn.^ Stat.^ § ^519^ (1990).
> Minn. Stat. § 519 (1990).
>
> **Unofficial Code:**
> Minn. Stat. Ann. § 519 (West 1991).
>
> 1. **Minn. Stat.**—name of the code
> 2. **§**—section symbol
> 3. **519**—section number
> 4. **West**—the publisher of the unofficial code in the second example
> 5. **1990 and 1991**—the year of the publications in both examples

Some states, such as California, identify portions of their codes by subject matter rather than by title. For those states, the subject matter code is included in the citation.

> **For Example:**
>
> Cal. Corp. Code § 200 (West 1986); Tex. Fam. Code Ann. § 2.101
>   (Vernon 1993).

4. Session Laws—BLUEBOOK R-12.4; ALWD-14.6 to 14.8   When a citation is not available in the official or unofficial codes, it is appropriate to cite to the session law. This may occur when a recently passed law has not yet been published in the official or unofficial codes. As with state statutes, the citation form for session laws varies from state to state. The abbreviations and formats for state session laws are presented in Table T.1 in the *Bluebook* and in Appendix 1 in the *ALWD*.

The basic elements of a federal session law citation are as follows:

1. Name or title of the act—optional (In the *ALWD* example, the name/title is italicized. In the *Bluebook* Quick Reference examples, the name/title are not italicized or underlined.)
2. Law abbreviation and number
3. Pinpoint reference when citing a specific section
4. Volume, statute, and initial page number
5. Pinpoint page reference when referring to a specific page
6. Date—year (in parentheses) of the cited volume of the Statutes at Large

> ■ *For Example:*
>
> Uniformed Services Former Spouses Protection Act, Pub. L. No. 101-510, § 554, 104 Stat. 1569, 1572 (1993).
>
> 1. **Uniformed Services Former Spouses Protection Act**—name or title of the act italicized or underlined
> 2. **Pub. L. No. 101-510**—law abbreviation and number
> 3. **§ 554**—pinpoint reference to a specific section
> 4. **104 Stat. 1569**—volume, statute, and initial page number
> 5. **1572**—pinpoint page reference to a specific page
> 6. **(1993)**—date

5.2 D   RULES OF EVIDENCE AND PROCEDURE—BLUEBOOK R-12.8.3; ALWD-17

The *Bluebook* rule governing citations to evidentiary and procedural rules differs from the *ALWD* rule. The *Bluebook* provides that the citation include the abbreviated name of the rule and the number of the rule.

> ■ *For Example:*
>
> | | |
> |---|---|
> | Fed. R. Civ. P. 4 | Rule 4 of the Federal Rules of Civil Procedure |
> | Fed. R. Evid. 407 | Rule 407 of the Federal Rules of Evidence |
> | Fed. R. Crim. P. 18 | Rule 18 of the Federal Rules of Criminal Procedure |

The *ALWD* rule states that the citation should include, in addition to the abbreviated name and rule number, the name of the publisher when the source is other than an official code and the year of the publication, both in parentheses.

> ▣ *For Example:*
>
> | | |
> |---|---|
> | Fed. R. Civ. P. 4 (2001) | Rule 4 of the Federal Rules of Civil Procedure |
> | Fed. R. Evid. 407 (West 2002) | Rule 407 of the Federal Rules of Evidence, published by West Group |
> | Fed. R. Crim. P. 18 (2001) | Rule 18 of the Federal Rules of Criminal Procedure |

5.2 E   ADMINISTRATIVE LAW—BLUEBOOK R-14; ALWD-19

The components of citations to administrative rules or regulations are as follows:

1. title (topic or agency) number in the code publication
2. abbreviated name of the publication (e.g., Code of Federal Regulations—C.F.R.; Federal Register—Fed. Reg.)
3. section number or page number of the rule or regulation
4. year of the publication

> ▣ *For Example:*
>
> 27 C.F.R. § 20.235 (1988)
> 48 Fed. Reg. 37,315 (1983)
>
> 1. **27 & 48**—title (topic or agency) number
> 2. **C.F.R. & Fed. Reg.**—abbreviated name of the publication
> 3. **§ 20.235 & 37,315**—section number or page number
> 4. **1988 & 1983**—year of the publication

5.3 SECONDARY AUTHORITY

This section presents an overview of rules of citation to be used when citing secondary authority; that is, sources a court may rely on that are not the law (not primary authority). The examples are to citation forms used in court documents and legal memorandums rather than law review articles. See Exhibit 5-1 for a chart listing the secondary authority sources and the reference for citation rules.

A detailed discussion of the citation rules for each type of secondary authority is beyond the scope of this text. Therefore, this section presents the citation format

Exhibit 5-1

■ Primary and Secondary Authority Citation Rule References

Primary Authority Citation Rules

Authority	*Bluebook* Rules and Practitioner's Notes (P)	*ALWD* Rules
Case Law	Rule 10 and P.1	Rule 12
Constitutions	Rule 11	Rule 13
Statutory Law	Rule 12 and P.5	Rule 14
Rules of Evidence and Procedure	Rule 12.8.3	Rule 17
Administrative Law	Rule 14	Rule 19

Secondary Authority Citation Rules

Authority		
American Law Reports (A.L.R.)	Rule 16.6.5	Rule 24
Dictionaries	Rule 15.7	Rule 25
Legal Encyclopedias	Rule 15.7	Rule 26
Periodicals (Law Reviews, Journals and so on)	Rule 16	Rule 23
Restatements	Rule 12.8.5	Rule 27
Treatises/Books	Rule 15	Rule 22

for the most commonly used secondary authorities. As with the previous sections, *there are differences between the* Bluebook *and the* ALWD. *Do not assume that you can substitute one for the other.*

5.3 A   ANNOTATED LAW REPORTS—BLUEBOOK R-16.6.5; ALWD-24

1. **Full Citation Format**   The components of an Annotated Law Report (A.L.R.) citation are as follows:

   1. full name of the author
   2. the word *Annotation* (**Note:** The *ALWD* omits the use of *Annotation* following the author name)
   3. title (italicized or underlined)
   4. volume number
   5. abbreviated name of the publication
   6. page number where the annotation begins (followed by the pinpoint page when a specific page is referred to; e.g., 852, 860)
   7. year of publication

> 🔲 *For Example:*
>
> Michael J. Weber, Annotation, *Application of Statute of Limitations to Actions for Breach of Duty in Performing Services of Public Accountant,* 7 A.L.R.5th 852 (1992).
>
> 1. **Michael J. Weber**—full name of the author
> 2. The word *Annotation*—included when using the *Bluebook;* not included when using the *ALWD*
> 3. *Application of Statute of Limitations to Actions for Breach of Duty in Performing Services of Public Accountant*—title (italicized or underlined)
> 4. **7**—volume number
> 5. **A.L.R.5th**—abbreviated name of the publication (no spaces)
> 6. **852**—page number where the annotation begins
> 7. **1992**—year of publication

2. Short Citation Format   Use *id.* when appropriate (see "*Id.* as a Short Citation" in Section 5.4 I). When *id.* is not appropriate, include the author's last name, the volume number, the A.L.R. series, *at,* and the pinpoint reference.

> 🔲 *For Example:*
>
> *Id.* at 861; Weber, 7 A.L.R.5th at 861.

5.3 B   LEGAL DICTIONARY—BLUEBOOK R-15.7; ALWD-25

1. Full Citation Format   A legal dictionary citation should include the following:

1. author (if any)
2. full name of the dictionary (underlined or italicized)
3. page of the definition (no comma after name of the dictionary and the page)
4. editor—required only in the *ALWD* format—followed by left parenthesis
5. edition
6. publisher—required only in the *ALWD* format
7. year of publication followed by right parenthesis

> 🔲 *For Example:*
>
> **Bluebook format:**
>
> *Black's Law Dictionary* 451 (7th ed. 1992).
>
> 1. *Black's Law Dictionary*—full name of dictionary (in italics or underlined)
> 2. **451**—page of the definition
> 3. **7th ed. 1992**—edition and year of publication

> **ALWD format:**
> *Black's Law Dictionary* 451 (Bryan A. Garner ed., 7th ed., West 1992).
>
> 1. ***Black's Law Dictionary***—full name of dictionary (in italics or underlined)
> 2. **451**—page of the definition
> 3. **Bryan A. Garner ed.**—name of editor
> 4. **7th ed.**—edition
> 5. **West**—publisher
> 6. **1992**—year of publication

2. Short Citation Format   Use *id.* when appropriate (see "*Id.* as a Short Citation" in Section 5.4 I). When *id.* is not appropriate, repeat the name and the page number.

> ◘ *For Example:*
>
> *Id.* at 451; *Black's Law Dictionary* at 451.

5.3 C   LEGAL ENCYCLOPEDIA—BLUEBOOK R-15.7; ALWD-26

1. Full Citation Format   A full citation to a legal encyclopedia should contain the following:

1. volume number of the encyclopedia
2. abbreviated name of the encyclopedia, usually either Am. Jur. 2d or C.J.S. (no underlining or italics)
3. title or topic name (italicized or underlined)
4. section symbol (§) and section number within the article
5. year of publication in parentheses

> ◘ *For Example:*
>
> 88 C.J.S. *Trial* § 105 (1980).
> 59A Am. Jur. 2d *Partnership* § 925 (Supp. 1995).
>
> 1. **88 and 59A**—volume numbers of the encyclopedia
> 2. **C.J.S. and Am. Jur. 2d**—abbreviated names of the encyclopedia
> 3. ***Trial* and *Partnership***—topic names (italicized)
> 4. **§ 105 and § 925**—section symbols and section numbers within the article
> 5. **(1980)** and **(Supp. 1995)**—years of publications

2. Short Citation Format   Use *id.* when appropriate (see "*Id.* as a Short Citation" in Section 5.4 I). When *id.* is not appropriate, repeat the full citation without the date.

> ◻ *For Example:*
>
> *Id.* § 925; *Id.* § 105; 59A Am. Jur. 2d *Partnership* § 925; 88 C.J.S. *Trial* §
> 105.

5.3 D   PERIODICALS—LAW REVIEW/JOURNAL CITATIONS—BLUEBOOK R-16; ALWD-23

1. **Full Citation Format**   Following are the components of a law review, a journal, or another periodical citation.

   1. full name of the author
   2. title of the article (italicized or underlined)
   3. volume number
   4. abbreviated title of the periodical
   5. page number where the article begins (followed by the pinpoint page when a specific page is referred to; e.g., 159, 165)
   6. year of the publication in parentheses

> ◻ *For Example:*
>
> Patricia W. Bennett, *After White v. Illinois: Fundamental Guarantees to a Hollow Right to Confront Witnesses,* 40 Wayne L. Rev. 159 (1993).
>
>   1. **Patricia W. Bennett**—full name of the author
>   2. ***After White v. Illinois: Fundamental Guarantees to a Hollow Right to Confront Witnesses***—title of the article
>   3. **40**—volume number
>   4. **Wayne L. Rev.**—abbreviated title of the periodical
>   5. **159**—page number where the article begins
>   6. **(1993)**—year of the publication

2. **Short Citation Format**   Use *id.* when appropriate (see "*Id.* as a Short Citation" in Section 5.4 I). When *id.* is not appropriate, include the author's last name, the volume number, the periodical abbreviation, *at,* and the pinpoint reference.

> ◻ *For Example:*
>
> *Id.* at 165; Bennett, 40 Wayne L. Rev. at 165.

5.3 E   RESTATEMENTS—BLUEBOOK R-12.8.5; ALWD-27

1. **Full Citation Format**   A citation to a restatement should include the following components:

1. full name and edition of the restatement (In the *ALWD,* the full name and edition is in italics or underlined, including a subtitle when the reference is to a subtitle.)
2. section symbol (§) and number of restatement
3. year of the publication in parentheses

> ⬘ *For Example:*
>
> *Bluebook:* Restatement (Second) of Judgments § 28 (1982).
> *ALWD: Restatement (Second) of Judgments § 28 (1982).*
> *Bluebook:* Restatement (Second) of Torts: Products Liability § 52 (1989).
> *ALWD: Restatement (Second) of Torts: Products Liability § 52 (1989).*
>
> 1. **Restatement (Second) of Judgments**—full name of the restatement and the edition; **Restatement (Second) of Torts: Products Liability**—full name of the Restatement, edition, and subtitle
> 2. **§ 28 and § 52**—section numbers
> 3. **(1982) and (1989)** year of the publications

2. Short Citation Format   Use *id.* when appropriate (see "*Id.* as a Short Citation" in Section 5.4 I); otherwise, repeat the full citation without the date.

> ⬘ *For Example:*
>
> *Id.* § 28; *Restatement (Second) of Judgments § 28.*

5.3 F   TREATISES/BOOKS—BLUEBOOK R-15; ALWD-22

1. Full Citation Format   Treatise and book citations should include the following:

1. volume number when there is more than one volume
2. full name of the author or editor when a name is given
3. full title of the publication as it appears on the title page, in italics or underlined
4. number of the section, paragraph, or page when you are referring to a specific number, paragraph, or page
5. editor when there is an editor, the edition or series number of the book when it is not a first edition, and the publisher (the *Bluebook* does not require the inclusion of the publisher) followed by left parenthesis
6. year of publication followed by right parenthesis

> ⬘ *For Example:*
>
> 6A Richard R. Powell, *Powell on Real Property* ¶ 899 (Patrick J. Rohan ed. Matthew Bender 1994).

1. **6A**—volume number
2. **Richard R. Powell**—full name of the author
3. *Powell on Real Property*—full title of the publication as it appears on the title page
4. **¶ 899**—number of the paragraph
5. **(Patrick J. Rohan ed., Matthew Bender 1994)**—editor, publisher, and year of publication (This is the first edition; therefore, there is no edition number.)

2. **Short Citation Format**   Use *id.* when appropriate (see *"Id.* as a Short Citation" in Section 5.4 I). When *id.* is not appropriate, include the author's last name, title, *at,* and the pinpoint reference.

▣ *For Example:*

id. ¶ 899; Powell, *Powell on Real Property* ¶ 899.

5.4   GENERAL RULES OF CITATION

This section presents an overview of basic rules of citation to be used when citing most legal sources. The general rule or rules governing each area are listed following the section title. See Exhibit 5-2 for a chart listing the general rules of citation and the references for citation rules. A detailed discussion of each rule is beyond the scope of this text.

5.4 A   TYPEFACE—BLUEBOOK R-2 & P1; ALWD-1.1

Bluebook Rule 2 requires different typeface conventions and the use of large and small capital letters for citations in law reviews and other writings, such as books. Practitioner's Note 1 requires the use of ordinary type (such as courier) and italics or underlining in court documents and legal memorandums. *ALWD* Rule 1.1 does not distinguish between the type of document and states that ordinary type and italics or underlining should be used in all legal writing. The use of italics and underlining is discussed in the next section.

5.4 B   ITALICS AND UNDERLINING BLUEBOOK P1; ALWD-1.3

These rules present a summary of the items that should be underlined or italicized. The rules governing each type of item should be checked for other provisions that may govern the use of underlining or italics.

The rules are referenced next to the subject below.
Items that should be *italicized* or <u>underlined</u>:

1. Case names—BLUEBOOK R-10.2; ALWD-12.2 and 12.21
2. Titles of publications and most documents—BLUEBOOK R-13, 15, and 16; ALWD-15.7(c), 22.1(b), 23.1(b), and 26.1(c)
3. Introductory signals, such as *See* and *Contra*—BLUEBOOK R-1.2; ALWD-45
4. Internal cross-references and short forms, such as *supra*—BLUEBOOK R-4; ALWD-10 and 11
5. Phrases indicating subsequent or prior history, such as *aff'd* and *rev'd*—BLUEBOOK R-10.7.1; ALWD-12.8 and 12.9
6. Words or phrases introducing related authority, such as *available at*—BLUEBOOK R-1.6, 15.5, 18.2, 18.6, and 20.1.5
7. Names of Internet sites—ALWD-40.1(b)
8. Words used for emphasis, words italicized in the matter quoted, and foreign words that are not common—BLUEBOOK R-5 and R-7

5.4 C   CITATION PLACEMENT IN SENTENCES AND CLAUSES—BLUEBOOK P2; ALWD-43.1

Citations are placed in legal documents as separate citation sentences or clauses or by incorporation within a sentence.

1. **Citation Sentence**   When a statement about the law is a complete sentence, the citation immediately follows the statement as a separate sentence that begins with a capital letter and ends with a period. In this situation, the placement of the citation indicates that it supports the entire statement about the law included in the sentence.

2. **Citation Clause**   When the citation supports only part of a sentence, it is placed as a clause immediately after the statement it supports. It is set off by commas.

> **□ *For Example:***
>
> Although the good faith exception to the exclusionary rule has been
> adopted by the United States Supreme Court, *United States v. Leon,*
> 468 U.S. 897 (1984), it has not been adopted by all of the states, *State
> v. Gutierrez,* 116 N.M. 431, 863 P.2d 1052 (1993).

In this example, the first citation supports the first clause of the sentence
and the second citation supports the second clause.

3. **Embedded Citations**   When the authority is mentioned in the sentence, the citation may be incorporated within the sentence.

> **□ *For Example:***
>
> In the case of *Coleman v. Alabama,* 399 U.S. 1 (1970), the Supreme Court
> held that a defendant has a right to counsel at a preliminary hearing.

Placing the citation in the sentence allows you to add variety to your writing.
Note that the citation is not repeated at the end of the sentence.

5.4 D   ABBREVIATIONS—BLUEBOOK R-6 AND TABLES T.5 TO T.17; ALWD-2 AND APPENDICES 3, 4, AND 5

1. **In General**   Various terms and sources, such as court names, legal periodicals,
and case names, are abbreviated in legal citations.

> **□ *For Example:***
>
> | **Term** | **Abbreviation** |
> |---|---|
> | Southern Reporter | S. in *ALWD;* So. in *Bluebook* |
> | United States Supreme Court | U.S. |
> | Cumberland Law Review | Cumb. L. Rev. |
> | Case name—Corporation | Corp. |

Note that the same abbreviations may be used for different words. According to *ALWD,* the *S* in the above example stands for "Southern" in *Southern
Reporter* and "States" in *United States.*

2. **Spacing**   In the section "Typical Legal Citations Analyzed" of the *Bluebook*
(pp. 5–9), dots (●) are inserted in the example to indicate a single space in the
citation. In the *ALWD,* a green triangle (▲) indicates a single space. Following
is a summary of the rules governing spacing.

   a. ***Single Capital Letters and Ordinals***—Do not place a space between single
   capital letters or single capital letters and an ordinal. An ordinal is a number
   used to designate a position in a series, such as 10th Circuit. Ordinals, such
   as 2d or 10th, are treated as a single capital letter.

> **For Example:**
>
> F.R.D.—Federal Rules Decisions; P.2d—Pacific Reporter Second Series.
> (There are no spaces between the single capital letters.)

b. *Single Capital Letters and Non-Single Capital Letters*—When the abbreviation includes a capital letter or letters and an abbreviation that does not include a single capital letter, include a space between the single capital letter and the other abbreviation.

> **For Example:**
>
> F. Supp.—Federal Supplement. (There is a space between *F.* and *Supp.* because *Supp.* is not a single capital letter.)
> N.D. Miss.—Northern District of Mississippi. (There is a space between *D.* and *Miss.* because *Miss.* is not a single capital letter. There is no space between *N.* and *D.* because they are single capital letters.)

c. *Abbreviated and Non-Abbreviated Words*—When an abbreviated word is combined with a non-abbreviated word, place a space on each side of the non-abbreviated word.

> **For Example:**
>
> J. Real Est. Taxn.—Journal of Real Estate Taxation. (There is a space on each side of *Real* because it is a non-abbreviated word combined with an abbreviated word.)

d. *Legal Periodicals*   In a legal periodical, use a space to separate the institutional or geographic abbreviation from the other parts of the abbreviation.

> **For Example:**
>
> U.S.F. L. Rev.—University of San Francisco Law Review. (A space separates *U.S.F.* and *L.* because *U.S.F.* is the institutional abbreviation. A space separates *L.* and *Rev.* because *Rev.* is not a single capital letter.)

e. *Section Symbol (§), Paragraph Symbol (¶), and Ampersand (&)*—Place a space after each of these symbols.

> **For Example:**
>
> 18 U.S.C. § 2113 (A space is placed on each side of the symbol.)

f. *Authorities Included in the Text of a Sentence*—The name of an authority is not abbreviated when it is incorporated in a sentence. According to

Bluebook Rule 10.2.1, widely known acronyms such as *Co.* and *Inc.* continue to be abbreviated.

> ◘ *For Example:*
>
> The case citation is *Bachman Chocolate Mktg. Co. v. Leigh Warehouse & Transp. Co.,* 1 N.J.239, 62 A.2d 806 (1949). (When used in a sentence, *Marketing, Transportation,* and *and* are not abbreviated: The court ruled against the manufacturer in *Bachman Chocolate Marketing Co. v. Leigh Warehouse and Transportation Co.,* 1 N.J.239, 62 A.2d 806 (1949).)

5.4 E   CAPITALIZATION—BLUEBOOK R-8 & P6; ALWD-3

1. **General Rule**   In a heading, title, or subtitle, capitalize the initial letter of the first word; the first word following a colon or dash; and all other words except articles, prepositions, and conjunctions.

> ◘ *For Example:*
>
> Michael Asimow, *Bad Lawyers in the Movies.* 24 Nova L. Rev. 533 (2000).

2. **Court and Party Designations**   *Bluebook* Practitioner's Note 6 provides that in addition to capitalizing the word *Court* when referring to a specific court, such as the California Supreme Court, also capitalize *Court* when the court receiving the document is referred to in the document.

> ◘ *For Example:*
>
> This Court has already denied defendant's petition on two previous occasions.

Practitioner's Note 6 also provides that party designations (*Plaintiff, Defendant, Appellant,* and so on) be capitalized when referring to the parties in a matter before the court.

> ◘ *For Example:*
>
> It is claimed by the Appellant that the letter should not have been admitted at trial.
>
> On six occasions, Plaintiff attempted to contact Defendant regarding Defendant's failure to answer the interrogatories.

3. **Specific Words**   Rule 8 of the *Bluebook* includes a page-and-a-half list of specific words and the rules governing their capitalization.

> ☐ *For Example:*
>
> Capitalize *Act* only when referring to a specific act; capitalize *Code* only when referring to a specific code, such as the 1990 Code; capitalize *Judge* only when it is the name of a specific judge or a justice of the United States Supreme Court.

4. **All Other Capitalizations** Both manuals refer to the *United States Government Printing Office Style Manual* for capitalization of other words. The *ALWD* also refers to *The Chicago Manual of Style.*

5.4 F QUOTATIONS—BLUEBOOK R-5; ALWD-47 TO 49

Quotations are stronger than summaries or paraphrases. Too many quotations, however, can cause the writing to be disjointed and may lead the reader to question whether the writer has analyzed the material at all or understands the material well enough to analyze it. Use quotations for emphasis. Use quotes primarily for statutory language, a law or legal principle presented by a court, or key portions of a court's reasoning.

1. **Quotation Marks** Quotations of fewer than 50 words should be placed in quotation marks (" "); these quotations are not indented. The citation is usually placed after the sentence that contains the quotation.

> ☐ *For Example:*
>
> The United States Supreme Court gave the following guidance when interpreting treaties: "In construing a treaty, as in construing a statute, we first look to its terms to determine its meaning." *United States v. Alvarez-Machain,* 504 U.S. 655, 663 (1992).
>
> The court noted that the text of the treaty must be "interpreted in good faith in accordance with the ordinary meaning to be given to the terms of the treaty in their context in light of its object and purpose." *Kreimerman v. Casa Veerkamp, S.A. de C.V.,* 22 F.3d 634, 638 (5th Cir. 1994).

Place periods and commas inside quotation marks. Other punctuation, such as semicolons, colons, question marks, and exclamation points, are placed outside quotation marks unless they are a part of the quotation.

> ☐ *For Example:*
>
> The court defined publication as "communication to a third party"; therefore . . .
>
> The victim then shouted, "I've been hit!" (The exclamation point is part of the quote; therefore, it is placed inside the quotation marks.)

2. **Indented Quotations** Quotations of 50 words or more (called block quotations) are set off from the rest of the text by one tab from the left and right margins and are single-spaced. They are not set off by quotation marks. Place the citation at the left margin of the next line of the text following the quotation. Do not place the citation with the block quotation. The block quotation should be set off from the rest of the text with a double space.

> **For Example:**
>
> With regard to the individual rights of tenants in common, the court noted the following:
>
> > *However, numerous other elements of control do follow the percentage of ownership. For example, if a cotenant obtains a loan and mortgages the property, he is able to mortgage only his percentage ownership interest. If one co-tenant rents the whole property to a third party, he must share the proceeds with his co-tenants in accordance with their respective percentages of ownership . . . .*
>
> *Garcia v. Andrus*, 692 F.2d 89, 92 (9th Cir. 1982).

Block quotations are punctuated as they appear in the original quote.

3. **Quote within a Quote** Enclose quotations within a block quotation in double quotation marks (" "). As mentioned in the previous subsection, block quotations are punctuated as they appear in the original quote.
   Enclose quotations within a short quotation in single quotation marks.

> **For Example:**
>
> "The statute requires that the annual statement 'must be filed within thirty (30) days of the end of the fiscal year.'"

4. **Citing a Quote within a Quote** When the source of a quote within a quotation is included within the quotation, do not repeat it in the citation.

> **For Example:**
>
> "The state corporation statute, section 57-9-21, requires that the annual statement 'must be filed within thirty (30) days of the end of the fiscal year.'" (In this situation, you do not cite section 57-9-21 again at the end of the quotation.)

When the source of a quote within a quotation is not cited within the quotation, place the citation in a parenthetical that follows the citation for the entire quotation.

> **For Example:**
>
> In discussing the time limits for appeal, the court in *El Dorado* noted
> "'[j]urisdiction of the matters in dispute does not lie in the courts until the

> statutorily required administrative procedures are fully complied with.'"
> *El Dorado Utils., Inc. v. Gallisteo Domestic Water Users Ass'n*, 120
> N.M. 165, 167, 899 P.2d 608, 610 (Ct. App. 1995) (quoting *In re Appli-
> cation of Angel Fire Corp.*, 96 N.M. 651, 652, 634 P.2d 202, 203 (1981)).

5. **Altering Quotations**   The reader must be alerted to any changes made to a
quotation. Following are the rules governing alterations.

   a. *Altering a Letter Case*—When you change the case of a letter from upper to
lower case or vice versa, enclose the letter in brackets.

> ❑ *For Example:*
>
> **Original quote:**
> The court does not have jurisdiction until the administrative procedures are
> complied with.
>
> **Alteration:**
> The Supreme Court noted that "[t]he court does not have jurisdiction until
> the administrative procedures are complied with."

   b. *Adding, Deleting, or Changing Letters*—Enclose the added, deleted, or changed
letter or letters in brackets.

> ❑ *For Example:*
>
> **Original quote:**
> Jurisdiction of the matter in dispute does not lie in the court.
>
> **Alteration:**
> Jurisdiction of the matter[s] in dispute does not lie in the court.

   c. *Substituting or Adding Words*—Place substituted or added words in brackets.

> ❑ *For Example:*
>
> **Original quote:**
> Jurisdiction of the matters in dispute does not lie in the courts until the ad-
> ministrative procedures are fully complied with.
>
> **Alteration:**
> Jurisdiction of the matters in dispute does not lie in the courts until the
> [statutorily required] administrative procedures are fully complied with.

   d. *Mistakes in Original Quote*—Indicate a mistake in the quoted material by
placing *[sic]* after the mistake.

> ❑ *For Example:*
> The preliminary hearing is a stage at which the defendant have [sic] a right
> to counsel.

e. ***Adding Emphasis***—Making any change in the typeface of the quotation, such as adding emphasis, should be indicated in parentheses following the citation.

> **For Example:**
>
> **Original quote:**
>
> "If one co-tenant rents the whole property to a third party, he must share the proceeds . . . ." *Garcia v. Andrus,* 692 F.2d 89, 92 (9th Cir. 1982).
>
> **Alteration:**
>
> "If one co-tenant rents the whole property to a third party, *he must share the proceeds* . . . ." *Garcia v. Andrus,* 692 F.2d 89, 92 (9th Cir. 1982) (emphasis added)

6. Omitting Words or Citations   On occasion, you may want to quote only the parts of a passage relevant to the issue being discussed rather than the entire passage. When you are omitting one or more words, the following rules apply.

a. ***Omission of One or More Words–Ellipsis (. . .)***—An ellipsis is three periods with a space between each period and a space before and after the periods. Use an ellipsis to indicate the omission of material from the middle of a quotation.

> **For Example:**
>
> "No will . . . shall be revoked, unless . . . by subsequent will or codicil."

To indicate the omission of words at the end of a quotation, use an ellipsis and the final punctuation of the quote.

> **For Example:**
>
> The statute provides that a will may be revoked by "cutting, tearing, burning, obliterating, canceling . . . ."

Do not use an ellipsis to indicate the omission of words at the beginning of a quotation when the quotation is part of a sentence.

> **For Example:**
>
> **Correct omission:**
> The court noted that a testator may revoke a will by "cutting, tearing, or cancellation with the intent to revoke."
>
> **Incorrect omission:**
> The court noted that a testator may revoke a will by ". . . cutting, tearing, or cancellation with the intent to revoke."

When language at the beginning of a quotation is omitted, capitalize the first letter and place it in brackets.

> **For Example:**
>
> **Original quote:**
> "This court has held in several cases that a defendant need not brandish the firearm in a threatening manner."
>
> **Correct omission:**
> "[D]efendant need not brandish the firearm in a threatening manner."

To indicate the omission of one or more paragraphs from a block quote, place 3 dots, centered and separated by seven spaces, on its own line.

> **For Example:**
>
> However, numerous other elements of control do follow the percentage of ownership. For example, if a co-tenant obtains a loan and mortgages the property, he is able to mortgage only his percentage ownership interest.
>
> . . .
>
> If one co-tenant rents the whole property to a third party, he must share the proceeds with his co-tenants in accordance with their respective percentages of ownership.

In that example, the dots on a separate line indicate the omission of a paragraph from the block quotation.

   b. *Omission of Citations or Footnotes*—A quotation may contain numerous citations or footnotes that you do not want to include in the quotation. Indicate the omission of a citation or footnote in a parenthetical.

> **For Example:**
>
> "It is clear, however, that in the United States, civil liability for assault and battery is not limited to the direct perpetrator, but extends to any person who by any means aids or encourages the act." *Rael v. Cadena,* 934 N.M. 684, 684, 604 P.2d 822, 823 (Ct. App. 1979) (citations omitted).

7. Paragraph Structure   When a quotation of fewer than fifty words is the first sentence of a paragraph from quoted text, the paragraph is enclosed in quotation marks, but it is not indented. When the quotation is 50 words or more (a block quotation) and the quotation begins with the first sentence of a paragraph from quoted text, indent a second tab on the left side of the block quotation. All subsequent paragraphs are likewise indented as they appear in the quoted text. In other words, indent the block quote like the paragraph or paragraphs from the quoted text.

☐ *For Example:*

With regard to the individual rights of tenants in common, the court noted the following:

> *However, numerous other elements of control do follow the percentage of ownership. For example, if a co-tenant obtains a loan and mortgages the property, he is able to mortgage only his percentage ownership interest. If one co-tenant rents the whole property to a third party, he must share the proceeds with his co-tenants in accordance with their respective percentages of ownership. . . .*

In that example, *However* is indented in the block quote because it is the beginning of a paragraph in the quoted text.

5.4 G   PAGE NUMBERS (PINPOINT CITATIONS)—BLUEBOOK R-3.3 TO 3.5; ALWD-5.2 TO 5.4

Whenever you quote material from a source, you must include a reference to the exact page or location of the information. Also, when you paraphrase or otherwise refer to specific information rather than quote it, you should include a reference to the exact page or location. That is referred to as a "pinpoint cite" or "jump citation." It allows the reader to refer to the exact page of the quotation rather than search through the entire source to find the quote. This applies to all reference sources, and information on how to cite specific sources are scattered throughout the rules that discuss primary and secondary sources. The general rules covering pinpoint citations are discussed here.

Place the page number on which the quote or reference appears immediately after the page on which the source begins.

☐ *For Example:*

"[I]t is not a search by a federal officer if evidence secured by state authorities is turned over to federal authorities on a silver platter." *Lustig v. United States,* 338 U.S. 74, 79 (1949). (Page 79 is the page of the quote.)

The Eighth Circuit addressed the derivative nature of proceedings brought on behalf of limited partnerships. *Allright Mo., Inc. v. Billeter,* 829 F.2d 631, 638 (8th Cir. 1987). (Page 638 is the page where the Eighth Circuit addressed the matter.)

It has been noted that those trained in the law are confused by the topic. Terry Christlieb, Note, *Why Superseding Cause Analysis Should Be Abandoned,* 72 Tex. L. Rev. 161, 162. (Page 162 is the reference page.)

When the citation includes a parallel citation, a reference to the page in the parallel citation must be included. Parallel citations were discussed in Section 5.2 A.3f "State Court and Parallel Citations."

> **For Example:**
>
> *Commonwealth v. Appleby,* 380 Mass. 296, 300, 402 N.E.2d 1051, 1054
> (1980).

When the quotation or reference is from the first page of the reference source, repeat the initial page number.

> **For Example:**
>
> *Lustig v. United States,* 338 U.S. 74, 74 (1949).

When the quotation or reference covers more than one page, separate the pages with a dash or *to.*

> **For Example:**
>
> *Lustig v. United States,* 338 U.S. 74, 74–79 (1949).

Always retain at least the last two digits of the second number.

> **For Example:**
>
> **Correct:**
> 74–79
>
> **Incorrect:**
> 74–9
>
> **Correct:**
> 104–09
>
> **Incorrect**
> 104–9

When the quotation or reference is from multiple pages that are not consecutive, list each page separated by a comma and one space. Do not use *and* or & before the final page.

> **For Example:**
>
> *Lustig v. United States,* 338 U.S. 74, 74, 76, 79 (1949).

When the quotation or reference is from a public domain format (also referred to as "vendor neutral"), the pinpoint citation may be to a specific paragraph rather than a page.

> **For Example:**
>
> *State v. Anaya,* 1997-NMSC-010, ¶ 28, 123 N.M. 14, 20, 933 P.2d 223,
> 229. (The paragraph of the quote is paragraph 28.)

Consult the rule of the jurisdiction governing neutral citations. Both the *Bluebook* and the *ALWD* include tables/appendices that set out each state's citation rules and formats.

5.4 H   STRING CITATIONS—BLUEBOOK R-1.1 & P.2.2; ALWD-43.3(A)

When a proposition is supported by more than one authority in a citation clause or sentence, the citation is referred to as a "string citation." Separate each authority cited with a semicolon.

> ⬛ *For Example:*
>
> The sudden emergency doctrine tends to elevate its principles above what is required to be proven in a negligence action. *Knapp v. Stanford,* 392 So.2d 196 (Miss. 1980); *Simonson v. White,* 220 Mont. 14, 713 P.2d 938 (1986).

5.4 I   SHORT CITATION FORMS (*ID., SUPRA* AND *HEREINAFTER*)— BLUEBOOK R-4, P4, & P7; ALWD-11.2 TO 11.4

Once a full citation to an authority is presented in a document, subsequent citations to the authority may be shortened. These shortened citations are usually referred to as "short citations" or "short form citations." Short citations are used primarily because they save space and are less disruptive to the flow of the text. Practitioner's Note 4 of the *Bluebook* provides that short citations be used when it is clear from the short form what is being referenced, the earlier full citation is in the same general discussion, and the reader can easily locate the full citation.

The rules included in the title to this section are the general rules governing short citations. The rules for each type of citation have sections on short citations; e.g., the rule governing case citations has a section on short citations, the rule governing book citation has a section on short citations, and so on. The discussion of each type of citation in Sections 5.3 and 5.4 of this chapter includes the short citation format. This section addresses general rules governing all short citations and provides examples of short citations.

1. ***Id.* as a Short Citation**   *Id.* means "the same" and is used the same way as *ibid.* You use *id.*, not *ibid.*, in legal writing. *Id.* is italicized or underlined. When it is underlined, the period is also underlined (<u>id.</u>). *Id.* is used in court documents and legal memorandums when you are referring the reader to the immediately preceding citation. In other words, you must be referring to the same citation as the last citation presented.

> ⬛ *For Example:*
>
> Numerous other elements of control do follow the percentage of ownership. *Garcia v. Andrus,* 692 F.2d 89, 92 (9th Cir. 1982). For example, if

> a co-tenant obtains a loan and mortgages the property, he is able to
> mortgage only his percentage ownership interest. If one co-tenant rents
> the whole property to a third party, he must share the proceeds with his
> co-tenants in accordance with their respective percentages of owner-
> ship. *Id.* at 94.

The use of *id.* indicates that the source of the statement is the preceding citation, *Garcia v. Andrus.* If the source was on the same page as the previous citation (page 92), *Id.* alone would be used, not "*Id.* at 94." If another citation follows *Garcia v. Andrus,* the use of *id.* following that citation to refer to *Garcia
v. Andrus* would be improper.

> ❑ *For Example:*
>
> Numerous other elements of control do follow the percentage of owner-
> ship. *Garcia v. Andrus,* 692 F.2d 89, 92 (9th Cir. 1982). For example, if
> a co-tenant obtains a loan and mortgages the property, he is able to
> mortgage only his percentage ownership interest. *Appeal of Schramm,*
> 414 N.W.2d 31, 32 (S.D. 1987). If one co-tenant rents the whole prop-
> erty to a third party, he must share the proceeds with his co-tenants in
> accordance with their respective percentages of ownership. *Id.* at 94.
> (The use of "*Id.* at 94" to refer to *Garcia v. Andrus* is improper.)

When *id.* is used with statutory or paragraph citations, the word *at* is not included when referring to a different statutory section.

> ❑ *For Example:*
>
> The full citation of the statute referred to is 18 U.S.C. § 1112 (1994);
> when the reference is to § 1113, the short citation is *Id.* § 1113, not *Id.*
> at § 1113.

Id. may be used for any legal authority except internal cross-references. Internal
cross-references are discussed in Section 5.4 J "Internal Cross-References."

2. ***Supra* as a Short Citation**   *Supra* as a short citation means "above" and is
used to refer to a reference source previously fully cited in a document. It cannot be used in place of *id.* In other words, it is not used to refer to an immediately preceding cited source. It is used to refer to a previously cited source in a
document when there have been other intervening cited sources. **Supra** *cannot
be used to refer to cases, statutes, session laws, ordinances, legislative materials (other than hearings), constitutions, and administrative regulations.* It is
italicized or underlined. When it is underlined, do not underline any accompanying punctuation. When using *supra,* put the author's last name first (or the title if the name is not available) followed by a comma, then *supra.* When the
reference is to a page other than the page in the earlier citation, follow *supra*
with a comma, then *at* and the page number.

> ◘ *For Example:*
>
> It is clear that a mixed motive does not invalidate zoning restrictions on adult entertainment as long as the predominate concern of the zoning body is legitimate. *See* Alfred C. Yen, *Judicial Review of the Zoning of Adult Entertainment: A Search for the Purposeful Suppression of Protected Speech,* 12 Pepp. L. Rev. 651, 655 (1985). Courts have noted that respect must be given to the community's need to preserve the quality of life. *Las Vegas v. Nevada Industries, Inc.,* 105 Nev. 174, 772 P.2d 1275 (1989). The key question is what is the predominate concern of the zoning body. Yen, *supra* at 657.

In that example, *supra* is used because there is a different citation between the Yen citation and the second reference to the Yen article. If the second Yen reference immediately followed the first full citation, *Id.* would be used.

> ◘ *For Example:*
>
> It is clear that a mixed motive does not invalidate zoning restrictions on adult entertainment as long as the predominate concern of the zoning body is legitimate. *See* Alfred C. Yen, *Judicial Review of the Zoning of Adult Entertainment: A Search for the Purposeful Suppression of Protected Speech,* 12 Pepp. L. Rev. 651, 655 (1985). The key question is what is the predominate concern of the zoning body. *Id.* at 657.

3. ***Hereinafter* as a Short Citation**   *Hereinafter* may be used in certain circumstances to shorten a long title that is cumbersome to cite repeatedly, such as when the source has no author and the title is long. It is also used when two or more authorities appear in a footnote and the use of *supra* would be confusing. Place the hereinafter designation in ordinary type in brackets ([ ]) immediately following the end of the first full citation to the authority. The shortened form should clearly identify the authority.

> ◘ *For Example:*
>
> *Assume the article in the previous example does not have an author:* It is clear that a mixed motive does not invalidate zoning restrictions on adult entertainment as long as the predominate concern of the zoning body is legitimate. *See Judicial Review of the Zoning of Adult Entertainment: A Search for the Purposeful Suppression of Protected Speech,* 12 Pepp. L. Rev. 651 (1985), [hereinafter *Adult Entertainment Zoning*].

5.4 J   INTERNAL CROSS-REFERENCES (*SUPRA* AND *INFRA*)—BLUEBOOK R-3.6; ALWD-10

Often, especially when a document is long or includes many footnotes, you may want to refer the reader to source material on a specific page or in a specific section or footnote of the document. For that purpose, *supra* is used to refer to material that appears earlier in the document; *infra* is used to refer to material that appears later. When used in that context, *supra* has a different function from its use as a short citation. When used as a short citation, it refers to a specific source, such as a law review article. As internal cross-references, *supra* and *infra* refer to parts of the document, not specific sources. The terms are either italicized or underlined, and it may be necessary to add an explanatory parenthetical to identify the reference.

> ◘ *For Example:*
>
> *See supra* pp. 9–11 (discussing the rights of third parties).
> *Supra* n. 7 (cases supporting third party claims).
> *Supra* Section III. B–F.
> *Infra* notes 8–9 and accompanying text.
> *Infra* pp. 23–25 and note 16.
> *Infra* Part II. A–B (discussing interrogatory questions).

5.4 K   SIGNALS—BLUEBOOK R-1.2 TO 1.5; ALWD-44 TO 46

Signals are terms used to indicate the manner in which the cited authority supports or contradicts the text. A signal is not used when the citation identifies the source of a quotation, directly supports a statement, or identifies the authority referred to.

> ◘ *For Example:*
>
> The United States Supreme Court has adopted the good faith exception to the exclusionary rule. *United States v. Leon,* 468 U.S. 897 (1984).

1. **Types of Signals**   Below is a list of citation signals followed by examples of their use:

   Accord.—Indicates other cases that state or support a proposition. It is placed after the citation given in support of the proposition.

   But cf.—Identifies authority that supports a proposition analogous to the contrary of the stated proposition.

   But see—Identifies authority that contradicts the stated proposition.

   Cf.—Indicates authority that supports a proposition different from but to analogous to the proposition stated.

   Compare . . . with—Compares authorities that may illustrate or reach a different result from the stated proposition. (The *Bluebook* and the *ALWD* differ somewhat in their use of *compare.*)

   Contra.—Identifies authority that directly contradicts the stated proposition.

   E.g.—Indicates that the cited authority is representative of or is an example of many other authorities that stand for the same proposition. It may be used with other signals, such as *see, e.g.* or *but see, e.g.*

See—Indicates that the cited authority clearly supports a proposition but does not directly state the proposition.

See Also—Shows additional authority that supports a proposition.

See Generally—Identifies authority that presents helpful background information related to the stated proposition.

2. **Presentation**   Capitalize the first letter of a signal that begins a sentence. Italicize or underscore signals and separate them from the rest of the citation with a space. Separate each authority within a signal with a semicolon. Both the *Bluebook* and the *ALWD* recommend the use of parenthetical explanations to describe the relevance of the cited authority.

> **For Example:**
>
> *See, e.g. Renton v. Playtime Theatres, Inc.,* 475 U.S. 41, 55 (1986); *Young v. American Mini Theatres, Inc.,* 427 U.S. 50, 59 (1976);
> *Goldstar (Panama) S.A. v. United States,* 967 F.2d 965, 968 (4th Cir 1992);
> *Accord Argentine Republic v. Amerada Hess Shipping Corp.,* 488 U.S. 428, 442 (1989) (Supreme Court determining that the convention set forth only substantive rules of conduct and did not create a private right).
> *Contra Knapp v. Stanford,* 392 So.2d 196, 198 (Miss. 1981) (the sudden emergency doctrine confuses the principle of comparative negligence).

3. **Order of Presentation**   Following is a summary of the order of presentation of authorities. For a detailed list, refer to the *Bluebook* and the *ALWD*. Present citations in the following order:
   1. *Constitutions*—Federal Constitution, followed by state constitutions (alphabetically by state), then foreign constitutions (alphabetically by country)
   2. *Statutes*—Federal statutes (chronologically by title number) followed by state statutes (alphabetically by state), then foreign statutes (alphabetically by country)
   3. *Cases*—Federal cases (starting with the highest court to the lowest court) followed by state cases (alphabetically by state from the highest to the lowest courts), then foreign cases (alphabetically by country)
   4. *Administrative and Executive Materials*—such as the *Code of Federal Regulations* or executive orders
   5. *Legislative Materials*—such as bills and legislative history
   6. *Secondary Authority*—see BLUEBOOK R-1.3 or ALWD-46.4(c) for the order of presentation of secondary authority

5.4 L   SECTIONS AND PARAGRAPHS (§ ¶)—BLUEBOOK R-3.4; ALWD-6

Following is a summary of citation rules when an authority is organized by sections or paragraphs.

Insert a space before and after the section or paragraph symbol—18 U.S.C. § 2111 (1994).

Do not use *at* when referring to a paragraph or section.

> ■ *For Example:*
>
> **Correct:**
> *Id.* § 2111
>
> **Incorrect:**
> *Id.* at § 2111

When the authority is divided into subsections or subparagraphs, use the punctuation of the original source to separate sections and subsections. If the source does not have any punctuation, place the subdivisions in parentheses—18 U.S.C. 842(a)(1). Note that there is no space between the main section 842 and the subsections (a)(1).

A section may include a letter as part of the designation. In that case, the letter does not refer to a subsection; therefore, do not separate it with punctuation (e.g., 42 U.S.C. 2000e-1(a) (1994), not 42 U.S.C. 2000(e)(1)(a) (1994)). The *e* is part of the section designation and does not refer to a subsection.

When citing consecutive sections or paragraphs, include the first and last sections and separate the sections with a hyphen, a long dash, or *to*. Retain all digits on both sides of the span. Use consecutive section or paragraph symbols to reference multiple sections or paragraphs.

> ■ *For Example:*
>
> **Correct:**
> ¶¶ 115-123; §§ 15 to 17
>
> **Incorrect:**
> ¶¶ 115-23; §§ 15 to 7

When citing multiple sections or paragraphs that are not consecutive, place a comma between the sections or paragraphs and do not place *and* or & before the final section or paragraph.

> ■ *For Example:*
>
> **Correct:**
> ¶¶ 115, 123, 129; §§ 15, 17, 19
>
> **Incorrect:**
> ¶¶ 115, 123, and 129; §§ 15, 17, & 19

When citing multiple subsections or subparagraphs of a single section or paragraph, use one section or paragraph symbol.

> ☐ *For Example:*
>
> § 231(a)-(f); ¶ 22(g)-(k) (multiple consecutive subsections and subpara-
>   graphs)
> § 231(a), (f), (k); ¶ 22(a), (g), (k) (multiple nonconsecutive subsections
>   and subparagraphs)

5.4 M   ELECTRONIC SOURCES—BLUEBOOK R-18; ALWD-38 TO 42

Both the *Bluebook* and the *ALWD* provide that when the authority is readily available in print, the citation should be to the print source; it is not necessary to reference the electronic source, such as Westlaw® or LexisNexis. That rule applies unless the documents are not available in a printed source or are difficult to obtain,
such as unpublished cases. The *Bluebook* and the *ALWD* differ in some electronic
citation details; therefore, it is recommended that the rules be checked when citing
these sources. For example, in the *ALWD*, citations to Westlaw or LexisNexis are
placed in parentheses with the words *available in WL or LexisNexis* (e.g., available in
LexisNexis in the Legal News database). In the *Bluebook*, Westlaw and LexisNexis
citations are not placed in parentheses and not preceded by *available in*. The examples in this section follow the *Bluebook* format.

In general, a citation to an authority should include information that clearly indicates the source. The rules governing electronic sources are quite detailed, and it
is beyond the scope of this text to present a discussion of each rule. Therefore, this
section contains a brief summary of the key points for citing electronic sources.

1. **Commercial Sources**   Rule 18.1 in the *Bluebook* recommends the use of commercial electronic databases over other Internet sources due to their reliability.
   In addition to the usual information given in a citation, such as a case name or
   statute number, the database identifier must be included. The identifier usually
   includes the database name (LEXIS and WL (for Westlaw)), the year, and the
   document number.

> ☐ *For Example:*
>
> **Unpublished cases:**
> *Christians v. Stafford,* No. 14-99-00038-CV, 2000. Tex. App. LEXIS 6423
>   (Tex. Ct. App. Oct. 26, 2000).
> *Devji v. Keller,* No. 03-99-00436-CV, 2000 Tex. App. WL 1862819, at * 2
>   (Tex. Ct. App. Dec. 21, 2000).

When you are referring to a specific screen or page number, place an aster-
isk before the number ("at *2" in the above example). When the reference is to
a specific paragraph number, precede the number with the paragraph symbol
and do not use *at* (¶ 15). In the above example, a specific screen page number
is referenced.

Congressional Bills: H. R. 1167, 106th Cong. (1999) WL 1999 CQ US HR 1167; H. R. 301, 107th Cong. (2001) LEXIS Archived Bill Text and Tracking Library, 106th Congress file.

Newsletter: Kim Biello, Susan Beck, Andrew Longstreth, *Bar Talk*, The American Lawyer, Sept. 2001, available in LEXIS Legal News Library, The American Lawyer file.

Law Review: Alfred C. Yen, *Judicial Review of the Zoning of Adult Entertainment: A Search for the Purposeful Suppression of Protected Speech*, 12 Pepp. L. Rev. 651 (1985), WL 12 PEPLR 651.

Exhibit 5-2

Rule References to General Rules of Citation

Topic	General Rules of Citation *Bluebook* Rules and Practitioner's Notes (P)	*ALWD* Rules
Abbreviations	Rule 6 and Tables T.5 to T.17	Rule 2 and Appendices 3, 4, 5
Capitalization	Rule 8 and P.6	Rule 3
Electronic Sources	Rule 18	Rules 38 to 42
Internal Cross-References (*supra* and *infra*)	Rule 3.6	Rule 10
Italics and Underscoring	P.1	Rule 1.3
Page Numbers (Pinpoint Citations)	Rules 3.3 to 3.5	Rules 5.2 to 5.4
Placement of Citations in Sentences and Clauses	P.2	Rule 43.1
Quotations	Rule 5	Rules 47 to 49
Sections and Paragraphs (§, ¶)	Rule 3.4	Rule 6
Short Citations (*id., supra, hereinafter*)	Rule 4, P.4, and P.7	Rules 11.2 to 11.4
Signals (e.g., *see, accord*)	Rules 1.2 to 1.5	Rules 44 to 46
String Citations	Rules 1.1 and P.2	Rule 43.3(a)(b)

2. World Wide Web Sources   An on-line citation should include the following: the full name of the author or owner; the title in italics; pinpoint references such as paragraph numbers (if any); the URL (Web address); and the date enclosed in parentheses.

> ◼ *For Example:*
>
> MSNBC, *MSNBC Home News, Oil Prices Sink after OPEC Dithers,* <http://www.msnbc.com/news/657546.asp> (Nov 15, 2001).

ALWD Rule 12.5 provides that if a case is available in a reporter or through an on-line database such as Westlaw, the Internet should not be cited.

5.5   KEY POINTS CHECKLIST: CITATION

❑ When checking citations, always consult an authority such as the *Bluebook* or the *ALWD.*

❑ Make sure the appropriate words in a citation, such as case names, article titles, and so on, are properly italicized or underlined.

❑ Check case citations to ensure that all of the elements are present—case name, reporter volume and page, pinpoint page if the citation is to a specific page, parallel citation (if any), court abbreviation if necessary, year of the decision in parentheses, and subsequent history (if any).

❑ Make sure all of the elements of statutory citations are present. Statutory citations usually include the name of the code or code abbreviation; the section symbol (§), title, chapter, or section numbers; and in parenthesis the publisher if it is a commercial publication and the year the volume was published.

❑ For any other citation, such as a secondary citation, check the rules to ensure that all of the elements of the citation are present and properly used.

❑ Check the rules and tables or appendices to ensure that words such as *Incorporated* and *South Eastern Reporter* are properly capitalized, abbreviated, and spaced.

❑ When signals such as *See Also* are included in a citation, check to ensure they are used properly.

❑ Check the use of *id.* and other short citations. Is the use of a short citation correct? If so, is the correct citation format used?

Chapter 6

Computer and Internet Research Web Sites

Contents

6.1 INTRODUCTION

As technology develops, more research is conducted using electronic resources. The two most frequently used commercial (fee-based) services are Westlaw and LexisNexis. Two of the smaller, less frequently used fee-based services are Loislaw and VersusLaw. Information on how to use the fee-based services is provided by the service provider.

In addition to the services mentioned above, there are other commercial web-based legal research services, including Commerce Clearing House (CCH®). The Web site addresses for Westlaw, LexisNexis, Loislaw, VersusLaw®, and CCH are as follows:

<http://www.westlaw.com>
<http://www.lexisnexis.com>
<http://loislaw.com>
<http://www.versuslaw.com>
<http://www.cch.com>

The remainder of this chapter presents an overview of the various non-fee-based Internet and other computer-based legal research sources.

6.1 A   ETHICS

There are literally thousands of non-fee-based Web sites on the Internet. Note that a non-fee-based service does not have a contractual relationship with the consumer of its information. There are no laws or regulations governing the accuracy of the content of non-fee-based Web sites. Such sites do not have a legal duty to provide information that is accurate or up to date. However, they do have an ethical obligation to provide clients with competent representation. *You must verify the accuracy of information you obtain from such sites and determine whether it is up to date.*

When selecting a non-fee-based site, there are no hard-and-fast rules for determining what constitutes a "good" site. Sites maintained by law schools are usually accurate and well maintained. Always consider the author/publisher and the content of the information and check the site to determine how frequently the information is updated. Beware that advocacy groups publish some sites, which means information may be limited or slanted in favor of the position advocated by the group. Links to documents that can help you evaluate Web sites are found at <http://www.vuw.ac.nz/~agsmith/evaln/evaln.htm> and at <http://www.lib.auburn.edu/madd/docs/eir.html>.

6.1 B   LIMITATIONS

In addition to the disadvantages of non-fee-based Internet research just mentioned, there are additional limitations. On many Web sites, when you are searching for statutory law, only the statute is available, not the annotations. Therefore, none of the valuable research information, such as A.L.R. annotations, law review articles, and case references, is included.

> ◘ *For Example:*
>
> If you are searching the United States Code for the bank robbery statute using <http://www.law.cornell.edu/uscode>, you will find the statute, but not the annotations.

Many sites require that you know the name or citation of the case when looking for case law. If you are trying to find any case that answers the question raised by the issue, *you may not be able to conduct the search based on search terms* (see the discussion of Boolean searching in Section 6.2 A). For many sites that allow Boolean searching, the search capability is not as sophisticated as that of fee-based services. Most non-fee-based sites do not provide you with the ability to update research.

> ◘ *For Example:*
>
> If you locate a case that is on point, most sites do not allow you to check the history or treatment of the case to determine whether the case has been overturned or affected by a subsequent case. The sites have no mechanism, such as *Shepard's*®, to identify cases, articles, and other secondary sources that have cited the case.

6.2   NON-FEE-BASED LAW-RELATED WEB SITES

Following is a discussion of various non-fee-based law-related web sites. Addresses of web sites are referred to as uniform resource locators or **URLs.** The URLs used in this text are current as of the book's date of publication. If you do not find a Web site at the URL listed, it does not mean that the site no longer exists. The site may be down temporarily due to technical problems or the URL may have changed. To determine whether the URL has changed, use a search engine to search for a key term in the address.

> **For Example:**
>
> If you are looking for Legal Pad and the site does not come up by using its URL, perform a search using *Legal Pad*. If you are looking for a school's law library, search under the name of the school and *law library*.

Also, you may have a specific URL, such as <http://www.willamette.edu/law/wlo/us-supreme>. This is the address of a specific page from the Willamette College of Law's Web site. Summaries of recent United States Supreme Court opinions are available here. Often specific page addresses change. If a specific page address does not come up, go to the home page. In this example, the home page is <http://www.willamette.edu>. The directory on the home page will lead you to the information you are seeking. In this case, the home page directory includes links to the Supreme Court opinions.

6.2 A   SEARCH TERMS

This section presents a brief discussion of how to conduct a legal research search on the Internet, followed by a discussion of non-fee-based Internet legal research sites. The initial steps for conducting a search, which will be discussed in Chapter 7, apply to the process for conducting a computer-assisted search: analyze the assignment, do preliminary preparation, identify key facts, and identify the issue. Computer searches are usually conducted using key words or terms from the issue (often referred to as **Boolean** searching or terms and connectors searches). The basic steps for determining the search terms are as follows:

1. State the issue you are researching as specifically as possible in the context of the facts.
2. Formulate the search query. Review the issue and select the significant terms. Ask yourself: "What terms in the issue are likely to be included in the constitutional provision, statute, or case being researched?"

> **For Example:**
>
> The issue is "Under federal statutory law, does bank robbery with a dangerous weapon occur when the weapon is a toy gun?" The assignment

> is to locate the federal law that governs bank robbery with a dangerous weapon. You are looking for a statute that includes the terms *bank, robbery, dangerous,* and *weapon.*

Once you have identified the terms, type them in the search query box and execute the search by clicking on the appropriate command, such as Search or Submit. Also, most Web sites that allow you to search using search terms also include instructions on how to conduct a search.

If you are conducting a broad search for general information on a topic, think of all of the terms the topic may be categorized under and conduct the search using any combination or all of the terms.

> ■ *For Example:*
>
> Assume the question involves child custody and you want to gain familiarity with that area of law. The first step is to list all of the terms child custody may be indexed under, such as *divorce, marriage, custody, parent and child, child custody, children,* and *domestic relations.* You will find the topic under at least one of those search terms.

6.2 B   GENERAL ACCESS AND LINKS

There are several sites that provide **general access** and links to legal research sites. The links are to Web sites that provide access to statutory law, case law, and other research sources. Some of the most comprehensive sites are as follows:

<http://www.findlaw.com> FindLaw® is one of the best and most comprehensive sites providing links to sources for federal and state statutory law, case law, government directories, law firms, legal organizations, law schools, legal practice materials, and numerous other sources.

<http://lawcrawler.findlaw.com> LawCrawler uses simple search terms or phrases to search the Internet for legal information sites. FindLaw is the parent site of LawCrawler.

<http://law.gsu.edu> This Georgia State University College of Law site provides access to U.S. federal resources. It allows you to conduct searches of major topics such as judicial opinions, federal regulations, and federal legislation (House and Senate Bills and the Congressional Record). On the home page, click "Law Library."

<http://www.abanet.org> This American Bar Association site includes links to legal research sources, law school libraries, branches of government, courts, and numerous other sources.

<http://www.legal-pad.com> This site includes legal clip art and a large number of links to law-related sites.

<http://lcweb.loc.gov> Through this Library of Congress Web site, you can locate any book that has been published.

<http://www.legaldocs.com> This site provides templates for legal documents in many areas, such as wills, trusts, sales, and real estate. Many documents are free. The law of the state where the document is to be used must be checked to ensure that the document complies with state law.

<http://www.llr.com> This site provides links to various legal research databases. Type *legal research* in the search box.

Most law schools have a Web site, and most sites provide links to the school's law library. The list of all law school Web sites is too extensive to include here. To find the site of a school you are interested in, use a search engine and insert the name of the law school (e.g., Harvard Law School).

You can conduct research through many law school library Web sites. Following is a list of law school sites that provide comprehensive legal research links, resources, and information.

<http://www.law.indiana.edu/v-lib> This Indiana Virtual Law Library includes links to sites of specialty areas of law, government resources, search engines, and law journals.

<http://www.law.cornell.edu/index.html> This Cornell University Law School site provides extensive resource guides and access to many different legal topics.

<http://www.washlaw.edu> In addition to links to numerous law- and legal research-related Web sites, this Washburn University School of Law site provides links to state and federal court and government sites.

<http://www.law.utexas.edu> This University of Texas School of Law site includes a legal resource guide on many different legal topics.

<http://www.kentlaw.edu> Information on how to find legal materials on the Internet is available at this Chicago-Kent College of Law site. Included are lists dealing with various areas, such as the federal government, computer law, and health law.

<http://www.law.emory.edu> This Emory University Law School site provides access to links to many federal circuit court decisions and other research material.

<http://www.law.villanova.edu> At this site, you can use locators to find official Web sites for federal and state courts and federal government information resources.

6.2 C   FEDERAL GOVERNMENT SOURCES

1. General Access Sources   The following sites are helpful in locating federal government on-line resources.

<http://www.firstgov.gov> FirstGov is the U.S. government's official Web portal. The site provides information and access links to various federal government on-line resources.

<http://www.fedworld.gov> FedWorld allows you to search for government reports and locate U.S. government Web sites, government documents, and government studies.

<http://www.uscourts.gov> This site is the home page for the federal courts.

<http://www.gpoaccess.gov/index.html> This is the address for the Government Printing Office. The site provides information on the executive branch, including the *Code of Federal Regulations*, the *Federal Register,* the *Congressional Record*, and government reports.

2. **Federal Courts Opinions**   The following sites provide access to the United States Supreme Court, the United States Circuit Courts of Appeal, and federal district court resources.

United States Supreme Court.

<http://www.findlaw.com/casecode/supreme.html> This FindLaw site includes Supreme Court cases and the United States Code.

<http://www.law.cornell.edu> On this Cornell Law School home page, place your cursor over "Court opinions"; from the drop-down box, select "U.S. Supreme Court Opinions." You may access transcripts, court orders, decisions, and so on.

<http://www.fedworld.gov> This FedWorld site allows you to locate opinions from 1937 to 1975 when you know the names of the parties but do not know the citation.

<http://www.law.cornell.edu/rules/supct/overview.html> The Supreme Court rules are available at this site.

<http://www.willamette.edu/law/wlo/us-supreme> Summaries of recent United States Supreme Court opinions and the text of the opinions are available at this Willamette College of Law site. Cases from 2002 to the present are available.

United States Circuit Courts of Appeal. Access to federal circuit court cases is available through several sources. A few are listed here.

<http://findlaw.com/casecode/courts> Through this FindLaw site, you can locate court cases.

<http://www.law.vill.edu/library/researchguides/fedcourtlocator.asp> This Villanova University School of Law site includes circuit court opinions and rules.

<http://www.law.emory.edu/fedcircuit> Circuit court opinions may be accessed through this Emory Law School site.

United States District Courts. The United States district courts are the primary trial courts in the federal system. Most federal district courts list their opinions on the court Web page. The home page for the federal courts, <http://www.uscourts.gov>, provides information about the courts and links to the district court Web sites.

3. **Federal Statutes, Court Rules, and Regulations**   The United States Code, federal court rules, and the *Code of Federal Regulations* are available at the following sites:

United States Code. The Cornell Law School site <http://straylight.law.cornell.edu/uscode> provides access to the United States Code. You can search by title and chapter, popular name, title of individual sections, and table of contents. The United States Code is also available at the Government Printing Office Web site, <http://www.gpoaccess.gov>.

Federal Court Rules. The federal court rules are included in the United States Code discussed in the previous section. Local court rules are usually available through the federal court's Web site, which may be accessed at <http://www.uscourts.gov>. The federal court rules are also available at many law school Web sites, including <http://www.law.cornell.edu>. Cornell Law School's Web site allows you to search the Federal Rules of Civil Procedure and Evidence using keywords.

Code of Federal Regulations **(C.F.R.).**

<http://www.law.cornell.edu/cfr>. This Cornell Law School site allows searches by title and section, the index of section headings, the Government Printing Office search engine, or the C.F.R. table of contents.

<http://www.gpoaccess.gov/cfr/index.html>. This Government Printing Office site includes the C.F.R. and a search engine for finding code sections.

Federal Register. The *Federal Register* is available at the Government Printing Office Web site <http://www.gpoaccess.gov/fr/index.html>.

4. **Legislation**   Information on federal legislation is available at <http://thomas.loc.gov>. Legislative history available at this site is maintained by the Library of Congress. The site includes information on legislation, the full text of the *Congressional Record,* and committee information.

   Legislative history maintained by the Government Printing Office is available at <http://www.access.gpo.gov>. Access is available to legislative history and presidential documents.

5. **Congress and Federal Agencies**   Following is a partial list of addresses for Congress and various federal agencies. The addresses for Web sites of agencies not listed here can be accessed through the Library of Congress Web site at <http://www.lcweb.loc.gov>.

<http://www.census.gov> U.S. Census Bureau
<http://www.cia.gov> Central Intelligence Agency
<http://www.cpsc.gov> U.S. Consumer Product Safety Commission
<http://www.uspto.gov> United States Patent and Trademark Office
<http://www.usdoj.gov> United States Department of Justice
<http://www.dol.gov> U.S. Department of Labor

<http://www.dot.gov> U.S. Department of Transportation
<http://www.epa.gov> U.S. Environmental Protection Agency
<http://www.faa.gov> Federal Aviation Administration
<http://www.fbi.gov> Federal Bureau of Investigation
<http://uscis.gov> U.S. Citizenship and Immigration Services
<http://www.irs.ustreas.gov> Internal Revenue Service
<http://www.nhtsa.dot.gov> National Highway Traffic Safety Administration
<http://www.sec.gov> U.S. Securities and Exchange Commission
<http://www.ssa.gov> U.S. Social Security Administration
<http://www.state.gov/index.html> State Department
<http://www.house.gov> United States House of Representatives
<http://www.senate.gov> United States Senate
<http://www.whitehouse.gov> The White House

6.2 D   STATE SOURCES

The amount of legal research material available over the Internet varies from state to state.

> **For Example:**
>
> Some states provide on-line access to state agency regulations; others do not.

Law-related material is usually available through state court, state government, local law school, or state bar association Web sites. Consider accessing those sites when conducting a search within your state. The legal materials most commonly available are state statutes, court opinions, law reviews, and agency regulations. Space limitations here prohibit listing the URL for each state. Following is a list of the URLs for sites that provide links to state sources.

<http://www.findlaw.com> Through findlaw you can access state statutes, case law, administrative law, law schools, professional legal organizations and some law reviews.
<http://www.lawsonline.com> Lawsonline provides links to state sources, including state codes.
<http://www.llr.com> At this site, you can access the recent opinions of the highest state courts.
<http://www.law.vill.edu> This Villanova University Law school site provides links to state courts and court opinions.
<http://www.law.indiana.edu/v-lib> At the Indiana Virtual Law library, you can find information on many state sources and links to many different specialty areas of law, such as family law.
<http://www.kentlaw.edu> Access to instructions on finding legal materials on the Internet are available at this Chicago-Kent College of Law site.

Lists provided include state government and specialty area sites such as health law.

<http://www.nass.org/acr/internet.html> This site provides links to official administrative codes and registers for all 50 states and the District of Columbia.

<http://www.ncsconline.org> This National Center for States Courts (NCSC) Web site includes a list of state courts. Law-related Internet sites are also available.

<http://www.hg.org/usstates-govt.html> This site provides access to state and local government information on uniform laws, on-line journals, and other topics.

6.2 E   SECONDARY AUTHORITY AND SPECIALTY AREAS

Many secondary authority and other sources such as A.L.R., West's Digests, and treatises are available only at fee-based Web sites such as Westlaw and LexisNexis. Many secondary sources such as *Shepard's* are available on fee-based Web sites and CD-ROM (see Section 6.3). However, there are many secondary source materials and other materials in specialty areas available at no charge on the Internet. A good source for information and links to sources for the specialty areas listed below may be found at the Amicus Attorney Web site, <http://amicus.ca/news/index.html>. Another site for accessing information and research sources in various specialty areas is the LawyerExpress site, <http://www.lawyerexpress.com>.

1. **Specialty Area Sources**   Following is a list of legal topics and related Web sites.

   a. *Arbitration and Mediation*—At the FirstGov Web site, <http://www.firstgov.gov>, you can locate numerous sources of information on arbitration and mediation. Conduct a search using either *arbitration* or *mediation*.

   b. *Administrative Law*—The FindLaw site <http://www.findlaw.com/01topics/00administrative/gov_laws.html> provides access to federal administrative codes, regulations, orders, and agency rulings. State and local administrative laws are available through the Municipal Code Corporation site at <http://www.municode.com>. Administrative law research may be conducted through the American Bar Association's Administrative Procedure Database at <http://www.law.fsu.edu/library/admin>.

   c. *Bankruptcy*—FindLaw (<http://www.findlaw.com>) provides access information on the various types of bankruptcy and bankruptcy law and links to bankruptcy courts. The Internet Bankruptcy Library at <http://bankrupt.com> provides access to publications and resource materials and links to bankruptcy resources.

   d. *Civil Litigation*—The Amicus Attorney site at <http://amicus.ca/news/index.html> includes links to numerous civil litigation support materials such as deposition techniques and tort law sources. A directory of expert witnesses is available at <http://www.claims.com>. A site that provides links to experts is <http://www.expertpages.com>. A site that includes information on damages is <http://www.lawcatalog.com>. For a list of sources dealing with damages, conduct a search using the keyword *damages*.

e. *Civil Rights*—The civil rights provisions of the United States Code may be found through FindLaw (<http://www.findlaw.com>). The American Civil Liberties Union (ACLU) Web site, <http://www.aclu.org>, provides extensive information on issues concerning civil rights.

f. *Consumer Law*—The Web site of the National Consumer Law Center at <http://www.consumerlaw.org> includes comprehensive information on consumer law.

g. *Corporate Law*—General information about corporate law is available through the LawyerExpress Web site (<http://www.lawyerexpress.com>) and the Amicus Attorney Web site (<http://amicus.ca/news/index.html>). State Business and Professional Codes are available through the Cornell University Web site at <http://www.law.cornell.edu>. Information on thousands of companies is available at <http://www.companiesonline.com>. The office of the secretary of state has information on incorporating in a state. Usually, forms and documents are available. Secretary of state offices can be contacted through the state government Web site or through <http://www.nass.org/sos/sos.html>.

h. *Criminal Law*—The Florida State University School of Criminology site at <http://www.criminology.fsu.edu> provides extensive information on criminal law. Links to criminal justice sites may be found at the Institute for Law and Justice site at <http://www.ilj.org>.

i. *Elder Law*—Information concerning Medicare, Medicaid, and rights of the elderly may be researched at <http://www.seniorlaw.com>.

j. *Environmental Law*—The Web site of the Environmental Protection Agency is <http://www.epa.gov>. Links to environmental law resources may be found at the WWW Virtual Library site at <http://www.vlib.org>.

k. *Estate Planning*—State probate statutes should be consulted when the question involves estate planning. Those statutes are available through FindLaw. Estate planning material may be located at the Amicus Attorney site, <http://amicus.ca/news/index.html>.

l. *Family Law*—The DivorceNet site at <http://www.divorcenet.com> provides information on state divorce laws. Information on numerous family law matters, such as property issues, custody, and tax planning, is available at <http://www.nolo.com>.

m. *Immigration*—The U.S. Citizenship and Immigration Services Web site is <http://uscis.gov>. Links to all types of material on immigration are available at <http://www.immigration-usa.com/is.html>. Immigration procedures, forms, books, and other materials are available at <http://www.us-immigration.com>.

n. *International Law*—International legal resources are available at the site of the Cornell Law School Legal Information Institute at <http://www.law.cornell.edu/topics> and at the United Nations System of Organizations site at <http://www.unsystem.org>.

o. *Intellectual Property and Copyright*—The United States Copyright Office Web site is <http://www.copyright.gov>. The United States Patent and

Trademark Office is <http://www.uspto.gov>. Information about copyrights is available at the Copyright Clearance Center, <http://www.copyright.com>.

p. *Legal Documents and Forms*—Legal documents and forms may be found through several sites. Two popular sites are <http://www.lectlaw.com/form.html> (the 'Lectric Law Library) and <http://www.legaldocs.com> (Legaldocs).

q. *Personal Injury*—Links to numerous sites that provide information on personal injury law are available at the Amicus Attorney site at <http://amicus.ca/news/index.html>. The National Highway Traffic Safety Administration (NHTSA) provides information on traffic safety and consumer complaints. Its address is <http://www.nhtsa.gov>. Data on consumer products is available at the U.S. Consumer Product Safety Commission's site at <http://www.cpsc.gov>. The Americans with Disabilities Act Document Center is located at <http://jan.wvu.edu/links/adalinks.htm>. Medical information is available at the Virtual Medical Center at <http://ww.martindalecenter.com>.

r. *Real Property and Landlord Tenant Law*—Along with many other specialty sites, the Amicus Attorney site at <http://amicus.ca/news/index.html> includes links to numerous sites that provide information on real property law. The National Association of REALTORS site is <http://www.realtor.com>. The site provides links to a wide variety of sources on real estate matters. Nolo Press maintains a landlord/tenant site at <http://www.nolo.com/home.html>.

s. *Tax Law*—The Web site for the Internal Revenue Service is <http://www.irs.ustreas.gov>. Links to numerous tax law resources are available through The Tax Prophet Web site at <http://www.taxprophet.com>.

t. *Uniform Commercial Code*—Comprehensive information on the Uniform Commercial Code is available at the Cornell University Law School Legal Information site at <http://www.law.cornell.edu>. On the home page, place your cursor over "Law about…" Then select "Commerce" from the drop-down menu. In addition to providing the Uniform Commercial Code, the site also contains links to state commercial code statutes and links to information about the code. The Amicus Attorney site, <http://amicus.ca/news/index.html>, also provides numerous links to resources on the commercial code.

2. Secondary Authority and Other Sources   In this section is a list of secondary authority and other source material sites that are available at non-fee-based Web sites.

a. *Law Reviews, Journals, and Periodicals*—Many law reviews, journals, and periodicals are available on-line. Many law schools publish their law reviews and journals. Examples include the *Harvard Law Review* at <http://www.harvardlawreview.org> and the *Cornell Law Review* at <http://organizations.lawschool.cornell.edu/clr>.

Directories that provide links to law reviews and law journals include FindLaw at <http://stu.findlaw.com/journals> and the University of Chicago D'Angelo Law Library at <http://www.lib.uchicago.edu/e/law/lawreviews.html>. The University Law Review Project provides information on the

availability of law reviews on the Internet; its URL is <http://www
.lawreview.org>.

b. *Legal Dictionaries*—Legal dictionaries are available at the following sites: <http://www.duhaime.org/dictionary/diction.aspx> and <http://www.lect-law.com/def/htm>.

c. *Uniform State Laws and Model Acts*—Uniform state laws and model acts are available at the Web site of the National Conference of Commissioners on Uniform State Laws; its URL is <http://www.nccusl.org>.

d. *Law Firms*—Information on law firms and ways to locate attorneys is available through FindLaw at <http://www.findlaw.com> and Martindale-Hubbell® at <http://www.martindale.com>.

6.2 F LISTSERVS

A listserv is an e-mail discussion group. A listserv links people with common interests so they can share information on a topic or area of expertise. To participate, you must subscribe to or join the group. Once you have joined a listserv discussion group, you can send (post) and receive messages from group members. When a message is posted, it is available to all members who subscribe to the group. In essence, the information is public; it is not like private e-mail.

There are hundreds of discussion groups on various legal topics. Listservs are valuable because they allow you to receive the input of colleagues who are interested in and often experts on a certain legal topic. If you have difficulty finding an answer to a legal question, you can post the question on the listserv and obtain an answer or guidance from other members of the group. However, you should verify the information received.

There are two types of listservs: unmoderated where all messages by group members are sent to the group and moderated where messages are sent to a moderator who reviews the message and decides whether to return it to the sender, edit it and send it on to the group, or send it on to the group as is. The activities of the moderator are usually governed by rules established by the group.

Two Web sites that provide information on legal listservs are a Washburn University School of Law site at <http://washlaw.edu> and the Weschester Library System site at <http://www.wls.lib.ny.us>.

6.2 G ORGANIZATIONS

Following is a list of law-related organizations and associations.

<http://www.aallnet.org> American Association of Law Libraries (AALL)
<http://www.abanet.org> American Bar Association (ABA)
<http://www.aclu.org> American Civil Liberties Union (ACLU)
<http://www.alanet.org> Association of Legal Administrators (ALA)
<http://www.aafpe.org> American Association for Paralegal Education (AAFPE)

<http://www.nala.org> National Association of Legal Assistants (NALA)

<http://www.nals.org> National Association for Legal Professionals

<http://www.nass.org/sos/sos.html> National Association of Secretaries of State (NASS)

<http://www.paralegals.org> National Federation of Paralegal Associations (NFPA™)

<http://www.un.org/english> The United Nations

State Bar organizations may be accessed by conducting a search using the name of the state bar, such as *New York State Bar.*

6.3   CD-ROMS

Many legal research sources are available on CD-ROM. These sources include *American Jurisprudence 2d, American Law Reports,* the *United States Code Annotated, Shepard's,* state statutory and case law, treatises such as Wright and Miller's *Federal Practice and Procedure,* and practice aids such as *American Jurisprudence Legal Forms.* For space-saving reasons, many law firms now purchase legal materials in CD-ROM form rather than paper texts.

An advantage of CD-ROMs is that they allow the researcher, through the use of a laptop computer, to conduct research at home, at court, or while traveling. The publisher usually updates its CDs with replacement discs at regular intervals, such as monthly or quarterly. A disadvantage is that the material is only as current as the update. Many law libraries have research sources on CD-ROM. You may find it easier to perform your search using a CD-ROM rather than a text if you are familiar with computerized research.

CD-ROMs, like texts, vary in their organization and search features. However, performing a search on most CD-ROMs is similar to performing a search on Westlaw or LexisNexis. That is, a search may be conducted by citation, natural language, terms and connectors, and so on. If the material is updated only monthly or quarterly, you may need to update your research using Westlaw or LexisNexis, which provide more timely information. For a list of law-related CD-ROM products, see the *Directory of Law-Related CD-ROMs* by Infosources Publishing at <http://www.infosourcespub.com>. This is a subscription service.

6.4   KEY POINTS CHECKLIST: COMPUTERS AND LEGAL RESEARCH

❑ It is important to know how to research using print resources because electronic resources may not be available or they may be too expensive to purchase. Electronic research systems are based on print resources, and a familiarity with print resources makes it easier to understand electronic research.

❑ A critical step in the research process is framing the issue in the context of the specific facts of the case. A well-framed issue, stated in the context of the facts, provides a researcher with the information necessary to conduct research using natural language or terms and connectors.

❏ Non-fee-based online research sources do not have a contractual duty to provide information that is accurate or up to date. You should verify the accuracy of any information that you obtain from such sites and determine whether the information is current.

❏ When using a CD-ROM, check to see how current the content is. It may be necessary to use another source to provide more up-to-date information.

Chapter 7

Preparing to Write—The Writing Process for Effective Legal Writing

Contents

 ## 7.1   INTRODUCTION

This chapter presents general directions for the legal writing process, including an approach to the writing process and guidelines to follow when engaging in the process. The legal writing process is a systematic approach that consists of three basic stages: the prewriting stage, the writing stage, and the postwriting stage. Charts listing tips and suggestions for each stage of the writing process are presented in Exhibits 7-1 through 7-3, followed by a discussion of each stage of the process.

General legal research suggestions and guidelines are presented in Exhibit 7-4. The suggestions are discussed in detail at the end of this chapter.

7.2   LEGAL WRITING PROCESS

A legal writing process is a systematic approach to legal writing. The process is an organized approach to legal research, analysis, and writing that helps you develop writing skills. It makes legal writing easier, and it is necessary for several additional reasons:

Exhibit 7-1

Sections of the Prewriting Stage

The Prewriting Stage

1. Assignment	A. Make sure that you understand the assigned task clearly. Identify the type and purpose of the writing assignment. If the assignment requires preparation of a document requiring legal research and analysis such as a legal research memorandum, be sure to identify the legal issue(s) to be researched. B. Identify the type of legal writing required: legal research and analysis memorandum, correspondence, case brief, court brief, and so on. C. Identify the audience: an attorney, a client, and so on.
2. Constraints	Identify any constraints placed on the assignment: A. Time—Is the performance of the assignment governed by a deadline? B. Length—Is the assignment governed by a length constraint; e.g., is it not supposed to exceed a certain number of pages? C. Format—What is the organization and format required for the type of legal writing required? Most law offices have guidelines governing the format of legal writing, such as research memorandums and correspondence. Courts often have rules governing the format of documents to be submitted to them.
3. Organization (Format)	Based on the format for the type of legal writing required, prepare and use an outline while gathering information, conducting research, and developing a rough draft. How to prepare and use an outline is discussed later in this chapter.
4. Preliminary Preparation	A. Gather information about the assignment. Review the case file and identify all of the key facts and terms relevant to the issue being researched. B. Preliminary Research. If necessary, conduct basic research to become familiar with the area(s) of law that govern(s) the issue(s) in the assignment.
5. Research	Identify the legal issue(s), the rule of law that governs the issue(s), and the law that interprets how the rule applies to the facts of the client's case (usually case law or secondary authority).

Exhibit 7-2

Guidelines and Suggestions for the Writing Stage

Writing Stage

1. Prepare the writing location.
2. Establish a timetable.
3. Do not begin to write until you are prepared.
4. Write during the time of day when you do your best work.
5. Begin with a part of the assignment you feel most confident about.
6. Begin writing; do not procrastinate.
7. Limit interruptions.
8. If you become stuck, move to another part of the assignment.
9. Do not try to make the first draft the final draft.

Exhibit 7-3

Postwriting Stage—Revising and Editing Checklist

Postwriting Stage—Revising and Editing

1. Make sure the writing is well organized.
2. Make sure the document is written in a manner the audience will understand.
3. Write clearly so that the content makes sense.
4. Write concisely. Eliminate any unnecessory words.
5. Make sure the writing is complete and all aspects of the assignment are covered.
6. Cite the legal authorities correctly.
7. Edit the document several times.
8. While editing, read the document aloud or have a colleague read it to you.
9. Have a colleague edit/proofread the document.

▶ Legal writing is highly organized and structured. The organized structure helps ensure that complex subject matter is clearly communicated.

■ *For Example:*

The IRAC (Issue, Rule, Analysis, Conclusion) analytical method is a structured approach to problem solving. The IRAC format, when followed in the preparation of a legal memorandum, helps ensure clear communication of the complex subject matter of analyzing a legal issue.

Exhibit 7-4

Guidelines and Suggestions for Conducting Research

Guidelines and Suggestions for Conducting Research

1. Prepare and use an expanded outline when conducting research.
2. Identify the issue first.
3. Research the issues one at a time.
4. Become familiar with the area of law.
5. Locate the enacted law that governs the question.
6. Locate the common/case law that may apply.
7. Make sure the research is current.
8. If you reach a dead end, reanalyze the issue.

The use of a legal writing process helps you conduct research and analysis within the structure and format of the type of legal writing assigned. A writing process saves time by providing a way to organize of your legal analysis and research material as you gathered it.

▶ If you do not have a writing process and merely gather research material and immediately begin to write, you will waste a great deal of time. You are not ready to write. If you begin to write without having organized your research and analysis or without having thought through what you are going to write, you will flounder. If you have gathered a mountain of research that requires a great deal of analysis, you will waste time determining what goes where and how to present the material. *A writing process forces you to think before you write.* It forces you to follow an organized structure from the beginning. When you sit down to write, you are ready. You will have thought through the project, and you will be organized.

▶ When you are researching or analyzing an assignment or engaging in legal writing, a writing process helps you capture ideas as they come to you. A process provides a framework for capturing ideas and recording them in their proper place as they occur. Without a process, your ideas may be lost. This topic is discussed under Subsection 7.2 A.3 in "Use of an Outline."

▶ A writing process also helps you overcome difficult areas of legal writing. You may get stuck in a difficult analytical area or encounter writer's block. A writing process helps you avoid those problems by providing a stepped approach. Often you become stuck or blocked because you missed a step or left something out. A process is a guide that includes all necessary steps and helps ensure that you leave nothing out.

There are many different processes and combinations of processes that you can adopt when engaging in legal writing. What works for one person may not work for you. You may ultimately adopt a process that includes steps from various approaches to legal writing, including some of those presented in this chapter. It does not matter what process you ultimately adopt, but it is essential that you adopt some writing process.

As mentioned in the introduction, the process of legal writing consists of three basic stages: the prewriting stage, the writing stage, and the postwriting stage. Each stage is discussed in the following sections.

7.2 A PREWRITING STAGE

The prewriting stage in the legal writing process is where an assignment is organized, researched, and analyzed. Novice writers often begin to write before they are prepared. One of the most important aspects of the writing process is performing the necessary preparation. Drafting is much easier when you are fully prepared to write. This stage of the writing process may be divided into four sections (see Exhibit 7-1 at the beginning of the chapter):

1. **Assignment**   You begin the writing process by identifying the type of assignment and its purpose. You must consider three questions when reviewing the assignment:
   ▶ Is the assignment clearly understood?
   ▶ What type of legal writing (document) is required?
   ▶ Who is the audience?

   a. ***Is the Assignment Clearly Understood?***—You may receive the assignment in the form of a written memorandum or through oral instructions from a supervising attorney. An early and important step in the prewriting stage is to be sure that you understand the task you have been assigned. If you have any questions concerning the general nature or specifics of the assignment, ask.

   If the assignment is to prepare a document requiring legal research and analysis, such as a legal research memorandum, be sure to clearly identify the legal issue(s) to be researched. The issue is the precise legal question raised by the facts of the case.

   If you misunderstand the assignment, you can waste a great deal of time undertaking the wrong task. Most attorneys welcome inquiries and prefer that a paralegal or legal assistant ask questions rather than proceed in the wrong direction. In this regard, if you are unclear about any aspect of the assignment, summarize the task orally with the supervisor. Another approach is to draft a brief recapitulation of the assignment and submit it for the supervisor's review and signature.

   b. ***What Type of Legal Writing (Document) Is Required?***—The next step is to determine the type of legal writing the assignment requires. This is important because each type of legal writing has a different function and different requirements. Before you begin, you must know what form of legal writing is required.

There are various types of legal writing and numerous ways to categorize them. The focus of this text is on the types of writing related to legal research and analysis, such as the following.

(1) **Legal Research Memorandum.**   A researcher may be assigned the task of researching and analyzing the law that applies to a client's case. The legal research memorandum is designed to inform the reader of the results of the research and analysis. The assignment may be as simple as identifying the statutory or case law that applies to a legal issue or as complex as identifying the issues in a case and analyzing the law that applies. Preparation of a legal research memorandum is discussed in Chapter 9.

(2) **Correspondence.**   There are several types of correspondence that you may be required to draft; for example, demand letters; settlement proposals; and notices of events, such as hearing dates. Your assignment may be to prepare the draft of a letter that will be sent to the client, informing the client of what law applies in his or her case and how the law applies. Neither a paralegal nor a legal assistant may give legal advice to the client, but he or she can prepare the draft of the correspondence that the attorney will send. Legal correspondence is addressed in Chapter 8.

(3) **Court Briefs.**   A court brief is a document filed with a court that contains an attorney's legal argument and the legal authority in support of that argument. There are primarily two categories of court briefs: trial court briefs and appellate court briefs.

Trial Court Brief. A court may require an attorney to submit a brief in support of a position he or she takes regarding a legal issue in the case. A trial court brief is usually submitted in support of or in opposition to a motion filed with the court.

> ❑ *For Example:*
>
> An attorney files a motion to dismiss a complaint, claiming that the statute of limitations has run. In support of the motion, the attorney files a legal brief that contains the legal and factual reasons why the court should grant the motion. The opposing side will also file a brief in opposition to the granting of the motion.

Appellate Court Brief. An appellate brief is a formal document filed with an appellate court. It presents the legal arguments and authorities in support of the client's position on appeal. It is designed to persuade the appellate court to rule in the client's favor.

Court briefs are discussed in detail in Chapter 10.

Each of those types of legal writing is structured differently. The organization and considerations involved in drafting the documents vary. The subsequent stages of the writing process are governed by an initial determination of the type of legal writing the assignment requires. Therefore, an early step in the prewriting stage is to identify the type of writing required.

Other types of legal writing may involve the drafting of legal documents such as contracts, wills, and pleadings. The specific considerations involved in the drafting of those documents are beyond the scope of this text. The writing process presented in this chapter, however, may be followed when preparing such documents.

c. *Who Is the Audience?*—An important step in assessing the requirements of an assignment is to identify the intended audience. Since the goal of legal writing is to clearly communicate information to the reader, the writing must be crafted so that it meets the needs of the reader.

Legal writing assignments may be designed to reach a number of different audiences. The intended reader may be a judge, an attorney, a client, or some other person. The ability of the reader to understand the writing will depend on his or her legal sophistication and the manner in which the document is written. You must identify the audience to ensure that the legal communication you craft is commensurate with the ability of the reader to understand the contents.

A legal writing designed to inform a client or another layperson of the legal analysis of an issue is drafted differently than a writing designed to convey the same information to an attorney. The use of fundamental legal terminology may be appropriate when the writing is to be read by a person trained in the law. On the other hand, if the reader has little or no legal training, nonlegal terms will be needed to convey the same information.

> **◻ *For Example:***
>
> **Communication to the supervising attorney:**
> The motion to suppress the evidence should be granted. Exigent circumstances that would have justified an unannounced entry were not present at the time the officers executed the warrant, and the judge who issued the search warrant did not authorize unannounced entry.
>
> **Communication of the same information to the client:**
> The court may not allow the prosecution to use at trial the evidence seized when the officers searched your house. The law requires officers to announce their presence before they enter your house to conduct a search. They are required to do this unless a judge gives them permission to enter without first announcing their presence. They may also enter unannounced if, when they arrive at your house, they believe that you are destroying evidence or present a danger to them. In your case, the judge did not authorize the officers to enter unannounced and nothing occurred when they arrived at your house to indicate that you were destroying drugs or you were a threat to them.

Another factor to consider is whether the writing is intended solely for internal office use. A writing that will be read only by individuals working in an office may contain information, comments, or assessments that would not be included in a writing intended to be read outside the office.

> **For Example:**
>
> "After analyzing the facts of the client's case and the applicable law, it may be necessary to convince the client to reconsider the amount of damages he believes he is entitled to recover and the possibility of settling this case. He needs to be informed about the amount of damages he can realistically expect to receive. He is adamant in his belief that he is entitled to over one million dollars, and he is not willing to consider settling for less. The range of recovery is more likely between ten thousand and one hundred thousand dollars."

2. **Constraints**   The next step in the prewriting process is to consider possible constraints that may affect the performance of the assignment. Three major constraints are presented in Exhibit 7-1.

   a. *Time*—The performance of an assignment may be governed by a time constraint. Most assignments have a deadline. You must determine what the deadline is. Once this is done, you can allocate a specific amount of time to each stage of the writing process.

> **For Example:**
>
> Suppose you have 15 days to write a legal research memorandum on an issue in a case. You should divide your time among the prewriting, writing, and postwriting stages of the writing process. A possible allocation could be six days for prewriting, five days for drafting, and four days for postwriting.

   If you fail to allocate your time or fail to stick to the allocation, you may become absorbed or stuck in one stage and fail to leave enough time to complete the assignment. It does no good to research and analyze an issue if you do not have time to translate the research and analysis into a written form.

> **For Example:**
>
> You may have 15 days to prepare a legal research memorandum. You become absorbed in the intricacies of the research and leave only two days to write the memo. This is not sufficient time to prepare a well-crafted product. As a result, you may miss the deadline for submitting the memorandum, or create a poorly written memorandum. In either event, your professional reputation is negatively affected.

   b. *Length*—The assignment may have a length constraint. If so, you should keep the length limitation in mind from the start. The amount of research material you gather is affected by this limitation. Of course, you must gather all applicable law. You must, however, screen the research to ensure that you do not gather excessive information. Keeping the length limitation in mind, consider how much of the material you are gathering can be included in the writing. Also, organize the writing to make sure that each section is allotted sufficient space.

> **□ *For Example:***
>
> The assignment is to prepare a legal research memorandum that does not exceed 15 pages. The organization must allocate sufficient space for each section of the memorandum. If the analysis ends up consisting of 14 pages, there will not be sufficient space for including the facts, the issue, and the conclusion.

   c. ***Format***—Most law offices have rules or guidelines that govern the organization and format of most types of legal writing, such as case briefs, legal research memorandums, and correspondence. Courts have formal rules governing the format and style of briefs and other documents submitted for filing.

> **□ *For Example:***
>
> Many courts have rules governing the size of the paper, the size of the margins, the length of briefs, and so on.

Because the assignment must be drafted within the constraints of the required format, that format must be identified at the beginning of the prewriting process.

3. **Organization (Format)**   *Organization in the prewriting stage is key to successful legal writing.* You must be organized when conducting research and analysis in the prewriting stage, and the assignment must be organized when it is written. This can be accomplished through the development and use of an outline. An outline is the skeletal structure and organizational framework of legal writing. Three aspects of outlines are as follows:

► value of an outline
► creation of an outline
► use of an outline

   a. ***Value of an Outline***—An outline is useful in the writing stage. It makes writing easier by providing an organized framework for the presentation of research and analysis. *An outline, however, is of greatest value when it is properly used in the prewriting stage.* There are several reasons for this:

   ► Creating an outline forces you to organize ideas and prepare an approach to the assignment at the beginning of the process. This helps you think through all aspects of the assignment and take a global view, thereby avoiding gaps and weaknesses in your approach. You focus your attention and organize your thinking before you jump into the assignment.

   ► Using an outline saves time. When an outline is used properly, all of the information from a research source is placed in the outline while research is being performed. You waste time when you have to retrieve a research source for a second or third time to gather information that you initially thought was not important or that you forgot to retrieve.

▶ An outline provides an organized framework for the structure of the assignment and for conducting research and analysis. It provides a context within which to place research and ideas as they are found. This use is discussed in more detail under Subsection 7.2 A.3 in "Use of an Outline."

▶ An outline breaks complex problems into manageable components. It provides an organized framework from which to approach complex problems.

b. *Creation of an Outline*—The goal when creating an outline is to prepare the skeletal framework of the document you are going to draft. The outline should provide an overall picture of how all of the pieces of the assignment relate to each other and fit together. The form of the outline is not important. Whether you use roman numerals (I and II), capital letters (A and B), narrative sentences, fragments of sentences, or single words does not matter. Use whatever form or style works for you. It is recommended that you do use indentations to separate main topics from subtopics.

> ❏ *For Example:*
>
> I. Introduction
> II. Issue
> III. Analysis
>   A. Rule of law
>   B. Case law
>   1. Name of case
>   2. Facts of case

The outline of the legal writing is governed by the type of writing you are preparing. Locate the standard format used in the office for the type of legal writing you are drafting. In the case of a legal research memorandum or correspondence, the law office may have a special format that you must follow. Use that format as the basis for the outline. Outline formats for correspondence, legal research memorandums, and court briefs are presented in Chapters 8 through 10.

If the writing is to be filed in court, such as an appellate brief, follow the format set out in the court rules. Whatever the basic format is, it may be necessary to make additions and expand the outline.

> ❏ *For Example:*
>
> Assume the firm's format for a legal research memorandum is as follows:
>
> 1. description of assignment
> 2. issue
> 3. facts
> 4. analysis
> 5. conclusion

This is a broad format that needs a lot of filling in to be useful. It may be necessary to fill in details for each section.

■ *For Example:*

An expansion of the analysis section may be as follows:

4. Analysis
    1. Introduction
    2. Rule of law
    3. Case interpreting the rule of law
        a. Name of case/citation
        b. Facts of case
        c. Rule of law or legal principle presented in the case that applies to the client's facts
        d. Application of rule/principle from the case to the client's facts

That outline example is referred to in this chapter as the analysis outline example.

When developing an outline, there are several points to keep in mind:

(1) **Keep the facts and issues of the assignment in mind while developing the outline.**   It may be necessary to expand the outline to accommodate additional facts and issues.

■ *For Example:*

The standard office outline may have only one issue. Your assignment may involve more than one issue. Your outline should be expanded to apply the standard office outline to each issue.

(2) **Be flexible when creating and working with an outline.**   Realize that it may be necessary to change the outline as you conduct research.

■ *For Example:*

Assume the assignment involves the drafting of a simple legal research memorandum that addresses one issue. The outline you decide to follow is the analysis outline example presented above. When you conduct your research, it becomes apparent that there are two aspects of the rule of law that apply to the issue and two court opinions that need to be included in the analysis. The memo outline must now be expanded as follows:

4. Analysis
    a) Introduction
    b) Rule of law
    c) Case interpreting the meaning of publication as used in the rule of law
        (1) Name of case/citation
        (2) Facts of case

>   (3) Interpretation of term
>   (4) Application of the interpretation to the client's facts
>   *d*) Case interpreting the meaning of written as used in the rule of law
>   (1) Name of case/citation
>   (2) Facts of case
>   (3) Interpretation of term
>   (4) Application of the interpretation to the client's facts

(3) Do not be surprised if you find that you must reorganize the outline as a result of your research. Research may provide a clearer picture of the relationship between issues and necessitate that you rethink the organization of the outline.

> ◘ *For Example:*
>
> As a result of your research, you realize that the sequence in which you planned to address the issues should be changed. The issue you thought should be discussed first should now come second.

(4) The basic organizational format for most legal writing is the IRAC format. First state the question or issue, then identify the rule of law that governs the issue, next analyze how and why the rule applies, and then end with a conclusion summarizing the analysis. You can follow this format when addressing each issue and subissue. If, for some reason, you are at a loss for a format to follow, use the IRAC format.

c. *Use of an Outline—The value of an outline is determined by its use.* If you prepare an outline and then set it aside while you are researching and analyzing the assignment, it is of limited value. Its only value when used in this manner is to help you organize your thinking and to provide the organizational framework for the writing that follows. An outline is of greatest value when it is actively integrated into the prewriting stage. It can serve as an invaluable guide during the research and analysis process.

> ◘ *For Example:*
>
> Follow the outline format when researching and analyzing: first identify the issue, next locate the rule of law that governs the issue, then identify the case law that interprets the rule of law in a fact situation similar to the client's case, and so on.

When integrated in the research and analysis process, an outline provides an organized context within which to place research and ideas. When so used, it will result in the development of a rough draft while research and analysis are being conducted. The result is a tremendous savings of time and effort. *The integrated use of an outline in the prewriting stage simplifies the writing stage, making it much easier.*

How, then, is an outline integrated into the research and analysis process in the prewriting stage? This can be accomplished in several ways. The practical approach suggested here is to use an expanded outline. This approach is composed of two steps.

Assume you are assigned the task of preparing a legal research memorandum addressing a single issue in a client's case. The cause of action is a slander tort claim. The broad issue is whether there was publication within the meaning of the law. Section 20-2-2 of the state statutes provides that civil slander is "the oral publication of a false statement of fact concerning an individual . . . ." The statute does not define *publication*. The facts of the case are that neighbor A, while visiting neighbor B's house, communicated to neighbor B a false statement of fact concerning the client.

That example is referred to in this chapter as the slander example.

The format for the body of a legal research memorandum adopted in the office is as follows:

I. Issue
II. Statement of facts
III. Analysis/application
  A. Rule of law—the rule of law that governs the issue—enacted/common law
  B. Case(s)—court interpretation of rule if necessary
    1. Name and citation
    2. Brief summary of facts showing case is on point
    3. Rule/principle/reasoning applied by the court that applies to client's case
    4. Application—discussion of how the rule of law presented in the court decision applies in the client's case
  C. Counteranalysis
IV. Conclusion—a summary of the analysis

Step 1 Convert the outline to a usable form—an expanded outline. The memorandum format used in the office is typed on one sheet of paper and is not very useful in this form. *The first step in the use of the outline is to convert it to a usable form—to expand the outline.* This is accomplished by taking several sheets of three-holed or binder paper (or creating separate pages if you are using a computer) and writing (or typing) the name of each section and subsection of the outline at the top of a separate page.

▢ *For Example:*

At the top of one sheet of paper or computer page, write or type the word *Issue*. At the top of another page, insert *Statement of facts*. At the top of another page, insert *Analysis—rule of law*. Continue with a new page for each of the following: *Analysis—case, Analysis—application of case to client's facts, Counteranalysis,* and *Conclusion.*

Some sections of the outline may require more than one page.

> ■ *For Example:*
>
> The *Analysis—case* section may require two pages: one page for *Analysis—case—citation and facts of case* and one page for *Analysis—case—rule/principle/reasoning*. Two or more pages may be required for a case because, in many instances, a great deal of information is taken from a case, such as lengthy quotes from the court's reasoning.

When more than one rule of law applies, there should be a separate page for each rule of law. When several cases apply, there are separate pages for each case. When there are separate issues, *each issue should be researched and analyzed separately* and there should be a separate expanded outline for each issue.

When completed, there should be a separate page for each section and subsection of the outline. The pages should be placed in a loose-leaf binder or entered in the computer in the order of the outline. In other words, the first page is the Issue page, followed by the Statement of facts page, then the Analysis—rule of law page, and so on. If you are using binder paper, insert blank sheets of paper between each section. This allows you to expand each section to accommodate additional notes, comments, and ideas. The end result is a greatly expanded outline for use in the prewriting stage.

Step 2 Integrate all research, analysis, and ideas into the outline while conducting research and analysis. As you conduct your research and ideas occur to you concerning any aspect of the assignment, enter them on the appropriate page of the expanded outline.

Ideas. When any idea occurs concerning the case, enter it on the page of the expanded outline that relates to that idea.

> ■ *For Example:*
>
> You may have a broad definition of the issue, such as the question "Was there slander?" As you conduct research and give more thought to the case, more refined formulations of the issue will become apparent, such as "Under § 20-2-2, does slander occur when one person orally communicates to a third party false statements of fact concerning an individual?" As soon as a formulation of the issue comes to you, write it on the issue page.

The word *ideas* used here includes all thoughts relating to the writing of the assignment, such as how to compose transition sentences.

> ■ *For Example:*
>
> While researching a case, an idea may come to you about how to write the transition sentence linking the case to the rule of law. Write the sentence at the beginning of the case section of the expanded outline or at the end of the Rule of law page.

Keep the expanded outline with you at all times, even at home. Often your mind will work on an aspect of a case while you sleep. You may wake up with an idea concerning the assignment or with the answer to a problem. If the expanded outline is handy, you can enter the idea or answer in the appropriate section.

The value of being able to immediately place ideas where they belong in the structure of the writing cannot be overemphasized. Following are some of the benefits.

▶ Ideas are not lost. When researching, you may have an idea and say to yourself "I'll remember to include this when I write the _______ section." Five minutes later the idea is lost. If you can immediately write the idea down where it belongs, you will not lose it.

▶ Confusion is avoided when ideas are recorded in the section where they will appear in the writing.

> ◘ *For Example:*
>
> While you are reading a case that interprets the rule of law, an idea occurs that relates to another aspect of the assignment, such as "This gives me an idea about the counteranalysis of this issue." You may jot down the idea on a separate piece of paper or think you will remember it. You say to yourself "I'll remember to include this when I write the counteranalysis." By the time you get down to writing, time has passed. You cannot remember what the idea was or, if you jotted it down, where the idea fits into the assignment. You have several pieces of paper containing notes and ideas, and you have forgotten what many of them relate to or how they relate.

▶ Writing is made easier. When you sit down to write, all ideas are at your fingertips, each in its proper place. You do not waste time performing the additional step of organizing ideas. You have already organized ideas as they came to you.

> ◘ *For Example:*
>
> If the Issue page of the expanded outline contains all of the ideas concerning the ways the issue can be stated, it is easier to craft the final draft. All of the possible variations are visually before you in one plac. Drafting it is just a matter of assembling it from the best of the variations.

Research. Just as you put ideas in the proper place in the expanded outline as they occur to you, you should enter all of the relevant research on the appropriate page as you conduct your research.

> 🔲 *For Example:*
>
> Referring to the slander example, when the slander statute § 20-2-2 is located, place it on the Rule of law page. Include the proper citation and a copy of the statute. In the outline on this page, include all information about the statute that you may need when writing. This ensures that you do not have to look up the statute more than once.
>
> When you find the case or cases on point, enter all of the information on the appropriate case page of the outline. This information should include the full citation, pertinent quotes concerning the rule of law or legal principle applied by the court, and the legal reasoning.

When researching case law, retrieve everything you need from the case and include it in the expanded outline. Why waste time looking up the same case twice? Place a copy of the case in the outline if necessary.

> 🔲 *For Example:*
>
> First, read through the entire case. Then, on the second reading, as you come upon a statement of the legal principle or legal reasoning that may apply to the client's case, stop reading. Enter the information from the case in the appropriate page of the expanded outline. Indicate the page of the case from which it was taken and quote the information if appropriate.

All too often the tendency when reading a case is to tell yourself that you will come back and note the pertinent information later. Often the reasoning or rule you want to use is not where you remembered it to be, and you waste time wading through the case trying to find it. If there is any possibility that you will use information from a case, *retrieve it as you find it* and place on the appropriate case page of the outline. You will save time by not having to reread portions of the case.

If it turns out that information you have retrieved will not be used in the legal writing, you simply do not use it. You are better off having everything about a case in your expanded outline when you sit down to write than having to stop, retrieve, and reread the case.

Transition sentences. Transition sentences connect the major sections of the writing and lead the reader smoothly through the legal analysis. They make the document more readable. It is easy to become so focused on the law, cases, and analysis that you forget the transitions. As the formulation of transition sentences come to you, place them on the appropriate page of the outline.

> 🔲 *For Example:*
>
> The rule of law that governs this issue is § 36-6-6, which prohibits oppressive conduct by majority shareholders. In the case of *Jones v. Thomas,* the court held . . .

> There should be a transition sentence linking the case to the rule of law:
> The rule of law that governs this issue is § 36-6-6, which prohibits op-
> pressive conduct by majority shareholders. *Since the statute does not
> provide a definition of the term* oppressive conduct, *case law must be
> referred to. A case on point is Jones v. Thomas, where the court held . . .*

Place the transition sentence on the Rule of law page of the outline.

If you use an expanded outline as suggested here, you are ready to write. All of your research and ideas are assembled and organized. In effect, you have prepared a rough draft, and the writing task is made much simpler: the organization is done, ideas are captured, research is assembled in the proper place, and many transition sentences are already crafted and in place. The writing task is reduced simply to converting the outline to paragraph and sentence form.

4. **Preliminary Preparation**   After the outline has been prepared, the next part of the prewriting stage is preliminary preparation. This section is broken down into two parts: (1) gathering information about the case and identifying key facts and terms and (2) conducting preliminary legal research if necessary.

Part 1—Gather Information and Identify Key Facts. Gather and review all of the information about the case; that is, the facts. *In every case, the legal re-search and analysis process involves determining how the law applies to the facts.* Facts of the client's case play a crucial role in legal research and analysis: the key facts are included in the issue; a determination of which law governs the issue is largely governed by the facts; how the law applies is governed by the facts. With-out the facts, the law stands in a vacuum.

With that in mind, you should begin the analysis process by considering the facts of the client's case. You should identify and review the facts at the outset. That preliminary step should include the following:

1. Make sure you have all of the facts. Ask yourself if you have all of the inter-views, files, statements, and other information about the case that you have been gathering.
2. Study the available facts to see if you should gather additional information before beginning legal analysis.
3. Organize the facts. Group all related facts. Place the facts in logical order, such as in the sequence in which they occurred (chronological) or according to topic (topical).
4. Weigh the facts. The value of some factual information, such as hearsay, may be questionable.

List all of the facts on the Facts page of the research outline.
Once you have gathered the information, the next step is to identify the facts that appear to be critical to the outcome of the case—the key facts. *Iden-tify the key facts on the Facts page of the research outline.*
Part 2—Conduct Preliminary Research. *Before conducting any re-search, check the office research files for previous memos or research that may*

have addressed the issue(s) you are researching. Doing so may eliminate the need for further research.

It may be necessary to conduct basic research in the area(s) of law that govern the issue(s) in the case. You may be unfamiliar with the area of law in general or with the specific aspect of the law that applies in the client's case. You may be able to obtain a general overview from a legal encyclopedia or a single-volume treatise. If you know the specific question or area at the outset, an A.L.R. reference or a multivolume treatise may be appropriate. Identification of key terms helps guide you to the areas you need to conduct the research.

When preliminary research is necessary, create a Preliminary research page in the outline. Include the results of the research on this page. Add all of the relevant information, including the official citation of the source. If the material is lengthy, copy it and attach it to the page.

5. **Research**   The last section of the prewriting stage is to conduct the research necessary to perform the assignment. This requires identifying the legal issue(s), the rule of law that governs the issue, and the law that interprets how the rule applies to the facts of the client's case (usually case law or secondary authority). This topic is discussed in detail with regard to correspondence, legal research memorandums, and court briefs in Chapters 8, 9, and 10, respectively. You should place the relevant portions of the research in the appropriate sections of the expanded outline, as discussed previously under Subsection 7.2 A.3 in "Use of an Outline."

7.2 B   WRITING STAGE

The second stage in the writing process is the actual drafting of the legal writing. In this stage, the research, analysis, and ideas are assembled into a written product. Many people find it difficult to go from the research stage to the drafting stage, from the prewriting stage to the writing stage—often called writer's block. Obstacles that make it difficult to begin writing are how to organize the research and determine what goes where, how the research relates, and how the research is connected. As discussed under Subsection 7.2 A.3 in "Use of an Outline," using an expanded outline in the prewriting stage makes it easier to begin writing.

A detailed discussion of what must be included when writing a legal research memorandum, a court brief, or legal correspondence is included in Chapters 8 through 10. General rules and guidelines that help with the writing process are presented here (also presented in chart form in Exhibit 7-2 at the beginning of the chapter).

Prepare the writing location. Make sure the work environment is pleasant and physically comfortable. Have on hand all of the resources you will need: paper, computer, research materials, and so on.

Establish a timetable. Break the project into logical units and allocate your time accordingly. This helps you avoid spending too much time on one section of the writing and running out of time. Do not become fanatical about the time schedule, however. You created the timetable; you can change it. Its purpose is to keep you on track and alert you to the overall time constraints.

Do not begin to write until you are prepared. Do all of the research and analysis before beginning to write. It is much easier to write a rough draft when the prewriting stage is complete.

Write during the time of day when you do your best work.

Begin with a part of the assignment you feel most confident about. You do not have to write in the sequence of the outline. Write the easiest material first, especially if you are having trouble starting.

Begin writing; do not procrastinate. Often one of the most difficult steps is beginning to write. Do not put it off. The longer you put it off, the harder it will become. Start writing anything that has to do with the project. Do not expect what you begin with to be great; just start. Once you begin writing, it will get easier.

Limit interruptions. Legal writing requires focus and concentration. Therefore, select a writing time and environment that allows you to be free from interruptions and distractions.

If you become stuck, move to another part of the assignment. If you are stuck on a particular section, leave it. The mind continues to work on a problem when a person is unaware of it. That is why solutions to problems often seem to appear in the morning. Let your subconscious work on the problem while you move on. The solution may become apparent when you return to the problem.

Do not try to make the first draft the final draft. The goal of the first draft should be to translate the research and analysis into organized paragraphs and sentences, not to create a finished product. Write the information in rough form. It is easier to polish a rough draft than to try to make the first draft a finished product.

7.2 C POSTWRITING STAGE

In the postwriting stage of the legal writing process, an assignment is revised, edited, and assembled in final form (see Exhibit 7-3 at the beginning of the chapter).

1. **Revising** The first draft will not be the final draft. All initial drafts should be reviewed with the intent of improving quality and clarity. Do not be surprised if the initial draft requires several redrafts. Do not set a limit on the number of redrafts required. Your goal in drafting the final product should be to convey the necessary information clearly, concisely, and completely. The number of redrafts is governed by this goal. Develop a checklist to use when reviewing a draft (see Exhibit 7-3 at the beginning of the chapter). Items you may want to include in the checklist are as follows:

   ▶ Is the writing well organized? Is it organized in a logical manner? Does each section logically follow the previous section?

   ▶ Is the document written in a manner the audience will understand? If the writing is addressed to a layperson, is the draft written in plain language the reader will understand?

   ▶ Is the writing clear? Does it make sense? Are the sections connected with transition sentences that clearly link the sections and guide the reader from one section to the next?

▶ Is the writing concise? Are there extra words that can be eliminated? Is the writing repetitive? If multiple examples are included to illustrate a single point, are all of the examples necessary?

▶ Is the writing complete? Are all aspects of the assignment covered? If there are multiple issues, is each issue and subissue thoroughly analyzed?

▶ Are the legal authorities correctly cited? Are all legal citations in the correct form? All legal research sources must be correctly cited. The rules and resources for ensuring the accuracy of your citations are discussed in Chapter 5.

When reviewing a draft, allow time to elapse between drafting and revising. This allows the mind to clear. You can then approach the revision with a fresh perspective, being more likely to catch errors and inconsistencies.

2. **Editing**   Editing is actually part of the revision process. The revision process discussed in the previous section addresses the broad intellectual and structural content of the legal writing, such as overall organization, clarity, and conciseness. Editing focuses on technical writing issues, such as punctuation, spelling, grammar, phrasing, typographical errors, and citation errors. When you need to check the accuracy of your writing, consult the current edition of a reference source such as a dictionary or the *Chicago Manual of Style*. A checklist to use when proofreading legal writing is presented in Exhibit 7-5.

Many of these specific areas are discussed in Chapters 1 through 4. A few general editing tips to keep in mind, however, are as follows:

▶ Be prepared to edit a legal writing several times. It may be necessary to edit a revision several times to catch all errors.

▶ Read the document aloud. When you silently read your own draft, your mind may automatically fill in a missing word or correct an error without your knowing it, and you will not catch the error. If possible, have a colleague read the document to you.

▶ Have another person edit the document. Have a colleague whose writing skills you respect edit the document.

7.3   GENERAL RESEARCH SUGGESTIONS

Research is usually the major part of prewriting. Following are general suggestions and guidelines concerning legal research as it relates to the prewriting stage. These suggestions and guidelines are presented in chart format in Exhibit 7-4 at the beginning of the chapter.

1. *Prepare and use an expanded outline when conducting research.* This topic is discussed in detail under Subsection 7.2 A.3 in "Use of an Outline."

2. *Identify the issue first.* Your first step should be to identify the issue, as you cannot begin to look for an answer until you know the question. The preliminary

Exhibit 7-5

Proofreading Checklist

Checklist to Use When Proofreading Legal Writing

Sentence Structure/Pattern
- ❏ Phrases and Clauses
- ❏ Subject/Verb Distance
- ❏ Sentence Length
- ❏ Excessive/Redundant Words
- ❏ Sentence Variety
- ❏ Run-on Sentences
- ❏ Sentence Fragments
- ❏ Mood Shifts
- ❏ Active/Passive Voice
- ❏ Action Verbs
- ❏ Repeated Prepositions
- ❏ Transitions

Paragraphs
- ❏ Topic Sentence
- ❏ Body
- ❏ Closing
- ❏ Transition Sentence
- ❏ Paragraph Length

Word Selection and Usage
- ❏ Noun/Verb String
- ❏ Nominalizations
- ❏ Legalese
- ❏ Archaic Words
- ❏ Sexist Language
- ❏ Excessive/Redundant Words
- ❏ Spelling
- ❏ Numbers

- ❏ Capitalization
- ❏ Abbreviations
- ❏ Italics/Underlining
- ❏ Formal Writing Conventions

Grammar
- ❏ Subject/Verb Agreement
- ❏ Noun/Pronoun Agreement
- ❏ Verb Tense and Superfluous Verbs
- ❏ Adverbs, Adjectives, and Conjunctions
- ❏ Parallel Construction
- ❏ Modifiers and Infinitives

Punctuation
- ❏ Commas
- ❏ Semicolon
- ❏ Colon
- ❏ Apostrophe
- ❏ Quotation Marks
- ❏ Period
- ❏ Question Mark
- ❏ Exclamation Point
- ❏ Ellipses
- ❏ Brackets
- ❏ Parentheses
- ❏ Hyphen
- ❏ Dash
- ❏ Slash

identification of the issue may be very broad, such as "Did negligence occur?" or "Was there a breach of contract when the goods were delivered ten days late?" This preliminary identification of the issue usually identifies the general area of law to be researched, such as contracts or negligence.

3. *Research the issues one at a time.* Thoroughly research one issue to its conclusion before proceeding to the next issue. If you find material on another issue, make a reference to it on the appropriate page in the expanded outline. Frustration and confusion can result from attempting to research several issues at once.

4. *Become familiar with the area of law.* If you are unfamiliar with the area of law that applies to the issue, obtain a general overview. Legal encyclopedias and treatises are sources you may consult to obtain an overview of an area of law.

5. *Locate the enacted law that governs the question.* Look first for any enacted law that governs the question, such as a statute or constitutional provision.

6. *Locate the common/case law that may apply.* Locate the relevant common/case law if there is no enacted law that governs or if the enacted law is so broadly drafted that case law is required to interpret the enacted law. Mandatory precedent should be located first, then persuasive precedent and secondary authority.

7. *Make sure the research is current.* Check supplements and "shepardize" cases to be sure that the authority located is current.

8. *If you reach a dead end, reanalyze the issue.* If you cannot find any authority, either primary or secondary, chances are the issue is too broadly or too narrowly stated. Restate the issue. If the issue is too broadly stated, restate it in narrower terms. Return to a basic research source for guidance, such as a legal encyclopedia. If the issue is too narrowly framed, restate it in broader terms.

7.4 KEY POINTS CHECKLIST: THE WRITING PROCESS

❑ Adopt a writing process. An organized approach is essential for legal writing. Develop a process that works for you. Follow the process recommended in this chapter or create your own.

❑ Work from an expanded outline in the prewriting stage. An expanded outline provides a framework for organizing your research and capturing your ideas.

❑ Consider the audience. Identify the audience early in the process. The style, depth, and complexity of the finished product are influenced by the type of audience.

❑ Consider time, length, and format constraints. Identify any constraints that affect the assignment. Design the approach to the assignment with these constraints in mind.

❑ Do not procrastinate. If you have trouble beginning to write, start with the easiest section. Sit down and begin. Do not worry about quality; just start.

❑ Break large assignments into manageable sections. Do not become overwhelmed by the complexity of an assignment.

❑ Do not try to make the first draft the final draft. Be prepared to compose several drafts. The goal is a quality product. Let the number of redrafts be determined by this goal.

❑ Update your research. Check all authorities to ensure that your research is current.

Chapter **8**

Legal Correspondence

Contents

◆ 8.1 INTRODUCTION

This chapter and Chapter 10 focus primarily on the preparation of documents that contain legal research and analysis and are designed for an audience outside the law office. This chapter examines the preparation of documents designed for an external audience other than a court. These documents are usually correspondence addressed to a client. However, you may draft correspondence to other audiences, such as witnesses, court personnel, and opposing counsel.

Correspondence is a major form of written communication between a law firm and the outside world. Other than documents submitted to courts and transaction documents such as contracts, correspondence is the *primary form* of writing designed for an audience outside the law office.

It is essential, therefore, that correspondence be well crafted because it helps establish and maintain a positive image of the law firm. Correspondence that contains grammatical and/or substantive errors or that is difficult to understand reflects poorly on the law firm, diminishing its reputation.

Since most legal correspondence is in letter rather than memo form, the term *letter* is used in this chapter to refer to legal correspondence. The three main categories of letters that include legal research and analysis to some degree are as follows:

1. letters that provide information—*informational letters*
2. letters that provide answers or legal opinions—*opinion letters*
3. letters that demand action—*demand letters*

Although the focus in this chapter is on letters that contain legal research and analysis, other types of letters are briefly mentioned. Following a discussion of the components common to the three categories mentioned above, each category is addressed in a separate section of the chapter.

8.2   BASIC COMPONENTS

Basic conventions apply to the various types of letters prepared in a law office, and basic components are usually present in all of the letters. However, each of these components may not be necessary or required in every letter you draft. This section introduces all of the components so that you will be familiar with them.

The content and manner of presentation of each of the components discussed here may vary from office to office. Compose your letters according to the guidelines adopted in your office. Refer to the letters in Appendix A for examples of the components discussed in the following sections.

The basic format and components of letters prepared in a law office are presented in Exhibit 8-1.

Exhibit 8-1

Basic Format and Components of Letters

Basic Format and Components of Law Office Correspondence

- ❑ Letterhead/Heading
- ❑ Date
- ❑ Method of Delivery
- ❑ Recipient's Address Block
- ❑ Reference (Re:) Line
- ❑ Salutation
- ❑ Body
- ❑ Closing
- ❑ Signature and Title
- ❑ Reference Initials
- ❑ Enclosure Notation
- ❑ Others Receiving Copies

8.2 A   LETTERHEAD

The letterhead usually contains the full name, address, telephone number, and fax number of the law firm. The letterhead is usually preprinted on the firm's stationery and centered at the top of the page. An example of a letterhead is as follows:

Tompkin, Belter and Ryan
751 Main Street
Friendly, New Washington 00065
(200) 444-7778 • FAX 444-7678 • www.thomaslaw.com

Subsequent pages contain an identification of the letter, which is usually called a header. These pages do not contain the letterhead. The header includes the name of the addressee, the date, and the page number. It is placed at the top left or right margin of the page. An example of a header is as follows:

Arlin Cook
May 5, 2006
Page Three

8.2 B   DATE

The full date is usually placed below the letterhead at the left or right margin. It may also be centered below the letterhead. The date should include the full date: the day, month, and year. Since most correspondence is filed chronologically, a date is essential. Note that many offices date-stamp correspondence when it is received in the office and file it according to that date.

8.2 C   METHOD OF DELIVERY

At the left margin below the date is the method of delivery. This notation is usually required only when the manner of delivery is other than U.S. mail. Examples are as follows:

Via Federal Express
Via Hand Delivery
Via Facsimile

8.2 D   RECIPIENT'S ADDRESS BLOCK

Below the date and method of delivery is the address block of the addressee. It is placed at the left margin. The address block should include the following:

- ▶ the name of the person to whom the letter is addressed
- ▶ the individual's title (if any)

- ▶ the name of the business (if applicable)
- ▶ the address

Following is an example of an address block.

Mirian Counter
President
Friendly Enterprises
139 Main Street
Friendly, NW 00065

8.2 E   REFERENCE (RE:) LINE

The reference line briefly identifies the topic of the letter. A reference line is usually placed at the left margin following the address block. Some firms require that the reference line include the case name and number when the letter concerns a pending lawsuit. Following is an example of a reference line.

Re: Request for production of documents
Smith v. Jones, Civil Action 03-1001

8.2 F   SALUTATION

Below the reference line is the salutation, or greeting. Legal correspondence is generally formal in tone, as is the greeting. An example of a greeting follows.

Dear Ms. Counter:

You may use the first name of the addressee if you know the person well. When in doubt, ask the supervisory attorney. If you do not know the name of the addressee, as when the letter is addressed to a business, contact the business and ascertain the individual's name. The use of *To whom it may concern* is very impersonal and invites a slow response. A person is more likely to respond quickly when he or she is specifically named.

8.2 G   BODY

The body is the heart of the letter—what the letter is about. The body is usually composed of an introduction, the main body, and requests or instructions.

1. **Introduction**   The body of the letter usually begins with an introductory sentence or paragraph (if necessary) that identifies or summarizes the main purpose of the letter.

> ◘ *For Example:*
>
> This letter is to advise you of the filing of a motion for summary judgment by the defendant. The hearing on the motion is scheduled to take place on March 4, 2006.
>
> This letter is to confirm our conversation today in which you stated that you would not be able to attend the hearing scheduled to take place on May 16, 2006.

2. Main Body Following the introduction is the main body of the letter. The main body explains in detail the purpose of the letter. Craft the main body with care to ensure that you communicate the required information clearly and concisely. It may be necessary to use an outline when a letter covers multiple or complex matters. As with a legal research memorandum or court brief, the body may require several drafts.

You must always consider the audience when drafting the main body. When you are drafting the letter to a layperson, such as a client, avoid the use of legalese and define and explain clearly any legal terms that you use.

When writing to a layperson, consider the sophistication of the reader. Ask yourself these questions:

▶ How familiar with legal matters is the reader?

▶ Does the reader often read material that involves complex subjects?

Although the addressee may not be familiar with the law, the individual may be highly educated or may often deal with complex or technical matters. In such cases, you may be able to craft a more complex letter and present the subject matter with greater legal or technical detail. If the reader does not as a matter of course engage in a lot of complex or technical reading or is not familiar with such matters, you should avoid including a detailed, complex discussion in the main body.

The content of the body will differ according to the type of letter you are drafting. The sections of this chapter that address information, opinion, and demand letters will discuss differences in the format and content of the body of these types of correspondence.

3. Requests/Instructions Include any requests or instructions for the recipient in the last section of the body.

> ◘ *For Example:*
>
> Please bring with you copies of the contract and any other written material related to the contract.
>
> Please keep a daily diary. Include in it a detailed description of all daily activities, such as how long you sleep, what physical activities you engage in during the day, and so on.

In some instances, a paralegal or legal assistant may draft and sign a letter to the client. A paralegal or legal assistant may sign a letter that provides general information. *Neither may sign a letter that gives a legal opinion or legal advice.* Most state laws and rules of ethics prohibit a paralegal or legal assistant from practicing law, and providing a legal opinion or legal advice constitutes the practice of law. Therefore, when preparing a letter that a paralegal or legal assistant will sign, do not include a legal opinion or provide legal advice.

8.2 H   CLOSING

The closing follows the body of the letter. The closing usually consists of some standard statement. Following are examples of closings.

- ▶ Thank you for your prompt consideration of this matter.
  Sincerely,
- ▶ Please contact me if you have any questions regarding this matter.
  Very truly yours,
- ▶ Thank you for your assistance.
  Best regards,

8.2 I   SIGNATURE AND TITLE

Following the closing is the signature and title of the person signing the letter.

> **For Example:**
>
> [Shannon Roark's signature]
> Shannon Roark
> Attorney at Law
>
> When the individual signing the letter is a paralegal or legal assistant, the paralegal or legal assistant status should be clearly indicated below the signature line, as in the following examples:
>
> - ▶ [Manuel Lucero's signature]
>   Manuel Lucero
>   Paralegal
> - ▶ [Inez Larson's signature]
>   Inez Larson
>   Legal Assistant

8.2 J   REFERENCE INITIALS

The final notation on the letter is a reference to the author of the letter and the typist. The author's initials are noted in all capitals, and the typist's are noted in lowercase letters; for example: JDR/mwt.

8.2 K   ENCLOSURE NOTATION

If enclosures such as contracts or documents are included with the letter, indicate their presence by typing *Enc.* or *Encs.* at the left margin following the signature.

> ■ *For Example:*
>
> [Shannon Roark's signature]
> Shannon Roark
> Attorney at Law
> Encs.

8.2 L   OTHERS RECEIVING COPIES

If another person or other persons are receiving copies of the letter, indicate this fact by typing *cc:* and the name of the individual(s) after the signature and title. This notation follows the enclosure notation when an enclosure notation is used. An example is as follows:

cc: Colin Nagle
Mae Carrey

If you are uncertain who should receive copies, check with your supervisor.

8.2 M   FORMAT STYLE

The basic format of a letter varies from firm to firm and is dictated by personal taste and style. Two basic styles are block and modified block. In block format, everything but the letterhead begins at the left margin. The information letter presented in Appendix A is typed in block style. In modified block, the date and the closing lines (closing and signature and title) begin near the horizontal center of the page. The first line of each paragraph is indented. The opinion letter in Appendix A is shown in modified block style.

8.3   GENERAL CONSIDERATIONS—ALL CORRESPONDENCE

Adopt the highest standards of accuracy, both substantive and stylistic, when drafting legal correspondence. As mentioned in the introduction to the chapter, correspondence helps determine the image, reputation, and success of a law firm. In many situations, the information provided in the correspondence constitutes the practice of law and subjects the firm to possible liability for claims of legal malpractice. Therefore, the quality of the product is critically important. You should do the following:

▶ Take the utmost care to ensure that any legal research and analysis is current and error free.

▶ Make sure the finished product is free from writing errors involving grammar, spelling, and punctuation.

▶ Be prepared to perform the number of edits and redrafts necessary to ensure
that the final product is professionally prepared.

Draft letters so clearly that they cannot be misinterpreted. A reader may not
like the information conveyed in the letter and may want to intentionally misinterpret the contents. The discussion in the following sections is designed to assist in
the preparation of letters that clearly convey information and that are difficult to
misinterpret.

8.4 TYPES OF CORRESPONDENCE

Although, as discussed in the previous section, the basic components of legal correspondence are the same, the content of the body of the correspondence varies according to the type of letter being drafted. There are many categories of legal correspondence, and the categorization is based on the purpose that each category is
designed to serve. This section addresses law office correspondence that communicates the results of legal research and analysis. The three basic categories of letters that communicate this information are information letters, opinion letters, and
demand letters (see Exhibit 8-2).

Exhibit 8-2

Types of Letters That Communicate the Results of Legal Research and Analysis

Law Office Correspondence That Communicate the Results of Legal Research and Analysis

Information Letters	Information letters provide general legal information or background on a legal issue. For example, the information may be a summary of the law or the requirements of a particular statute.
Opinion Letters	Opinion letters provide information concerning the law, an analysis of that information, and a legal opinion or legal advice.
Demand Letters	Demand letters are designed to persuade someone to take action favorable to the interest of the client or cease acting in a manner that is detrimental to the client. These letters include a summary of the applicable law in support of the requested action.

This section focuses on the body of these categories of letters and the way each letter differs in the presentation of legal research and analysis. The following sections address the preparation of letters where the recipient is a nonlawyer. Most of the correspondence a paralegal or legal assistant is called on to prepare is for that audience.

8.4 A   INFORMATION LETTER

A paralegal or legal assistant is often asked to draft a letter providing information to a client or another layperson. The components of an information letter usually include the elements mentioned in Section 8.2 "Basic Components." The body of the information letter, however, varies according to the type of information conveyed. There are many types of information letters. Some of the types and examples of parts of the body of types are as follows:

► letters that confirm an appointment or that communicate the date and time of scheduled events

> *For Example:*
>
> This letter is to advise you that the court hearing on the motion to modify child support will be held on May 6, 2006, in the courtroom of . . .
> This letter is to confirm our appointment at 9 a.m., May 22, 2006.

► letters that inform a client of the current status of a case

> *For Example:*
>
> The defendants filed an answer on June 6, 2006. On June 14, 2006, we sent them a request to produce documents concerning the contract and are awaiting their response to that request. We will contact you when we receive their response.

► letters that present a firm's bill
► letters that give the results of an investigation

> *For Example:*
>
> After performing a thorough investigation, we were unable to locate any witness who actually saw the accident. We interviewed the witnesses at the scene, canvassed the neighborhood, and contacted all store owners in the area. If you happen to remember the license plate of any vehicle that passed by or have any additional information, please let us know.

► letters that provide general legal information or background on a legal issue (The information may be a summary of the law involved in a client's case or the requirements of a particular statute. This type of information letter is

Exhibit 8-3

Body of Information Letter—Recommended Format and Components

Recommended Components of the Body of an Information Letter

Introduction/Opening	A sentence or paragraph explaining the purpose of the letter
Answer/Explanation	A detailed presentation of the legal information or background on a legal issue
Closing	A standard closing statement or, if the answer/explanation is lengthy, a summary of the answer

usually very complex, often involving communicating the results of legal research and analysis. The body of this type of information letter is discussed in the remainder of this section. An example of an information letter is presented in Appendix A.)

The body of an information letter that provides the results of legal research and analysis usually consists of an introduction/opening, an answer/explanation, and a closing (see Exhibit 8-3).

1. **Introduction/Opening**   The introduction states the purpose of the letter.

> **For Example:**
> The purpose of this letter is to inform you of a request that has been filed by the defendant and the law the court will consider when addressing the request.
> The purpose of this letter is to inform you of a recent law that was passed that affects your business.

2. **Answer/Explanation**   This section presents the results of legal research and analysis.

> **For Example:**
> Section 97-355-21 of the corporation statutes was recently amended. Under the provisions of the amendment, you must file your annual report no later than twenty days after the end of the fiscal year. As you know, the statute prior to the amendment allowed forty days to file the report.

The body of the information letter in Appendix A provides a detailed illustration of an answer/explanation.

3. Closing   The closing of the letter is similar to the closing of any legal correspondence, as discussed in Section 8.2 "Basic Components."

> **□ *For Example:***
>
> Since you prepare the annual report for your corporation, I believe it is important that you be advised of the change in the law. If you have any questions, please contact me.

In some instances, especially when the answer/explanation is lengthy or complex, it may be necessary to include a summary or a conclusion in the closing. The information letter in Appendix A provides a good example.

This type of information letter merely presents a summary of the law or the legal status of a case. It communicates basic information; *it does not give a legal opinion on a question or provide legal advice*. That role is performed by an opinion letter.

8.4 B   OPINION LETTER

An opinion letter is like an information letter in that it provides information concerning the law. It is different in that it also often includes an analysis of that information and provides a legal opinion or legal advice. The purpose of an opinion letter is to inform the reader about how the law applies to the facts. An opinion letter is usually generated by a question a client has asked or raised by the facts of the client's case. Therefore, the focus of this section is on opinion letters addressed to a client.

You may be assigned the task of researching, analyzing, and preparing a legal research memorandum that addresses the question that will be answered in an opinion letter. The purpose of the assignment is usually to provide the attorney with the information he or she needs to prepare the letter. You may be assigned the additional task of preparing a rough draft of the opinion letter. Many of the considerations involved in preparing an opinion letter are the same as those involved in preparing a legal research memorandum. If you are assigned the task of preparing an opinion letter, refer to this chapter and Chapter 9 for guidelines.

An opinion letter provides the reader with a legal opinion and legal advice; therefore, *it constitutes the practice of law and must be signed by an attorney*. The attorney is subject to legal liability for harm that occurs as a result of the client acting upon erroneous information contained in the letter. If you are preparing the draft of an opinion letter, take care to ensure that your research and analysis are accurate.

Since the purpose is to inform the client of the law and to provide legal advice, the opinion letter is drafted in the same objective tone as the legal research memorandum. The difference is that the client is usually a layperson who is unfamiliar

Exhibit 8-4

Body of Opinion Letter—Recommended Format and Components

Recommended Components of the Body of an Opinion Letter

Introduction/Opening	A sentence or paragraph identifying the question or questions that will be answered
Facts	A brief presentation of the background and key facts relative to the question(s) being addressed
Answer/Conclusion	A brief answer to the question; similar to the brief answer section of a legal research memorandum
Explanation	An explanation of how the law applies to the facts raised by the question; crafted in a manner that the client will understand
Closing/Conclusion	The last paragraph of the explanation section; contains a standard closing statement or, if the explanation is lengthy, a summary of the explanation; also includes a statement of what action, if any, the client should take or what will occur next

with legal terms and legal writing. In this case, you should avoid legalese and keep legal quotations and citations at a minimum. If the reader is familiar with the law and with legal writing, you may use more legal terms, quotations, and citations. In some instances, the attorney may direct that the client be provided with the legal research memorandum rather than an opinion letter.

Although an opinion letter and a legal research memorandum are similar in many respects, they are different in format. An opinion letter follows the format discussed in Section 8.2 "Basic Components." A legal research memorandum follows the format discussed in Chapter 9. The body of the letter includes the basic elements of the legal research memorandum, but the elements are presented with less technical detail and fewer legal terms.

As with most legal writing, there is no standard format for the body of an opinion letter. The body of most opinion letters, however, follows the format presented in Exhibit 8-4.

1. **Introduction/Opening** The introduction establishes the focus of the letter and identifies the question or questions that will be answered. The opening usually begins with a reference to the question and the context within which the client raised the question.

> ☐ *For Example:*
>
> On January 2, 2006, you hired me to represent you in your criminal case. When we met in my office on that date, you asked me to determine whether we could obtain a suppression of the evidence (the heroin) seized when the police officers executed a search warrant by entering your residence unannounced.

Notice that the question is stated in broader terms than it would be in a legal research memorandum. Draft the question so that the client will understand the question. You do not have to state it as completely or as formally as is discussed in Chapter 9. You do not need to follow the Law + Question + Key Facts format. In the preceding example, there is no reference to the rule of law.

Include language in the introduction that indicates that the opinion and advice apply only to addressee and to the specific facts included in the letter. You should also mention that the opinion is based on the law as of the date of the opinion.

> ☐ *For Example:*
>
> This opinion is provided for your use and solely for your benefit. It applies only to the facts presented in the facts section of this letter and the law as of the date of the letter.

2. **Facts**   Present the facts in an opinion letter in the same objective manner as you would in a legal research memorandum. Apply the techniques presented in Chapter 9 when preparing this section. Include only the key facts and the background facts to keep the section as short as possible. See the facts section of the opinion letter presented in Appendix A.

3. **Answer/Conclusion**   This section of an opinion letter presents a brief answer to the question. It is similar to the brief answer section of the legal research memorandum. Refer to the section "Brief Answer" in Chapter 9 when preparing the answer/conclusion. By placing the answer near the beginning of the letter, the reader immediately knows the result without having to read the explanation. This is helpful when the reader is busy and may not be able to read the explanation until later.

The answer should be clear and concise. Since the answer is usually a legal opinion, you should state it as an opinion.

> ☐ *For Example:*
>
> The court will probably not suppress the evidence based on the officers' failure to announce their presence prior to entering your residence when they executed the warrant.
> Add any needed specifics or limitations after the answer.
> The outcome could be different if Officer Galen changes his testimony and states he did not see you holding a rifle in your front room when they

> approached the house. Officer Kaler stated that he did not see you in the front room as they approached the house. In light of Officer Kaler's statement, Officer Galen could change his statement.

4. **Explanation**   The explanation section is similar to the analysis section of a legal research memorandum. The difference is that the explanation must be crafted in a manner that is not so technical that the client has difficulty understanding it. Also, the explanation section is usually not as long or as complex as an analysis section of a legal research memorandum. When preparing this section, note the following guidelines:

- ▶ If there is more than one issue, discuss the issues in the order they are presented in the introduction.
- ▶ If possible, limit the letter to as few issues as possible; i.e., two to three. If there are multiple issues, the letter may become too complex or long and the reader may have difficulty understanding or keeping track of the subject matter. Separate the issues and prepare more than one letter if necessary.
- ▶ Draft the content keeping in mind the legal sophistication of the reader. The client may not be familiar with the law and with technical writing, and an explanation that is as detailed as the analysis section of a legal research memorandum may not be appropriate. Keep quotations and citations to a minimum. Rather than quote a statutory or case law, rephrase it in a manner that a layperson can understand. If you must use a legal term, make sure its meaning is clear. Define any legal terms that are used.
- ▶ Provide a complete explanation. The client must be fully informed. Do not omit important information because the client is unsophisticated in the law. Present all key information in a manner that fully and clearly informs the client.

Following is an example of an explanation section of an opinion letter.

The Fourth Amendment to the United States Constitution and article II, section 9, of the state constitution prohibit "unreasonable searches and seizures." These amendments do not prohibit all searches and seizures, however, just those that are "unreasonable."

The law provides that anything seized as a result of an unreasonable search may not be admitted into evidence in a trial. The state supreme court has ruled that officers must announce their presence before entering a residence when executing a search warrant. The court has stated that an unannounced entry is unreasonable and violates the United States and state constitutions.

There are, however, exceptions to the rule that officers must announce their presence before executing a warrant. One exception is when the officers arrive at the place to be searched and there is evidence that the person or persons present at the scene are a danger to the officers. *Smith v. Jones* is a court case remarkably similar to your case. In this case, when the police arrived at the residence to be searched, they saw the defendant enter the house with a rifle in his hands. The state supreme court ruled that this evidence provided the officers with authority to execute the warrant and enter the residence to be searched without first announcing their presence.

Based on the ruling in the *Smith v. Jones* case and the similarity between the facts of that case and the facts in your case, the trial court probably will not suppress the evidence seized at your residence and will allow its admission at trial.

5. **Closing/Conclusion**   The closing is usually not a separate section of an opinion letter. Rather, it is usually the last paragraph of the explanation section. It is similar to the closing of any legal correspondence, as discussed in Section 8.2 "Basic Components." In addition, the closing of an opinion letter should summarize what, if any, action the client should take or what will occur next.

> **⬛ *For Example:***
>
> I hope this letter answers your questions. Please note that although the officers may have acted properly when they entered your residence unannounced, there is a question as to whether the warrant was properly issued in the first place. When we complete our investigation into this matter, we anticipate that we will file a motion to suppress the evidence because the warrant should not have been issued at all. We will discuss this at our appointment scheduled on Friday, November 9. Please contact me if you have any questions.

An example of an opinion letter is presented in Appendix A.

8.4 C   DEMAND LETTER

Another basic type of letter that often communicates legal information is a demand or advocacy letter. This letter is designed to persuade someone to take action favorable to the interests of the client or cease acting in a manner that is detrimental to the client. This communication may be as simple as demanding payment on a debt or as complex as requesting that a course of conduct be taken, such as rehiring an employee. In many instances, a demand letter includes a summary of the applicable law in support of the requested action. This section addresses the considerations involved in preparing a demand letter that includes a reference to the law and an analysis of the law. An example of a demand letter is presented in Appendix A.

Your assignment may be to prepare a legal research memorandum, summarizing the law that will be used as the basis for the demand letter and the preparation of a draft of the letter. *Like the opinion letter, a demand letter is signed by the attorney.*

The basic format and components of a demand letter are similar to those discussed in Section 8.2 "Basic Components," and like an opinion letter, there is no

Exhibit 8-5

Body of Demand Letter—Recommended Format and Components

Recommended Components of the Body of a Demand Letter

Introduction/Opening	An identification of the writer or client followed by the statement of the purpose of the letter
Facts	A brief presentation of the background and key facts relative to the subject being addressed
Explanation	A presentation of the legal authority in support of the relief requested; crafted in a manner that the recipient will understand.
Closing/Conclusion	The last paragraph of the explanation section; contains a standard closing statement or, if the explanation is lengthy, a summary of the explanation; should restate the relief requested and indicate what the next course of action may be

standard format for the demand letter. A major difference is that a demand letter is not designed to address a legal question but, rather, to encourage action or seek relief. Therefore, it does not contain an answer/conclusion section in the body because it does not address a question that requires a brief answer. The demand letter also differs from an opinion letter in that it is designed to advocate a position and persuade the reader; therefore, it is written in a persuasive manner.

The body of a demand letter follows the same basic format and is composed of elements similar to the body of the opinion letter (see Exhibit 8-5).

This section explores the differences between the body of a demand letter and the body of an opinion letter. The discussion focuses on demand letters sent to nonlawyers. The attorney usually drafts a demand letter that will be sent to another attorney.

1. **Introduction/Opening**   The introduction of a demand letter is somewhat different from the opening of an opinion letter. It begins with the identification of the writer or the client.

For Example:

Our office represents Mr. Jeremy Hill in the above-referenced case.
Mr. Jeremy Hill has retained this office with regard to . . .

A statement of the purpose of the letter follows the identification. It establishes the focus of the letter and identifies the problem addressed and the relief sought.

> **◻ *For Example:***
>
> Your efforts to collect payment from Mr. Hill on his automobile loan are in violation of the Collections Act, and we demand that they cease immediately.

2. **Facts**   The content of the facts section is the same as in an opinion letter except that the facts should be presented in a persuasive manner similar to the way they are presented in a court brief. See Subsection 10.2 B.2 "Statement of Facts—Persuasive Presentation" in Chapter 10.

> **◻ *For Example:***
>
> On January 7, 2006, Mr. Hill signed a loan with your company to pay for the purchase of an automobile. From the date of the loan until two months ago, he has paid, on time and in full, every installment on the loan. For the past two months, due to the illness of his oldest child, Mr. Hill has been able to pay only one-half of the required monthly payment. He contacted your office on the fifth of last month and informed the loan officer that for the next three months, he would be making reduced payments. He was informed that he should be making full payments.
>
> For the past three weeks, your collections department has telephoned Mr. Hill after 7 p.m. six nights a week, demanding full payment. In each instance, Mr. Hill has politely informed the caller that he is paying all he can and requested that the calls cease. The calls have not ceased.

3. **Explanation**   This section presents the legal authority in support of the relief requested. Since the reader is a nonlawyer, draft the section with this fact in mind. Refer to the discussion about the explanation section of an opinion letter for guidelines. This section of a demand letter differs from the explanation section of an opinion letter in that you should draft the section in a persuasive manner. Subsection 10.2 B.3 "Argument—Persuasive Presentation" in Chapter 10 can help you in this regard.

> **◻ *For Example:***
>
> The Collections Act provides that efforts to collect debts shall be made in a reasonable manner. The state supreme court, in the case of *Irons v. Collections, Inc.,* ruled that telephone calls to a debtor's residence after 7 p.m. or more frequently than three times a week are unreasonable and violate the Act when the debtor objects to the calls. Your office has contacted Mr. Hill after 7 p.m. six nights a week for the past three weeks. The calls have continued despite Mr. Hill's objections and requests that they cease.

4. **Closing/Conclusion**   Like the closing of an opinion letter, the closing of a demand letter is usually not a separate section. It is usually the last paragraph of the explanation section and is similar to the closing of any legal correspondence. The closing should restate the relief requested and indicate the next course of action.

> ◫ *For Example:*
>
> Your calls to Mr. Hill are unreasonable, clearly in violation of the Collections Act, and must cease immediately. If the calls do not cease, we will take the appropriate steps necessary to obtain the relief provided in the Act.
>
> If you have any questions regarding this matter, please contact me.

8.5   KEY POINTS CHECKLIST: LEGAL CORRESPONDENCE

❏ Prepare correspondence accurately and professionally. Letters may affect the reputation of a firm, and poorly drafted letters do not inspire a client's confidence.

❏ Draft the correspondence with the legal sophistication of the reader in mind. Avoid legalese, and if you must use legal terms, define them clearly.

❏ Keep legal citations and quotations to a minimum. Use quotations only when they are easy to understand and add clarity to the subject matter. Paraphrase the material when it is written in a manner that is difficult to comprehend.

❏ When drafting an opinion letter, indicate that the letter is limited to the facts of the case, based on the current law, and intended solely for the benefit of the addressee.

❏ If there are multiple issues, divide the subject into separate manageable topics. Prepare and send separate letters covering the topics.

❏ Do not include legal advice or recommend a course of action when the correspondence is to be signed by someone other than an attorney. Such information constitutes the practice of law and must be signed by an attorney.

❏ Keep a file of letters and other documents you have prepared. Organize the file by topic, such as demand letters and opinion letters. Rather than writing a new letter, it is often faster and easier to edit an old letter or use it as a guide for the correspondence you are drafting.

Chapter 9

Legal Research Memorandum

Contents

9.1 Introduction
9.2 Prewriting Stage
9.3 Sections of the Legal
     Research Memorandum

9.4 General Considerations
9.5. Key Points Checklist: Legal
     Research Memorandum

9.1 INTRODUCTION

A legal research memorandum provides an objective, critical analysis of a legal problem. It is an informative document that summarizes the research and analysis of a legal issue or issues raised by the facts of a client's case. It contains a summary of the law and explains how the law applies to the facts of the case. It presents an objective legal analysis and includes the arguments in favor and in opposition to a client's position. Preparation of a legal research memorandum is a multistep process involving the integration of legal research, analysis, and writing. Two examples of legal research memorandums are presented in Appendix B.

A legal research memorandum prepared for office use is referred to by many different names; for example, interoffice legal research memorandum, interoffice memorandum of law, legal research memorandum, office research memorandum, objective memorandum, and legal memo. In this chapter, the term *office memo* is used to refer to a legal research memorandum.

The major purposes and functions of an office memo are as follows:

1. to identify and record the law that applies to a specific issue or issues raised by a client's facts

2. to analyze and explain how the law applies to an issue
3. to assess the strengths and weaknesses of a client's case
4. to present a conclusion and proposed solution based on the analysis

In this chapter, the writing process addressed in Chapter 7 is used as the framework for the preparation of an office memo. As discussed in that chapter, the three stages of the process are the prewriting stage, the writing stage, and the postwriting stage.

9.2   PREWRITING STAGE

A prerequisite to beginning the prewriting stage is the assembly of all available files and information concerning a client's case. All of the relevant files and information must be complete. Once that is accomplished, the following matters should be addressed.

9.2 A   WHO IS THE AUDIENCE?

An office memo is usually designed for office use only. Therefore, the reader of the memo (the audience) will be familiar with the law and the use of legal terminology is appropriate. Determine the writing preferences of the person for whom the office memo is being prepared, such as preferences regarding style.

> *For Example:*
>
> Some attorneys prefer a summary of the requirements of the statutory or case law. Some prefer that the law be quoted.

If the memo will be read outside the office, you should exclude comments, recommendations, and so on, that are intended only for office use, such as "The client's expectations are unreasonable."

9.2 B   CONSTRAINTS ON THE ASSIGNMENT

The next section of the prewriting stage requires the identification of any constraint that may affect the preparation of the office memo. Ask yourself if there are any time or page limitations. You should take those matters into consideration before you begin writing. Time constraints govern the allocation of time for research, analysis, and drafting. Length constraints may limit the depth of research and analysis.

9.2 C   ORGANIZATION OF THE ASSIGNMENT

The most important section of the prewriting stage is the organization of the memo. In organizing an office memo, the format or outline of the memo is identified and an expanded outline is created and used.

Exhibit 9-1

Basic Legal Research Memorandum Format

Recommended Format for a Basic Legal Research Memorandum

Heading
Statement of Assignment
Issue
Brief Answer
Statement of Facts
Analysis
 Rule of Law
 Case law (if necessary)—interpretation of rule of law
 Application of law to facts of case
 Counteranalysis
Conclusion
Recommendations

Legal Research Memorandum

Most law offices have a preferred format to follow. This format serves as a basic outline and starting point for the organization of the assignment. In this chapter, the focus is on the format and outline of an office memo and the requirements and considerations involved in the preparation of each section of the outline.

There is no standard format for an office memo. Formats vary from office to office, and attorneys within an office may have different preferences. Follow the format preferred by your supervisor. The format presented in Exhibit 9-1 includes all of the basic sections of an office memo that you may encounter.

Certain sections, such as the Statement of Assignment and the Brief Answer, are not included in all formats and may not be included in the format adopted in your office. They are included here so that you can become familiar with them. Other sections, such as the Issue and Analysis, are required in all office memos. In addition, note that the organization of the format may vary from office to office.

For Example:

Some offices may prefer that the facts section precede the issue section. Usually, the issue section follows the statement of assignment section and precedes the facts section.

The recommended formats for a basic office memo and a complex office memo are presented in Exhibits 9-1 and 9-2, respectively. Following discussion of the formats, the requirements and considerations involved in the preparation of each section are addressed in detail.

There is no definition of what constitutes a complex legal research memorandum. Generally, however, a complex office memo consists of more than one issue and is relatively long (over 10 pages). The formal outline of a complex office memo is merely an expansion of the basic office memo format. The components and considerations involved in the preparation of a complex office memo are the same as those involved in the preparation of a basic office memo. The sections are the same in basic content, although the number of sections is expanded.

> ◻ *For Example:*
>
> A complex memo may consist of three issues. The procedures recommended for identifying, stating, and analyzing each issue are the same as those involved in the preparation of a basic memo. Each issue is addressed separately, and the process for addressing each issue is the same as that followed when addressing the single issue in a basic office memo.

The format for a complex legal research memorandum is presented in Exhibit 9-2.

The office memo format may require the inclusion of a table of authorities or a table of contents. These usually follow the statement of the assignment.

> ◻ *For Example:*
>
> **TABLE OF CONTENTS**
>
> | | | Page |
> |---|---|---|
> | I. | Issues | 2 |
> | II. | Facts | 3 |
> | III. | Analysis Issue I | 5 |
> | IV. | Analysis Issue II | 10 |
> | V. | Recommendations | 18 |
>
> **TABLE OF AUTHORITIES**
>
> | CASES | Page |
> |---|---|
> | *Smith v. Jones,* 354 F.2d 786 (9th Cir. 1970) | 7 |
> | *Tod v. Doe,* 559 N.E.2d 31 (Ind. App. 1988) | 13 |
>
> | CONSTITUTIONAL PROVISIONS | |
> |---|---|
> | Art. 3 Ind. Constitution | 6 |
>
> | STATUTES | |
> |---|---|
> | Ind. Code § 35-42-3-2 | 6 |
> | Ind. Code § 35-42-3-8 | 13 |

✚ 9.3   SECTIONS OF THE LEGAL RESEARCH MEMORANDUM

The elements of a legal research memorandum are discussed in this section: heading, statement of assignment, issue, brief answer, facts, analysis, conclusion, and recommendations.

Exhibit 9-2

Complex Legal Research Memorandum Format

Recommended Format for a Complex Legal Research Memorandum

Heading
Statement of Assignment
Issue I
Issue II
Issue III
Brief Answer Issue I
Brief Answer Issue II
Brief Answer Issue III
Statement of Facts
Analysis Issue I
    Rule of Law
    Case law (if necessary)—interpretation of rule of law
    Application of law to facts of case
    Counteranalysis
    Conclusion Issue I
Analysis Issue II
    Rule of Law
    Case law (if necessary)—interpretation of rule of law
    Application of law to facts of case
    Counteranalysis
    Conclusion Issue II
Analysis Issue III
    Rule of Law
    Case law (if necessary)—interpretation of rule of law
    Application of law to facts of case
    Counteranalysis
    Conclusion Issue III
Recommendations (separate recommendation sections may follow conclusion of each issue)

9.3 A   HEADING

Most office memos begin with a heading. The heading is usually brief and at a minimum contains the following:

► a heading in all capital letters indicating the type of document; i.e., MEMORANDUM OF LAW

► the name of the person to whom the memo is addressed

► the name of the person who prepared the memo
► the date
► information identifying the subject of the memo; may include the case name, the client's name, the case number, the office file number, and the subject matter of the memo; usually follows *Re:*

There are various styles for the heading.

■ *For Example:*

MEMORANDUM OF LAW

To: Susan Day, Attorney
From: Travis Clug, Paralegal
Date: December 1, 2006
Case: *Smith v. Garage Doors, Inc.*
Office File No.:   Civ. 05-1136
Docket No.:   Civ. 05-378
Re: Whether a contract for the sale and installation of a garage door is a sale of goods covered by the commercial code or is a sale of a service.

LEGAL RESEARCH MEMORANDUM—CONTRACTS

Title: *Smith v. Garage Doors, Inc.,* Civ. 05-378
Office File: Civ. 05-1136
Requested by: Susan Day, Attorney
Submitted by: Travis Clug, Paralegal
Date Submitted: 12/1/06
Re: Contract law, Commercial Code § 42-2-205
                     Sale of goods/sale of service

OFFICE RESEARCH MEMORANDUM

To: Susan Day, Attorney
From: Travis Clug, Paralegal
Date: December 1, 2006
Re: *Smith v. Garage Doors, Inc.,* Civ. 05-378.
                     Whether a contract for the sale and installation of a garage door is a sale of goods or a sale of a service; Commercial Code § 42-2-205.

9.3 B   STATEMENT OF ASSIGNMENT

This section may also be referred to as the Background or Purpose. Some offices require a section that discusses what the writer has been assigned to do. This section usually follows the heading and may include some background information. Its purpose is to provide the reader with a description of the topic covered and the parameters of the assignment.

> ⬚ *For Example:*
>
> STATEMENT OF ASSIGNMENT. You have asked me to prepare a legal
>   memorandum on the question of whether the sale and installation of a
>   garage door by Garage Doors, Inc., is a sale of a service or a sale of
>   goods covered by Commercial Code § 42-2-205.
> STATEMENT OF ASSIGNMENT. You have asked me to research the
>   question of whether the search of our client's automobile was an illegal
>   search when she was stopped for a minor traffic offense and did not
>   consent to the officer's request for permission to search the backseat of
>   her vehicle. Pursuant to your request, this memo includes an analysis
>   of the relevant state and federal law.

9.3 C　ISSUE

In an office memo, present the issue or issues at the beginning of the memo following the heading and the statement of assignment. Doing so establishes the focus of
the memo. A well-crafted memo informs the reader at the outset of the following:

- ▶ the law that applies
- ▶ the precise legal question
- ▶ the significant facts of the case

In other words, the issue identifies the specific question to be addressed and places
it in the context of the applicable law and the facts of the case. The issue sets the
scope of the memo, thereby saving the reader from having to determine it by reading the analysis section.

There are several matters to keep in mind when preparing the issue section of
the memo:

- ▶ The issue should be correctly identified.
- ▶ The issue should be completely and correctly stated.
- ▶ An expanded outline should be used when preparing the section.
- ▶ Issues are addressed separately when preparing complex office memos.

1. **Identify the Issue**　The issue is the precise legal question raised by the facts
   of the client's case. One of the most important tasks in the legal analysis
   process is the correct identification of the legal issue. You cannot solve a client's
   legal problem until it is correctly identified. If the issue is misidentified, everything that follows—time spent researching, analyzing, and writing—is wasted.
2. **Correctly State the Issue**　The issue should be completely and correctly presented. That is, it should include the applicable law, the question raised by the
   key facts, and the key facts. When the issue is stated correctly, the reader knows
   the focus of the memo at the outset and is saved from having to identify the
   precise question while reading the analysis section.

> ☐ *For Example:*
>
> Assume the issue involves a question of whether a will is valid when one of the witnesses does not actually see the testator sign the will. If the issue is stated "Was the will validly executed?" the reader would have to read the analysis section of the memo to determine why it may not have been validly executed. There could be several reasons why the will may not have been validly executed: it may not have been witnessed correctly, there may not have been enough witnesses, or it may have been signed improperly. If the issue is stated "Under Probate Code § 29-5-7, is the execution of a will valid if one of the witnesses is present in the room when the testator signs but the witness does not actually see the testator sign?" the issue is correctly and completely stated. The reader knows the precise question being addressed, the key facts, and the applicable law. The reader does not have to obtain this information from the analysis section of the memo.

3. **Use the Expanded Outline**   The use of an expanded outline can greatly simplify identifying and drafting the issue. On the issue page of the expanded outline, write every formulation of the issue as it comes to mind. The initial draft may be as simple as "Was the will valid?" As you conduct research and gain a greater understanding of the applicable law, more complete formulations will become apparent.

> ☐ *For Example:*
>
> Under the state probate code, is a will validly executed if a witness is merely present in the room when the testator signs?
>
> Under the probate code, is the execution of a will valid if one of the witnesses is present in the room when the testator signs but the witness does not actually see the testator sign?

When you begin to write the issue section of the memo, all of your ideas concerning the issue and all of the drafts of the possible ways the issue may be stated are before you in one place. Crafting the final statement of the issue is merely a matter of selecting and combining the necessary elements from the various drafts. The use of the expanded outline is discussed in detail in Chapter 7.

4. **Address Issues Separately**   Office memorandum assignments, such as a complex memorandum, often involve more than one issue. When addressing such assignments, it is preferable that each issue be listed sequentially in the issue section of the memo. In the analysis section of the format, each issue is addressed separately and completely. An outline of the analysis format is presented in Exhibit 9-3.

When there are multiple issues, they should be listed in the issue section in the order in which they are discussed in the analysis section. Issue I should be the first issue addressed in the analysis section, Issue II should be the second issue

Exhibit 9-3

Complex Memorandum—Analysis Section Format

Recommended Format for the Analysis Section of a Complex Office Legal Memorandum

Analysis Issue I
   Rule of Law
   Case law (if necessary)—interpretation of rule of law
   Application of law to facts of case
   Counteranalysis
   Conclusion Issue I
Analysis Issue II
   Rule of Law
   Case law (if necessary)—interpretation of rule of law
   Application of law to facts of case
   Counteranalysis
   Conclusion Issue II
Analysis Issue III, and so on

Legal Research
Memorandum

addressed, and so on. The issues also should be listed in logical order. If the analysis of one issue is dependent on or affected by the analysis of another issue, the issue that affects the other issue should be presented first. For example, if the analysis of Issue B is in some way affected by the analysis of Issue A, Issue A should be addressed first in the memo.

For Example:

Assume a client alleges that she entered into a contract to purchase dresses from a dressmaker and the dressmaker installed defective zippers in the dresses. The dressmaker claims that the contract between them was not a valid contract, and even if there was a valid contract, the zippers were not defective. There are two separate issues. Present and discuss the issue of whether there is a valid contract first because if there is no contract, there can be no breach. The issue section would appear as follows:

Issue I   Existence of contract
Issue II   Breach of contract

If the issues are not dependent on or affected by other issues, present them in chronological order.

For Example:

Assume a client was involved in an automobile accident. The defendant ran a red light and hit the client's car. After the wreck, the defendant approached the client's car, screaming and threatening the client. The defendant then pushed the client. At least four possible causes of action are present. They should be presented in the order in which they occurred:

Issue I   Negligence—the car wreck
Issue II   Assault—approaching client's car, threatening and screaming
Issue III   Battery—pushing the client
Issue IV   Infliction of emotional distress—arising from the combined acts of assault and battery

Exhibit 9-4

Checklist—Issue Section

Checklist to Use When Preparing Issue Section

❏ Is the issue correctly identified?
❏ Is the applicable rule of law included?
❏ Is the citation of the rule correct?
❏ Is the legal question clearly stated?
❏ Are the key facts included?
❏ If there are multiple issues, are they presented in the proper order, such as logical or chronological?

A checklist for the issue section is presented in Exhibit 9-4.

9.3 D   BRIEF ANSWER

The brief answer section of the office memo is composed of a brief, precise answer to the issue(s). In one or two sentences, it answers the question and includes a brief summary of the reasons in support of the answer. Its purpose is to provide a quick answer to the issue. It should not include information that is not discussed in the analysis section of the memo.

Usually, this section begins with a one- or two-word answer, such as *Yes, No, Maybe,* or *Probably not.* The answer is followed by a brief statement of the grounds in support of the answer.

☐ *For Example:*

Issue: According to the provisions of the Ski Safety Act § 679-33, does a resort have a duty to warn skiers of ice hazards on expert runs?

<table>
<tr><td>Brief Answer:</td><td>No. The act provides that resorts have the duty to warn of hazards, and skiers are responsible for snow and ice conditions. The state supreme court has ruled that resorts have a duty to warn of snow and ice hazards only on intermediary and novice ski runs. The court specifically held that there is no duty to warn of any ice hazard on an expert run.</td></tr>
<tr><td>Issue I</td><td>Under the holographic will statute, Colo. Rev. Stat. § 15-11-503, is a holographic will valid if it is handwritten by a neighbor at the direction of the testator, but not written in the testator's handwriting?</td></tr>
<tr><td>Issue II</td><td>Under the holographic will statute, Colo. Rev. Stat. § 15-11-503, is a holographic will valid if one of the witnesses to the testator's signature is a beneficiary of the will?</td></tr>
<tr><td>Brief Answer Issue I:</td><td>Yes. The statute requires a holographic will to be handwritten by the testator. The state court of appeals has held that the statute should be interpreted liberally to effect the intent of the testator. If there is clear and convincing evidence that the writing took place at the direction of the testator, the will is valid even if it is not written in the testator's handwriting.</td></tr>
<tr><td>Brief Answer Issue II:</td><td>No. The statute requires that the testator's signature be witnessed by two disinterested witnesses.</td></tr>
</table>

A checklist for the brief answer section is presented in Exhibit 9-5.

Exhibit 9-5

Checklist—Brief Answer Section

Checklist to Use When Preparing Brief Answer Section

- ❏ Does the brief answer follow the office format; e.g., a one- or two-word answer followed by a short statement of the reasons?
- ❏ Is it brief? Does it summarize the reasons in one or two clear sentences?
- ❏ Is there a separate answer for each issue?

Exhibit 9-6

Considerations—Fact Section

Considerations to Keep in Mind When Preparing the Facts Section

Importance of the facts	Do not underemphasize the importance of the facts. The law is applied in the context of the facts of the dispute.
Contents of the section	Include the key and background facts.
Organization of the section	Organize the facts chronologically or topically or a combination of the two.
Manner of the presentation of the facts	Present the facts accurately and objectively and free of legal conclusions.

9.3 E   STATEMENT OF FACTS

Following the brief answer section is the presentation of the facts of the case. The purpose of the facts section is to inform the reader of the factual context of the issue. There are four considerations to keep in mind when preparing this section (see Exhibit 9-6).

1. **Facts Section—Importance**   Some writers underemphasize the facts section of a legal research memorandum because they fail to understand the importance of the facts. The facts and, therefore, the facts section of the memo are important for several reasons:

   ▶ Every legal dispute involves a question of how the law applies to the facts of the case. Legal questions are not decided in a vacuum. The law is applied in the context of a dispute raised by the facts of the case. The rule of law selected is determined by identification of the law that applies to the facts.

   ▶ The facts section may serve to refresh the reader's memory. The reader may be working on other issues in the case or on several other cases and may not recollect the specific factual context of the issues addressed in the assignment. The facts section saves the reader from having to review the file to determine the facts.

   ▶ In many law offices, legal research memorandums are kept in research files categorized by areas of law. They are available for reference and for use in other cases involving similar issues. Subsequent researchers may not be familiar with the facts of a case. By reading the facts section, subsequent readers should be able to obtain all of the facts necessary to understand the analysis. They should not have to review the case file.

   ▶ The facts section protects the writer from possible criticism. If additional facts come to light that affect the analysis of the issue and lead to a different conclusion, a well-drafted facts section provides a record of the factual basis of the writer's conclusion. It protects the writer from criticism that he or she misanalyzed or misapplied the law.

2. **Facts Section—Content**   The facts section of the legal research memorandum should not simply repeat the facts included in the memo assignment; it should include a brief statement of the background and the key facts. Preparation of this section requires identification of the facts necessary to provide the reader with a complete understanding of the factual context of the issues analyzed in the memo. This section may require fewer facts than those included in the memo assignment, or it may require more.

All facts referenced or included in the analysis section of the memo should be included in the facts section. The writer's goal should be to provide, as briefly as possible, enough facts so the memo is a self-contained document; that is, the memo should be sufficiently complete so that any reader who is not familiar with the facts of the case does not have to refer to the case file. To accomplish that end, the facts section should include background facts and key facts.

▶ *Background facts:* Background facts are necessary because they put the key facts in context. That is, they give the reader the information necessary to gain an overall understanding of the context within which the key facts occurred.

▶ *Key facts:* Key facts are those facts upon which the outcome of the case is determined. A key fact is so essential that if it were changed, the outcome of the case would probably be different.

3. **Facts Section—Organization**   The facts section should be organized in a manner that enables the reader to clearly understand the events that relate to the issue(s) addressed in the memo. There are basically three organizational formats for presenting the facts:

▶ chronological
▶ topical
▶ a combination of chronological and topical

The format selected is usually governed by the nature of the facts.

a. *Chronological Order*—A chronological organization of the facts usually is adopted when the facts are a series of events related by time or date.

■ *For Example:*

Assume the memo involves the following fact situation: On December 1, the client, Mr. Billings, was driving in the 600 block of First Street when the defendant, Mr. Doe, ran a red light at the intersection of First and Rose Street. As a result, Mr. Doe's vehicle collided with Mr. Billings' vehicle. Mr. Billings suffered a broken leg, and his wallet was stolen at the scene. On the way to the hospital, the ambulance was involved in a collision when it yielded at a stop sign. Mr. Billings suffered additional injuries, including a separated shoulder, in this collision. At the emergency room, his back was sprained when he was being helped onto the examining table by the hospital staff. Mr. Billings wants to know who he can sue for his various injuries and whether he can recover from Mr. Doe for the loss of his wallet.

That example is referred to as the auto collision example in the remainder of this chapter.

The best way to present the facts of the case in the preceding example is chronologically. The facts that give rise to the various causes of action occurred in a linear sequence, and they are most clearly understood when narrated chronologically.

When facts occur in a linear sequence of events, such as in the auto collision example, the best form of presentation is chronological.

b. *Topical Order*—Some fact situations do not lend themselves to a chronological presentation. In such situations, the facts are related more by topic than by time sequence.

☐ *For Example:*

The memo involves the following divorce situation. The client, Mrs. Cardona, is the petitioner in a divorce action. Mr. and Mrs. Cardona disagree on the property distribution. They own three pieces of real property, parcels A, B, and C. All three parcels are held in both of their names as joint tenants.

Parcel A includes the family home. The property is paid for. Forty percent of the mortgage was paid from an inheritance Mrs. Cardona received from her father. The remainder was paid by both Mr. and Mrs. Cardona from income from their respective employments. The assessed value is $150,000.

Parcel B is a rental property. They purchased the property shortly after the marriage. The mortgage on the property is being paid from the rent payment and contributions from the income of both Mr. and Mrs. Cardona. Their current equity is $100,000. Ten thousand dollars of the equity was a contribution by Mr. Cardona from his separate property.

Parcel C is recreational property. It was purchased five years after the marriage. It includes a small cabin and storage shed. Their equity in the cabin and shed is $75,000. Mrs. Cardona contributed $12,000 of the equity from lottery ticket winnings. The balance of the equity represents equal contributions from Mr. and Mrs. Cardona.

In that example, a presentation of the facts by topic is most appropriate. The dates of purchase and the dates payments were made on the various parcels may be available, but a presentation of these facts by date would not lead to the clearest presentation of the facts. In the facts section, all of the facts relating to each parcel should be presented separately, by parcel, regardless of the time sequence. All of the facts relating to parcel A should be presented together, all of the facts relating to parcel B should be presented together, and all of the facts relating to parcel C should be presented together. The facts are more clearly understood when all of the facts relating to each parcel are presented together; therefore, each parcel should be addressed separately in the facts section of the memo.

c. ***Combination of Chronological and Topical Order***—It may be appropriate to present the facts both chronologically and topically.

□ *For Example:*

In the previous example, assume parcel B was purchased by the husband three years prior to the marriage; parcel A, immediately after the marriage; and parcel C, five years later. Assume, also, there is personal property: an automobile purchased two years after the marriage and a boat purchased three years after the marriage.

In addition to the matters concerning the three parcels, there are other issues in the divorce involving the other property. The appropriate presentation of the facts is a combination of the chronological and topical schemes.

In that situation, the real and personal property may be presented in the facts section in a chronological sequence according to the order of purchase, such as parcel B first, then parcel A, followed by the automobile, the boat, and finally parcel C. Note that all of the information concerning each parcel of property is included when the parcel is discussed even though some factual events may have occurred after the purchase of another parcel.

□ *For Example:*

All of the information concerning parcel B is included in the discussion of parcel B even though some of that information may have occurred after the purchase of parcel A. Mr. Cardona's $10,000 contribution of separate property may have taken place after parcel A, the automobile, and the boat were purchased.

It would be confusing in that example to present all of the facts only in chronological order. It is clearer to present the property in chronological order and in the discussion of each piece of property, to present all of the facts regardless of when they occurred.

The goal in the organization of the facts section is the clear presentation of the facts. The organizational format that best meets that goal should be used.

4. **Facts—Presentation—Ethics**   Rule 3.3(a)(1) of the Model Rules of Professional Conduct provides that a lawyer should not make false statements of law or fact to a tribunal. Therefore, when drafting the facts section of a memo, you should present the facts accurately and objectively and avoid legal conclusions.

a. ***Accuracy***—Accuracy in presenting the facts means that all of the facts are presented, including those unfavorable to the client.

> ▣ *For Example:*
>
> If in the auto collision example, Mr. Billings was speeding when the defendant ran the red light, this fact should be included. Although it may not be a key fact that affects the outcome of the negligence claim, it is, at minimum, a background fact that should be included.

Accuracy also means not adding or changing facts. It is not proper to add a fact even if the existence of the fact seems obvious.

> ▣ *For Example:*
>
> In the auto collision example, it is not proper to state that the defendant knew he was running a red light if there are no facts indicating his actual awareness of that fact. It is improper to add such a fact even if it seems obvious.

   b. *Objectivity*—State the facts objectively, which means you should present the facts in a neutral, not slanted, manner.

> ▣ *For Example:*
>
> *Slanted presentation:*
> Mr. Banker obviously knew what he was doing when he advised Mrs. Widow to buy a risky stock when the market was at its peak. Unfortunately, Mrs. Widow relied on his bad advice to her detriment.

The use of *obviously, risky, unfortunately, bad,* and *detriment* slants the presentation of the facts in favor of Mrs. Widow. The facts should be stated neutrally.

> ▣ *For Example:*
>
> *Neutral presentation:*
> The stock was at a two-year high when Mr. Banker advised Mrs. Widow to buy the stock. Mrs. Widow relied on his advice and purchased the stock. The value of the stock subsequently fell, and Mrs. Widow suffered a loss of $1,000.

   c. *Legal Conclusions*—When composing the facts section, avoid legal conclusions.

> ▣ *For Example:*
>
> Mrs. Roe was driving negligently through the school zone. (The phrase *driving negligently* is a legal conclusion.)

Exhibit 9-7

⊞ Checklist—Facts Section

Checklist to Use When Preparing the Facts Section

❏ Are sufficient background facts presented to inform the reader of the factual context of the assignment? Will the reader be required to refer to the case file to understand the analysis of the issues?

❏ Are all of the key facts included? Will the reader have to refer to the case file to obtain the key facts?

❏ Are the facts organized chronologically, topically, or chronologically and topically combined?

❏ Are the facts presented accurately and objectively?

❏ Are legal conclusions excluded from the fact presentation?

❏ Is the Fact section complete?

State the facts without legal conclusions.

⊞ *For Example:*

Mrs. Roe was driving thirty-five miles per hour through the school zone. The posted speed is fifteen miles per hour.

A checklist for the facts section of an office memo is presented in Exhibit 9-7.

9.3 F   ANALYSIS

The purpose of an office memo is to provide a legal analysis of the issue(s) in a case. The memo informs the reader of the law that governs the issue(s) and the way it applies in the client's case. *The analysis section is the part of the memo where the law is presented, analyzed, and applied to the issue(s).* It connects the issue with the conclusion. It is the heart of an office memo.

The analysis section is often referred to as the discussion section. The conventional analytical format, the most efficient way through which to approach a legal question, is the IRAC format; that is, Issue, Rule, Analysis, and Conclusion. Under the IRAC approach and the office memo format introduced in Exhibits 9-1 and 9-2, the issue is presented at the beginning of the memo; the rule of law, analysis, and application of the rule of law to the facts are covered in the analysis section; and the conclusion summarizes the analysis. The reasons for following this approach are as follows:

▶ The reader must know the question in order to know the context in which the rule is analyzed.

Exhibit 9-8

◪ Basic Four-Part Format—Analysis Section

Recommended Format for the Analysis Section of a Legal Research Memorandum

Part A.   Rule of law
Part B.   Case law (if necessary)—interpretation of rule of law
    1. Name of case
    2. Facts of case—sufficient to demonstrate that case is on point
    3. Rule or legal principle from case that applies to client's case
Part C.   Application of law to facts of case
Part D.   Counteranalysis

▶ The rule that applies to the question must be identified before the rule can be analyzed and applied to the facts of the case.

▶ Application of the rule to the facts must take place before a conclusion can be reached.

Although IRAC is the basic format for addressing legal issues, it is only a broad outline of the format. A more detailed outline of the analysis section is necessary to effectively approach an office memo assignment and to prepare an office memo.

1. Analysis—Format   The recommended format of the analysis section is presented in Exhibit 9-8.

In the prewriting stage of the writing process, each subsection of the analysis section should be assigned at least one page in the expanded outline: a page for the rule of law, a page for each case, at least one page for the application of the law to the facts, and at least one page for the counteranalysis.

If the memo is a complex memo involving multiple issues, the same basic format is followed for each issue (see Exhibit 9-9).

If more than one rule of law applies to a specific issue, the outline should include a reference to each rule.

◪ *For Example:*

Issue I—Analysis
    Part A. Rule of law
        1. Section 59-703 of the commercial code
        2. Section 45-211 of the usury statute

If more than one case is required to interpret the rule of law, such as when more than one element of the rule requires case law interpretation, the outline should include a reference to each case.

> ☐ *For Example:*
>
> Issue I—Analysis
>   Part A. Rule of law—section 59-703 of the commercial code
>   Part B. Case law
>   1. Case 1. *Smith v. Jones*—interpreting the term *sale* as used in § 59-703
>   a. Facts of case—sufficient to demonstrate that case is on point
>   b. Rule or legal principle from case that applies to client's case
>   Part C. Application of law to facts of case
>   Part D. Counteranalysis
>   2. Case 2. *Row v. Downs*—interpreting the term *merchant* as used in § 59-703
>   a. Facts of case—sufficient to demonstrate case that is on point
>   b. Rule or legal principle from case that applies to client's case
>   Part C. Application of law to facts of case
>   Part D. Counteranalysis
>   Part A. Rule of law—section 45-211 of the usury statute
>   Part B. Case law
>   1. *Stiles v. Dean*—interpreting the term *loan* as used in § 45-211
>   a. Facts of case—sufficient to demonstrate that case is on point
>   b. Rule or legal principle from case that applies to client's case
>   Part C. Application of law to facts of case
>   Part D. Counteranalysis

The elements of the basic format for the analysis section of an office memo are discussed next. *Once the considerations involved in preparing the analysis of a single issue are mastered, complex memo assignments that address multiple issues or separate subissues are approached by applying the basic process to the analysis of each issue or subissue.*

2. **Analysis—Part A Rule of Law**   Inasmuch as the analysis section of an office memo addresses how the law applies to the issue(s) and facts of the client's case, the starting point is a presentation of the rule of law or the legal principle that applies. This is necessary because the law must be presented before it can be applied.

The governing law may be enacted law, such as a constitutional provision or a legislative act, or common law, such as a court-adopted rule of law.

Considerations to keep in mind when preparing the rule of law portion of the analysis section are listed in Exhibit 9-10.

a. **Rule of Law—Introduction**—The analysis section begins with the presentation of the rule of law. Do not start immediately with a presentation of the

Exhibit 9-9

■ **Complex Memo—Analysis Section Format**

Recommended Format for the Analysis Section of a Complex Legal Research Memorandum

Issue I—Analysis
    Part A.   Rule of law
    Part B.   Case law (if necessary)—interpretation of rule of law
        1. Name of case
        2. Facts of case—sufficient to demonstrate that case is on point
        3. Rule or legal principle from case that applies to client's case
    Part C.   Application of law to facts of case
    Part D.   Counteranalysis

Issue II—Analysis
    Part A.   Rule of law
    Part B.   Case law (if necessary)—interpretation of rule of law
        1. Name of case
        2. Facts of case—sufficient to demonstrate that case is on point
        3. Rule or legal principle from case that applies to client's case
    Part C.   Application of law to facts of case
    Part D.   Counteranalysis

Issue III—Analysis (same format as Issues I and II)

rule; use introductory language. The introductory language is italicized in the following examples.

■ *For Example:*

The rule of law governing the sale of securities is section 59-903 of the New Washington Commercial Code. The section provides . . .
In New Washington, the doctrine of strict liability was established in the case of Elton v. All Faiths Hospital, 931 N. Wash. 395, 396 (1976), where the court stated . . .

   b. *Rule of Law—What to Include*—When presenting the rule of law, paraphrase or quote only the relevant portions of the law. In some instances, the rule of law is very lengthy and only portions of the law apply to the issue being addressed. This is often true when the applicable law is statutory law, the

Exhibit 9-10

Rule of Law—Considerations

**Considerations to Keep in Mind When Preparing
the Rule of Law Portion of the Analysis Section**

Introduction	Use introductory language to introduce the rule of law; e.g., "The law governing the witnessing of wills is . . . ."
What to include	Paraphrase or quote only the relevant portions of the law.
Multiple rules of law	Use introductory language and present the relevant portion of each rule.
Citation	Provide the citation for the rule of law. If it is enacted law, cite the statute, ordinance, rule, and so on; if it is case law, cite the court opinion.

statute is composed of many subsections, and only one subsection applies. In this case, include only the relevant portion of the law.

For Example:

Statutory law:

The rule of law governing oppressive conduct is § 50-14-5, which provides:
   A. The district courts may liquidate the assets and business of a
      corporation:
      1. in an action by a shareholder when it is established that: . . .
         (b) the acts of the directors . . . are illegal, oppressive, or
             fraudulent . . . .

NOTE: Subsection (a) is omitted because its provisions do not apply to the issue being discussed.

For Example:

Common law:

The rule of law governing a ski resort's duty to warn of snow and ice conditions was established in the case of *Jones v. Mountain Ski Resort*, 943 N. Wash. 857, 877 (1988), where the court stated, "Resorts have a duty to warn of snow and ice conditions in the following situations: . . . when the snow or ice condition is a latent hazard . . . ."

NOTE: Portions of the opinion are omitted because they do not apply to the issue being discussed.

    c. ***Rule of Law–Multiple Rules***—The analysis may require consideration of more than one rule of law. In this case, the format is similar to that discussed previously. Use introductory language and present the relevant portions of each rule.

> ◘ *For Example:*
>
> The New Washington Commercial Code section 50-101 establishes which contracts must be in writing. In our case, two subsections of that section apply: section 50-101B, which requires that "An agreement that is not to be performed within one year from the making . . ." must be in writing, and section 50-101C, which provides that "Contracts for the sale of goods in the amount of $500 or more . . ." must be in writing.

When the rule of law involves both general and specific sections of a statute, the relevant general portion of the statute should be presented first, followed by the specific portion of the statute.

> ◘ *For Example:*
>
> Section 50-501 creates an implied warranty of merchantability if the seller is a merchant with respect to goods of that kind. The term *merchant* is defined in section 50-401 as "A person who deals in goods of that kind . . . ."

    d. ***Rule of Law–Citation***—Whenever the reference is to a rule of law or a legal principle, you must present the authority in support of your statement of the rule. If the source for the rule is enacted law, cite the enacted law; if the source is case law, cite the case. Note that in the previous four examples, the reference includes the source for the rule of law—either statutory or case law. Without a reference to the authority, it is merely your word that the rule of law presented in the memo is actually what the law provides. The reader needs to know the source in order to check for accuracy and answer any questions concerning the law.

3. **Analysis–Part B Rule of Law Interpretation–Case Law** Three considerations you should keep in mind when addressing the interpretation of the rule of law discussed in the memo are presented in Exhibit 9-11.

    a. ***Rule of Law Interpretation–No Interpretation Required***—In some instances, the rule of law, whether it is statutory or case law, can be applied directly to the facts of the client's case. Further case law is not required to determine how the rule applies.

> ◘ *For Example:*
>
> The rule of law establishes a 15 mph speed limit in school zones, and the client was ticketed for driving 30 mph in a school zone. In this situation, case law is not needed to determine how the law applies. The law can be applied directly to the facts: driving 30 mph in the school zone is a violation of the law.

Exhibit 9-11

⬛ Rule of Law Interpretation—Considerations

**Considerations to Keep in Mind When Addressing
Interpretation of the Rule of Law**

Is interpretation required?	Does the rule of law require interpretation? Can the law be applied directly to the facts without interpretation?
What is the role of case law?	Is the rule of law so broadly stated that case law must be consulted to determine how it applies?
What is the process for presenting case law?	If case law is required, when presenting each case, use a format like the one laid out in Exhibit 9-12.

In such instances, proceed to Subsection 9.3 F.4 "Analysis—Part C Application of Rule of Law to Client's Case."

Note, however, that you should perform at least a cursory check of the case law. Doing so ensures that there is not some special interpretation of the rule or a term used in the rule that is not apparent from a plain reading of it.

b. *Rule of Law Interpretation—Role of Case Law*—Usually, the rule of law that governs the issue being analyzed has some unexpected, unobvious quirk or is so broadly stated that case law must be referred to determine how it applies. Case law, in effect, provides the link between the rule of law and the issue raised by the facts of the client's case. Court opinions determine and explain how the law is interpreted and applied in specific fact situations.

⬛ *For Example:*

The First Amendment protects freedom of speech. The amendment does not define what constitutes speech. If the client's case involves the question of whether a symbolic act such as burning a state flag is protected under the First Amendment's freedom of speech provisions, case law must be consulted. The Supreme Court has interpreted how the First Amendment applies in this specific fact situation. Acts such as burning a state flag are considered symbolic speech mend are protected under the First Amendment.

Suppose a statute prohibits oppressive conduct by majority shareholders against minority shareholders, and *oppressive conduct* is not defined in the statute. Court decisions may define what constitutes oppressive conduct in specific fact situations, and reference to court decisions is necessary to determine how the law applies.

Exhibit 9-12

Format for Presenting Case Law

Recommended Format for Presenting the Case Law That Interprets How the Rule of Law Applies

Name and Citation of Court Opinion	First, provide the name and citation of the case.
Facts of the Case	Next, provide those facts from the case that are sufficient to demonstrate that the case is on point.
Rule of Law	Then identify the rule of law or legal principle adopted by the court that applies to the issue addressed in the memo.

c. *Rule of Law Interpretation—Process for Presenting Case Law*—When presenting the case law that interprets how the law applies to a fact situation such as a client's, the recommended format is to present the name and citation of the case first, then the facts of the case, followed by the rule of law or the legal principle applied by the court (see Exhibit 9-12).

(1) **Name and Citation of Court Opinion** When presenting the case, identify the case name and citation first. The reader should know the name of the case at the beginning of the discussion. This eliminates any possible confusion about which case is being discussed.

For Example:

The case that defines the term *publication* as used in the statute is *Smith v. Jones,* 956 N. Wash. 441, 881 N.E.2d 898 (1995).

(2) **Facts of the Case** The next step is to provide sufficient information concerning the facts and rule of law applied in the case to demonstrate that the case is on point. To accomplish this, you must include enough information about the court opinion to demonstrate that the similarity between the key facts and the rule of law of the opinion and those of the client's case is sufficient for the court opinion to govern or provide guidance in deciding how the law applies.

For Example:

Assume the client's case involves the question of whether a majority shareholder in a closely held corporation engaged in oppressive conduct when he refused to issue dividends while granting himself, as CEO of the corporation, semiannual bonuses in an amount triple his

annual salary. Section 90-9-4 of the state corporation statutes prohibits oppressive conduct by majority shareholders against minority shareholders. The statute does not define *oppressive*. The case on point is *Cedrik v. Ely,* 956 N. Wash. 776, 881 N.E.2d 451 (1995).
The introduction of the case may read as follows: The case that defines what constitutes "oppressive" conduct in a fact situation such as that presented in our case is *Cedrik v. Ely,* 956 N. Wash. 776, 881 N.E.2d 451 (1995). In that case, just as in our case, a majority shareholder of a closely held corporation granted himself bonuses in excess of triple his salary. In *Cedrik,* the majority shareholder also refused to issue dividends. In defining what constitutes "oppressive conduct" under § 90-9-4, the court stated . . . . *Id.* at 778.

When presenting a case in an office memo, it is not necessary to include all of the information that would be included in a case brief. In a legal research memorandum, for example, only the facts sufficient to show that the case is on point should be presented. A case brief should include more detail, such as background facts and other information.

(3) Rule of Law   The last step when discussing a case that is on point is to identify the rule of law or the legal principle adopted by the court that applies to the issue being addressed in the office memo.

For Example:

The state collections statute provides that efforts to collect payment for a debt must be made in a "reasonable manner." *Reasonable manner* is not defined in the statute. In the client's case, the collector called the client three times a day, often after 9 p.m. The case on point is *Cerro v. Collectors, Inc.,* 955 N. Wash. 641, 880 N.E.2d 401 (1994). The presentation of the *rule of law* applied by the court would read as follows: In the Cerro case, the court stated that "reasonable contact" as used in the collections statute means no more than one telephone call a day to the debtor's residence. The court went on to state that no calls should be placed before 6 a.m. or after 7 p.m. *Id.* at 645.

Two considerations should be kept in mind when presenting the rule of law from the case:
1. Quote the language of the court whenever practical. Quotations are stronger than paraphrases. Sometimes the language does not lend itself to quotation, such as in situations where the rule is composed of several parts or steps that are presented in more than one paragraph of the opinion.

Do not use too many quotations. Quotations should be used to quote the law or legal principle presented by the court and key portions of the court's reasoning. They should not be used in place of an analysis. You have failed to analyze the case law properly if your analysis consists almost entirely of quotations of a court's presentation of the law and its reasoning.

2. When presenting the law, cite the page of the court opinion where the rule is presented.

> **□ *For Example:***
>
> In defining what constitutes "oppressive conduct" under § 90-9-4, the court stated, "Oppressive conduct occurs when a majority shareholder engages in wrongful conduct which inures to the benefit of the majority and the detriment of the minority." *Id.* at 778.

In summary, the sequence when presenting a case is as follows:

1. case name and case citation
2. relevant facts from the case that demonstrate that the case is on point
3. the rule of law or principle adopted by the court that applies to the issue in the client's case

It is logical to discuss a case using that format for the following reasons:

▶ It is more readable when the reader knows the name of the case first; then what happened, the facts; then the rule of law applied by the court.

▶ It is logical to discuss the rule of law last because the next step is application of the rule to the issue(s) and facts of the client's case. The memo flows more smoothly when the *application* of the rule immediately follows the *presentation* of the rule.

That sequence is only a recommendation, however, not a hard-and-fast rule. In some instances, it may be better to address the rule of law from the opinion first, then present the name and facts from the case. Follow a sequence that works best for the memo you are drafting.

4. Analysis—Part C Application of Rule of Law to Client's Case   The purpose of the office memo is to demonstrate how the rule of law and the case law apply to guide or govern determination of the issue being addressed in the memo. A critical element of the analysis section, therefore, is application of the law to the issue(s) raised by the facts of the client's case. You will encounter two situations when applying the rule of law to the facts of the case:

▶ The rule does not require interpretation through the use of case law.

▶ The rule requires interpretation through the use of case law.

a. *Application of Rule That Does Not Require Case Law Interpretation*—As discussed in Subsection 9.3 F.3 "Analysis—Part B Rule of Law Interpretation—Case Law," there are some instances when case law is not required to determine how the rule of law applies to the issue being analyzed. It is clear from the face of the rule how it applies. In such instances, simply apply the rule directly to the issue being addressed in the office memo.

> **For Example:**
>
> Municipal ordinance 91-1 establishes 25 mph as the maximum speed in residential areas of the municipality. The client was ticketed for driving 55 mph in a residential neighborhood. The application of the ordinance is clear. The client violated the ordinance.

   b. ***Application of Rule That Requires Case Law Interpretation***—In most instances, there is a question of how the rule of law or an element of the rule applies to the issue(s) being analyzed. In such cases, it is necessary to refer to case law to learn how the law applies. Once the case on point is discussed, as addressed in the previous section, *the rule of law or the legal principle adopted by the court must be applied to the facts of the client's case.* This is the next step of the analysis process. It immediately follows presentation of the rule of law from the case on point.

> **For Example:**
>
> In this case, the court defined *oppressive conduct* as "wrongful conduct that inures to the benefit of the majority and the detriment of the minority." *Id.* at 675. (The court ruled that the majority shareholder's act of granting himself a bonus triple his annual salary while refusing to allow dividends was wrongful, inured to his benefit and the detriment of the minority shareholders, and was, therefore, "oppressive conduct" within the meaning of the statute.)
>
> In our case, just as in the *Cedrik* case, the defendant (the majority shareholder) gave himself bonuses in excess of triple his salary while refusing to allow the issuance of dividends. If the court follows the definition of "oppressive conduct" established in the *Cedrik* case, the defendant engaged in oppressive conduct.
>
> In the *Cerro* case, the court held that "reasonable contact" as used in the collections statute means no more than one telephone call a day to the debtor's residence, and no call should be placed before 6 a.m. or after 7 p.m. *Id.* at 645.
>
> The collection agency contacted our client more than three times a day for seven straight days, and several of the calls were made after 9 p.m. If the trial court follows the rule adopted in *Cerro,* the outcome should be in our favor. The collections statute has clearly been violated.

     Remember, you must include in the analysis a discussion of how the law applies to the issue(s) and facts of the client's case. It is useless to introduce the rule of law and discuss how the rule is interpreted through the presentation of a case on point, then fail to apply the law to the facts of the client's case.

5. Analysis—Part D Counteranalysis   The next part of the analysis section is the counteranalysis. The analysis of a legal issue is not complete unless counterarguments to the analysis are explored. The process of addressing the counterarguments is called counteranalysis. Note the following when preparing the counteranalysis:

▶ In the analysis section, the counteranalysis should follow part C, the application of the law to the issue and facts of the client's case. The reader, then, is immediately apprised of any counterargument and can easily compare and contrast the arguments and counterarguments and evaluate the merits of each.

▶ If rebuttal is necessary, it should follow the counteranalysis. Rebuttal may be required if you believe it is necessary to explain why the counterargument does not apply or if you want to evaluate the merits of the counterargument.

> **For Example:**
>
> The opposing side may argue that oppressive conduct did not occur, and the *Cedrik* case does not apply, because the majority shareholder in our case earned the triple bonuses by working long hours and weekends. In *Cedrik,* just as in our case, the majority shareholder worked long hours, and the court noted "Even though the majority shareholder is entitled to receive extra compensation, he is not entitled to receive an amount of compensation that results in the total denial of benefits to the minority shareholders." *Id.* at 778.

A checklist for the analysis section is presented in Exhibit 9-13.

Exhibit 9-13

Checklist—Analysis Section

Checklist to Use When Preparing the Analysis Section

❑ Does the analysis section follow the proper format? The format is Rule of Law + Case Interpreting the Rule of Law (if necessary) + Application + Counteranalysis.

❑ If application of the rule of law is not clear, is case law presented that is on point and that interprets how the rule of law applies?

❑ Is the proper citation presented for each rule of law and authority included in the analysis?

❑ Is there a separate analysis section for each issue addressed in the memo?

❑ Is the rule of law presented in the analysis applied to the issue raised by the facts of the client's case?

❑ Is there a counteranalysis and a rebuttal to the counteranalysis if necessary?

9.3 G   CONCLUSION

Part C of the analysis section, application of the rule of law to the client's case, is a discussion of how the rule of law or the legal principle applies to the issue. This application of the law to the issue is really a miniconclusion: it concludes how the law applies. In effect, a conclusion is presented in the analysis section. Because the analysis section includes a brief conclusion, some law firms do not require a separate conclusion section. It is recommended, however, that you include a separate conclusion section composed of a general summary of the entire memo.

The conclusion section should not introduce new information or authorities, nor should it merely repeat the brief answer. It should summarize the conclusions reached in the analysis section. The conclusion should be crafted to include a reference to and a summary of all of the law discussed in the analysis section, both the enacted and case law. It requires, however, fewer introductory and transitional sentences. Ideally, the conclusion should briefly inform the reader of what law applies and how it applies. *The reader should be able to obtain from the conclusion a general understanding of the law and its application without having to read the entire memo.*

The advantage of this type of conclusion is that researchers working on similar cases can determine from the conclusion whether a memo from the office memo files applies to their case. They should be able to obtain all essential information by reading just the conclusion. Researchers save time by not having to read the entire memo if all that is needed is a summary of the law and an analysis.

> ❑ *For Example:*
>
> Section 30-3-9 of the criminal code prohibits the possession of proscribed drugs. The case of *Smith v. Jones* provides that when an individual does not have actual possession, he may be in constructive possession if there is either direct or circumstantial evidence establishing that the defendant had both knowledge and control of the drugs. In our case, there is no evidence, either direct or circumstantial, that the client had either knowledge or control of the drugs he was charged with possessing. If *Smith v. Jones* is followed, there is not sufficient evidence to support charges of possession under § 30-3-9.
>
> Article II, section 7, of the state constitution prohibits illegal searches and seizures. In the case of *State v. Idle,* the court held that an individual is seized within the meaning of the law when the actions of the law enforcement officers are such that a reasonable person would not believe that he was free to leave. In our case, the client was handcuffed and ordered to sit in the backseat of a police car. He was not placed under arrest. A reasonable person would not believe he was free to leave in this situation; therefore, if the test adopted in *State v. Idle* is followed in our case, our client was under arrest.

Note that in these examples, the reader is able to obtain all essential information concerning the applicable law by reading the conclusion. Also, note that introductory

Exhibit 9-14

■ Checklist—Conclusion Section

Checklist to Use When Preparing the Conclusion Section

- ❑ Does the conclusion include a brief summary of the analysis of each issue?
- ❑ Is all of the law discussed in the Analysis section summarized in the conclusion, both enacted and case law?
- ❑ Is new information or authority excluded from the conclusion?

sentences are not used to introduce the law and transitional sentences are not utilized to connect the statutory and case law. The importance and use of introductory and transitional sentences in the other sections of an office memo are discussed in Section 9.4 "General Considerations."

When there are multiple issues, the conclusion is usually presented immediately after the analysis of each issue. When there are only two issues and the analysis is not complex, one conclusion that summarizes the analysis of both issues may be presented at the end of the memo.

A checklist for the conclusion section is presented in Exhibit 9-14.

9.3 H   RECOMMENDATIONS

Not all law firms require that a recommendations section be included as part of the basic format of an office memo. Also, in some formats, recommendations are included in the conclusion section. Generally, a separate section for any comments or recommendations should follow the conclusion section. Recommendations are not part of the analysis or conclusion sections; they frequently address matters to be considered and steps to be taken as a result of conclusions reached in the analysis section. The recommendations section should include any comments or recommendations you have concerning the client's case or matters discussed in the memo.

Areas that may be addressed in the recommendations section are as follows:

1. What the next step should be

■ *For Example:*

Based on the analysis of the issues, it is apparent that the risk of liability is great. It may be advisable to seek a settlement in this case.

2. Identification of additional information that may be necessary due to questions raised in the analysis of the issue

> 💠 *For Example:*
>
> It appears from the case file that the neighbors were not asked if they heard any strange noises. Inasmuch as the analysis of this issue reveals that this information is critical, it is recommended the neighbors be reinterviewed.

3. Identification of additional research that may be necessary on the issue

> 💠 *For Example:*
>
> Additional research may be required because the necessary research sources are not locally available, the analysis is preliminary due to time constraints, or the factual investigation of the case has not been completed.

4. Identification of related issues or concerns that became apparent as a result of the research and analysis

> 💠 *For Example:*
>
> Assume the memo addresses a negligence issue concerning an automobile accident. If the analysis of the negligence issue reveals other possible causes of action in the case, such as assault or negligent infliction of emotional distress, the reader should be advised of the existence of these additional causes of action.

9.4 GENERAL CONSIDERATIONS

Following are some general considerations to keep in mind when preparing an office research memorandum. A separate section is devoted to these matters because they often apply to more than one section of a memo and you should consider them when approaching a memo assignment.

9.4 A HEADING

Although an office memo is written in paragraph form, use headings for each section. Headings provide the overall structure of the assignment, guide the reader, and apprise the reader of what is covered in each section. The reader may want to read a specific section, such as the analysis, in which case a heading allows him or her to locate that section quickly. Headings also serve as a guide for preparation of the table of contents if one is needed. Use the format presented in Exhibit 9-1 or 9-2 as a guide for the appropriate headings.

Legal Research Memorandum

9.4 B   INTRODUCTORY SENTENCES

Introductory or topic sentences should be used to inform the reader of what is to follow. Avoid immediately jumping into the discussion of a topic, such as the presentation of the law.

> ◘ *For Example:*
>
> **No introduction:**
> Section 59-3-2 of the criminal code provides that possession of cocaine is illegal. In *Smith v. Jones,* the defendant . . .

Provide an introduction when discussing a topic.

> ◘ *For Example:*
>
> **Includes an introduction:**
> *The rule of law prohibiting the possession of cocaine* is criminal code § 59-3-2, which states that possession of cocaine is illegal. The statute does not define possession; therefore, case law must be referred to. *The case that provides guidance as to what constitutes possession in a fact situation such as ours is Smith v. Jones.* In this case, . . . (The introductions are italicized in this example.)

9.4 C   TRANSITION SENTENCES

Use transition sentences to connect sections, subsections, and related topics. The following example lacks a transition.

> ◘ *For Example:*
>
> The rule of law governing possession of drugs is § 59-3-2. Section 59-3-2c makes it illegal to possess cocaine. *Smith v. Jones* provides that possession occurs when . . .

A transition should be used in that example to connect the statutory law with the case law. The reader should be informed as to why case law is being presented. The following example uses a transition sentence.

> ◘ *For Example:*
>
> The rule of law governing possession of drugs is § 59-3-2. Section 59-3-2c makes it illegal to possess cocaine. *The statute does not define what constitutes possession; therefore, it is necessary to refer to case law for guidance.* (The transition sentence is italicized in this example.)
> A case that defines what constitutes possession in a fact situation such as ours is *Smith v. Jones.* In this case, . . .

9.4 D   PARAGRAPHS

Paragraphs add coherence and make a memo more readable. Each area or topic should be addressed in a separate paragraph.

> **■ *For Example:***
>
> In the analysis section of a memo, the discussion of the rule of law, the case that serves as a guide to the interpretation of the rule of law, the application of the rule to the issue, the counteranalysis, and the rebuttal to the counteranalysis should each be addressed in a separate paragraph or paragraphs.

9.4 E   PERSUASIVE PRECEDENT

Persuasive precedent is case law a court is not bound to consider or follow but may consider or follow when reaching a decision. When presenting persuasive authority, you must indicate the reason you are relying on this type of authority and lay a proper foundation for its use.

> **■ *For Example:***
>
> Section 90-9-6 prohibits oppressive conduct by a majority shareholder. The statute does not define what constitutes oppressive conduct, and the courts of this state have not addressed the question.
> The state of New Washington, however, has a statute identical to our statute, and the New Washington courts have addressed the question of what constitutes oppressive conduct under the statute. In the case of *Darren v. Darren*, . . .

In the preceding example, the reader is *informed as to why the out-of-state law (persuasive precedent) is referred to*: the statute does not define the term, and the state courts have not addressed the question. A *foundation for the presentation of the persuasive precedent is laid*: the statute of the state referred to is identical to our state statute, and the other state's courts have addressed the question. In the following example, a foundation is laid for the use of a court interpretation of one statute to interpret another statute.

> **■ *For Example:***
>
> Our courts have not defined the term *oppressive conduct* as used in § 90-9-6. Section 45-5-6C of the Small Loan Act prohibits "oppressive conduct" in small loan transactions. The state court of appeals, in the case of *Irons v. Fast Loans, Inc.*, has defined what constitutes oppressive conduct under the Small Loan Act, and we can look to that definition for guidance in interpreting § 90-9-6.

9.4 F   CONCLUSIONS

In many instances, after researching and analyzing a legal problem, you may not be able to provide a definite yes or no answer as to how it may be resolved.

> ◘ *For Example:*
>
> If there is no mandatory precedent and persuasive precedent or secondary authority is relied on, you may not be able to provide an answer as to how the court is likely to resolve the issue. If the case law that applies is very old and policies have changed, the case law may or may not be followed.

In such instances, you should present your conclusions and explain your reservations.

> ◘ *For Example:*
>
> In conclusion, the courts of this state have not addressed this question. The majority of states that have addressed this issue follow the rule adopted by the New Washington supreme court in the case of *Tyler v. Tyler.* As stated in the analysis of this issue, the progressive approach of the New Washington court reflects the approach our supreme court has taken in resolving similar issues and will likely be adopted by the court.

9.4 G   REVISIONS/REDRAFTS

When preparing an office memo, you must produce a professional product. This demands thorough research and analysis of all issues assigned and all aspects of each issue. It also requires assembling the research and analysis into an organized, error-free final product. Be prepared to compose a number of redrafts.

9.4 H   ADDITIONAL AUTHORITY

If several cases are on point, it is not necessary to thoroughly discuss each one. Present and discuss thoroughly the most recent case on point and refer to the others.

> ◘ *For Example:*
>
> The case that defines what constitutes "oppressive" conduct in a fact situation such as that presented in our case is *Cedrik v. Ely,* 956 N. Wash. 776, 881 N.E.2d 451 (1995). In this case, the majority shareholder gave himself three bonuses that were triple his salary. At the same time, he refused to allow dividends to be issued. In defining what constitutes

> "oppressive conduct" under § 90-9-4, the court stated, "Oppressive conduct occurs when a majority shareholder engages in wrongful conduct which inures to the benefit of the majority and the detriment of the minority." *Id.* at 778. See also *Tyre v. Casey,* 953 N. Wash. 431, 878 N.E.2d 49 (1993) (oppressive conduct found when no dividends were issued and majority shareholder received several bonuses and was provided an extravagant expense account); *Ireland v. Ireland,* 952 N. Wash. 288, 873 N.E.2d 553 (1992) (oppressive conduct found when no dividends were issued and majority shareholder was given a house as a bonus).

9.5 KEY POINTS CHECKLIST: LEGAL RESEARCH MEMORANDUM

- ❏ A legal research memorandum should be a self-contained document. Include in the memo all of the information necessary for the reader to understand the context of the legal analysis. Subsequent readers should not be required to refer to the case file to understand the issue, facts, or analysis.
- ❏ Present the fact situation objectively and include both background facts and key facts.
- ❏ Follow the format adopted where you work. You may be familiar with or prefer a different format; if appropriate, recommend changes. If your suggestions are not adopted, follow the format used in the office.
- ❏ Make sure you understand the assignment. If you are unclear about any aspect of the assignment, ask the supervisory attorney. Do not waste time finding answers to the wrong question or performing the wrong task.
- ❏ Follow the standard format for the analysis section of a memo: Rule + Case Law (interpretation of the rule) + Application of Rule + Counteranalysis. That format is based on the standard IRAC model.
- ❏ The presentation of a case in a case brief is different from the presentation of a case in an office memo. When introducing a case in the analysis section of a memo, it is not necessary to include all of the information you would include in a case brief.
- ❏ In the analysis section, discuss how the rule of law applies to the issue and what the facts of the client's case are.
- ❏ Conduct a counteranalysis. If there is no counterargument, mention the fact that there is no counterargument or different position supported by the case law.
- ❏ Provide enough information in the conclusion to inform the reader of all of the applicable enacted and case law.
- ❏ Use introductory and transition sentences. Do not jump from one topic to another. Provide a smooth transition between subjects.
- ❏ Before presenting persuasive precedent or secondary authority, indicate why you are not relying on mandatory authority.

❑ Do not be disturbed if you do not reach a definite conclusion as to how the law applies. There are many gray areas and issues that have not been ruled upon. Your job is to inform the reader of the existing law and provide a well-reasoned analysis of its application. Predicting the legal outcome always involves some measure of uncertainty.

❑ Do not try to make the first draft the final draft. Write the information in rough form. It is easier to polish a rough draft than to try to make the first draft the finished product.

Chapter 10

Court Briefs

Contents

10.1 INTRODUCTION

This chapter focuses on the considerations involved in the preparation of legal analysis documents designed for submission to a court: trial court and appellate court legal memorandum briefs. A trial court brief is often referred to as a memorandum of law or a memorandum of points and authorities. In this chapter, a legal memorandum brief submitted to a trial court is referred to as a trial brief and a brief submitted to a court of appeals is referred to as an appellate court brief. An example of a trial court brief and an appellate court brief is included in Appendix C.

10.2 GENERAL CONSIDERATIONS

Both trial and appellate court briefs are similar in many respects to legal research memoranda (memorandums), and the fundamental principles that apply to the preparation of research memorandums also apply to the preparation of court briefs. The similarities are outlined here.

10.2 A SIMILARITIES—COURT BRIEFS AND LEGAL RESEARCH MEMORANDUMS

1. **Legal Writing Process**   It is necessary to adopt and use a legal writing process when preparing a research memorandum; the same is true when preparing a court brief. The basic writing process is the same for both court briefs and legal research memorandums:

   Prewriting Stage
   >Assignment—type of brief, audience, and so on
   >Constraints—time, length, format (court rules)
   >Organization—creation of an expanded outline
   >>Use of an expanded outline

   Writing Stage
   Postwriting Stage
   >Revising
   >Editing

   Refer to Chapter 7 for instructions and information about using a writing process.

2. **Basic Format**   Court briefs follow the same basic format as research memorandums. Both include a presentation of the issue(s), the relevant facts, a legal analysis, and a conclusion. Refer to Chapter 9 for information and guidelines concerning the preparation of these components.

3. **Analysis Approach**   Court briefs follow the same basic organizational approach to the legal analysis of an issue as research memorandums: the rule of law is presented first, then the interpretation of the rule of law through the case law (if interpretation is necessary), then the application of the law to the issues presented by the facts of the case, followed by the conclusion. The basic format of this approach is presented in Exhibit 10-1.

   Refer to Chapter 9 when preparing the analysis and conclusion sections of a court brief.

10.2 B DISSIMILARITIES—COURT BRIEFS AND LEGAL RESEARCH MEMORANDUMS

As noted above, court briefs, both trial and appellate, are similar in many respects to research memorandums. They are similar primarily in basic format and content. The major difference is in the presentation of the format and content. A research memorandum is designed to present an objective analysis of the law. The goal is to provide a neutral analysis that thoroughly addresses all sides of an issue and provides the attorney with guidance on how the court may resolve the issue.

Whereas a research memorandum is designed to inform objectively, a court brief is designed to convince. A court brief is an advocacy document designed to persuade the court to adopt a position or take an action that is favorable to the client.

Exhibit 10-1

■ **Legal Analysis—Court Brief Organizational Approach**

Organizational Approach to the Legal Analysis of an Issue in a Court Brief

Rule of law—Present the rule of law or the legal principle that applies. Case law (if necessary)—Follow the rule of law with presentation of the case law that interprets how the rule of law applies.

1. name of case
2. facts of case—sufficient to demonstrate that case is on point
3. rule or legal principle from case that applies to client's case

Application of law to facts of case—After presentation of the case law, apply the law or principle in the case to facts of client's case. Include an explanation of why the opposing position does not apply. Conclusion—Provide a summary of the legal analysis.

Therefore, although the elements of a research memorandum and court brief are basically the same, court briefs differ in that they are designed to advocate a position and persuade the reader.

The following subsections address the guidelines, factors, and considerations involved in the preparation of persuasive court briefs. To eliminate repetition, this section addresses the factors involved in the persuasive presentation of both trial and appellate court briefs. Therefore, the detailed discussion of court briefs presented in "Trial Court Briefs" and "Appellate Court Briefs" does not include information on persuasive writing factors. The information presented applies to the preparation of both trial and appellate court briefs and should be kept in mind when preparing those briefs.

Ethics. Rule 3.3(a)(1) of the Model Rules of Professional Conduct provides that a lawyer should not make false statements of law or fact to a tribunal. Broadly interpreted that means that matters should not be presented in a manner that may mislead the court. Also, Under Rule 3.3(a)(3) of the Model Rules, an attorney has an ethical duty as an officer of the court to disclose legal authority adverse to the position of the client that is not disclosed by the opposing counsel. Therefore, when preparing a persuasive presentation of a legal position or argument, you must keep in mind the importance of the rules of professional conduct. Although designed to persuade, a court brief must present the issue(s), facts, and analysis accurately, clearly and concisely. It should not mislead, distort, or hide the truth. The guidelines for how that is accomplished are presented in the following subsections.

1. **Issues—Persuasive Presentation**   Once you have identified the issue, introduce each of its elements—the law, the question, and the key facts—in a persuasive manner.

a. *Law Component of the Issue*—You should state the law component of the issue persuasively.

> ☐ *For Example:*
>
> Assume a case involves oppressive conduct by a majority shareholder against the minority shareholders in the hypothetical state of New Washington. The corporation consists of three shareholders. The majority shareholder holds 60 percent of the stock and is employed as president of the corporation. The minority shareholders are not employed by the corporation.
>
> In the case, the defendant, the majority shareholder, controls the board of directors and refused to allow the issuance of dividends for a ten-year period. During this period, he gave himself an annual 40 percent raise each year and an annual bonus equal to 50 percent of his salary. The minority shareholders filed a suit claiming that the majority shareholder's actions constitute oppressive conduct.
>
> Section 53-6 of the New Washington statutes authorizes the court to dissolve the corporation when the majority shareholder engages in oppressive conduct.
>
> That example is referred to in this chapter as the corporation example.

In a research memorandum, the law component of the issue in that example is stated objectively: Under the New Washington corporation statute, NWSA § 53-6, did oppressive conduct occur when . . .? In a court brief, however, the law is presented persuasively: Under the New Washington corporation statute, NWSA § 53-6, *which prohibits oppressive* conduct, did . . .? (The persuasive language is italicized.)

Note that the persuasive presentation of the law component emphasizes the prohibitory nature of the statute.

> ☐ *For Example:*
>
> If your position is that the statute has limited application, the law should be presented in a manner that focuses on that limitation: Under NWSA § 51-7, which *limits the requirement of a written contract to . . .*
>
> If you want to emphasize the applicability of the statute, the law should be presented in a manner that focuses on applicability: Under NWSA § 51-7, *which requires that a contract be in writing when . . .*

b. *Question Component of the Issue*—Present the question component of the issue in a persuasive manner that suggests a result.

> ☐ *For Example:*
>
> *Objective presentation:* . . . did oppressive conduct occur when . . .
>
> *Persuasive presentation:* . . . was the majority shareholder's conduct oppressive when . . .

> . . . did the majority shareholder engage in oppressive conduct when . . .
> (Note that in the objective presentation, the focus is on the conduct. In
> the persuasive presentation, the statement immediately links the con-
> duct to the majority shareholder.)

The language used should focus on the result desired.

> **For Example:**
>
> The key language is italicized. . . . does the statute *allow* oral contracts for . . .
> . . . does the statute *require* oral contracts for . . .
> . . . does the statute *prohibit* oral contracts for . . .

    c. **Fact Component of the Issue**—State the key facts of the issue in a manner
designed to focus the reader on the facts favorable to the client and to persuade the reader to favor the client's position.

> **For Example:**
>
> **Objective presentation:**
> . . . did oppressive conduct occur when dividends were not issued for a
> ten-year period and the majority shareholder received annual salary in-
> creases and bonuses?
>
> **Persuasive presentation:**
> . . . did the majority shareholder engage in oppressive conduct when he
> refused to issue dividends for a ten-year period while giving himself
> large annual salary increases and bonuses?

> **For Example:**
>
> **Objective presentation:**
> . . . when the defendant entered the property after being advised not to enter?
>
> **Persuasive presentation:**
> . . . when the defendant intentionally entered the property even though he
> was warned not to enter?

Note that in both examples, the persuasive presentation focuses on the defendant and links the defendant directly to the improper conduct.

    A checklist for use in the persuasive presentation of the issue(s) is pre-
sented in Exhibit 10-2.

2. **Statement of Facts—Persuasive Presentation**   The statement of facts section
of a court brief presents the facts of the case. This section is often called the
statement of the case. In a court brief, as in a research memorandum, the statement
of facts should include both the background facts and the key facts. In a court
brief, introduce the facts credibly and persuasively and in a light most favorable to

Exhibit 10-2

Issues—Persuasive Presentation—Checklist

Checklist to Use When Preparing the Issue Section

- ❑ Law Component—Is the law correctly presented, stated persuasively, and accurately cited?
- ❑ Question Component—Are the law, question, and key facts included and stated persuasively?
- ❑ Fact Component—Are the key facts and background facts included and stated persuasively?

the client's position. That is accomplished by emphasizing favorable facts and de-emphasizing or neutralizing unfavorable facts.

There are several techniques you can use to emphasize favorable facts and neutralize unfavorable facts. Some of these are discussed in the following subsections.

a. *Placement*—Readers tend to remember information presented at the beginning and end of a section, and they usually give most of their attention to opening and closing sentences. Therefore, introduce the facts favorable to the client's position at the beginning and the end of the factual statement. In the middle of the section, present the facts unfavorable to the client's position that you wish to de-emphasize.

For Example:

The defendant is the majority shareholder and controlling member of the board of directors of XYZ Corporation. He has refused to authorize the issuance of dividends for ten years. During this time, the defendant has been the president of the corporation. As president, he has granted himself a 40 percent raise each year. In addition, he has given himself an annual bonus equal to 50 percent of his salary. It is claimed by the defendant that he is entitled to the salary increases and bonuses because he works long hours, is underpaid, and is the person in charge. The defendant has rebuffed the plaintiff's repeated requests to discuss the defendant's grants to himself of salary increases and bonuses and failure to issue dividends. The defendant has informed the plaintiff that he does not intend to issue dividends.

In that example, the facts least favorable to the defendant, his failure to issue dividends and receipt of salary increases and bonuses, are presented at the beginning. His conduct immediately captures the reader's attention. His conduct is also mentioned again at the end of the presentation. The reader's first and last impressions are focused on the acts least favorable to the defendant.

The facts favorable to the defendant, that he is entitled to the salary increases and bonuses, are de-emphasized by their placement in the middle of the fact statement.

If the facts statement is composed of several paragraphs, place the favorable material at the beginning of the presentation and close with a summary or rephrasing of the favorable key facts. Place the unfavorable facts in the middle of the presentation and mention them only once or as few times as possible.

Note that the goal is a persuasive presentation of the facts. That goal should not be so rigidly pursued that clarity is lost.

> *For Example:*
>
> It may not be practical to state the favorable facts immediately at the beginning of a paragraph. To ensure clarity, you may need to present transitional or introductory sentences first, then follow with the favorable facts.

b. *Sentence Length*—Use short sentences to emphasize favorable information and long sentences to de-emphasize unfavorable information. Shorter sentences generally draw the attention of the reader; are easier to understand and remember; and, therefore, are more powerful.

> *For Example:*
>
> The defendant is the majority shareholder and controlling member of the board of directors of XYZ Corporation. He has refused to authorize the issuance of dividends for ten years. During this time, the defendant has been the president of the corporation. As president, he has granted himself a 40 percent raise each year.

The sentences in that example are short and clear, and they draw the reader's attention. Longer sentences that string together several facts tend to downplay and reduce the impact of each fact.

> *For Example:*
>
> It is claimed by the defendant that he is entitled to the salary increases and bonuses because he works long hours, is underpaid, and is the person in charge.

In that example, if each of the defendant's actions were presented in separate sentences, they would stand out and be clearer.

c. *Active Voice*—Use active voice to emphasize favorable information and passive voice to de-emphasize unfavorable information. When active voice is used, the subject of the sentence is the actor. When passive voice is used, the subject is acted upon. Active voice draws the attention to and emphasizes the actor. Passive voice draws attention away from and de-emphasizes the actor.

> ### For Example:
>
> **Passive voice:**
> It is claimed by the defendant that he is entitled to the bonuses . . . (The use
>   of passive voice draws attention away from the actor, the defendant.)
>
> **Active voice:**
> The defendant claims he is entitled . . . (The sentence is less wordy and
>   focuses the attention on the actor.)

The use of active and passive voice is discussed in Chapter 1.

d. *Word Choice*—Ideally, the words you choose should introduce the client's facts in the most favorable light and the opponent's facts in the least favorable light. You should present the client's position in the most affirmative manner and the opponent's position in the most questionable manner.

> ### For Example:
>
> The plaintiff states that . . .
> The defendant alleges . . .

Notice that the plaintiff's presentation sounds stronger, since it is presented as a statement. The defendant's position is presented as a charge—an "allegation" rather than a statement of fact. There are numerous ways to present positions in a strong or weak manner. Make sure you check your word choice.

It is easy, however, to get carried away and state the facts in such a slanted way that your bias is obvious.

> ### For Example:
>
> The defendant stubbornly and unreasonably refuses to issue dividends.

In that example, the presentation of the facts is clearly biased and heavy-handed. It would be better to note just that the defendant has refused to issue dividends. When in doubt, avoid inflammatory language and exercise restraint.

Refer to the techniques presented in the preceding text when preparing a persuasive presentation of the facts. A checklist for use with the guidelines for the persuasive presentation of the statement of facts is included in Exhibit 10-3.

Many of the considerations involved in preparing the Statement of Facts section of a legal research memorandum are the same as those involved in preparing the statement of facts section of a court brief. Therefore, Section 9.3 E "Statement of Facts" in Chapter 9 also will prove helpful when preparing this section of a court brief.

3. Argument—Persuasive Presentation   The persuasive tone and orientation of a court brief is initially established in the presentation of the issue and facts statements. The persuasive techniques discussed previously (such as word

Exhibit 10-3

Statement of Facts—Persuasive Presentation—Checklist

Checklist to Use When Preparing the Statement of Facts Section

- ❏ Placement of Facts—Are the facts favorable to the client's position placed at the beginning and end of the factual statement?
- ❏ Sentence Length—Are short sentences used to emphasize favorable information and long sentences used to de-emphasize unfavorable information?
- ❏ Active/Passive Voice—Is active voice used to emphasize favorable information and passive voice used to de-emphasize unfavorable information?
- ❏ Word Choice—Are words chosen that introduce the client's facts in the most favorable light and the opponent's facts in the least favorable light?

choice, sentence length, and active and passive voice) also apply and should be used when crafting the argument section of a court brief.

The argument section is the heart of a court brief. It is the equivalent of the analysis section of a legal research memorandum. Unlike the analysis section of a legal research memo, however, the argument section of a court brief is not an objective presentation of the law. It should be crafted in a persuasive manner. The goal of the argument section is to persuade the court that your position is valid. That is accomplished by a persuasive presentation of the following:

▶ the law in support of your position

▶ the analysis of the law

▶ the argument that your analysis is valid and the opposition's analysis is invalid

The following text presents a summary of the techniques you can use to ensure that the argument component of a court brief is presented in a persuasive manner. Several helpful guidelines apply to both trial and appellate court briefs. Sections 10.3 and 10.4, "Trial Court Briefs" and "Appellate Court Briefs," respectively, introduce additional information concerning the format and content of the argument section. The content focuses on the differences between trial and appellate court briefs.

a. *Organization*—The organization of the argument section is similar to that of the analysis section of the research memorandum: *the rule of law is introduced, followed by an interpretation of the law (usually through case law), then an application of the law to the issue raised by the facts of the case.* The opposing position is addressed in the presentation of the argument instead of in a separate counteranalysis section.

(1) Issue Presentation. When there is more than one issue or when there are issues and subissues, discuss the issue supported by the strongest argument first. There are several reasons for this:

▶ First impressions are lasting. The tone of the argument is set at the beginning. By presenting the strongest argument first, you set a tone of strength and credibility.

▶ When you introduce the strongest argument first, the court is more likely to be persuaded that your position is correct and look more favorably on your weaker arguments.

▶ Judges are usually very busy. On some occasions, a judge may not read or give equal attention to all sections of a brief, especially when the brief is long. In such instances, the judge may not read your strongest argument if you do not present it first or near the beginning of the brief. For that reason, if there are several arguments in support of a position, omit the weak ones. Arguments or positions that are weak or that have little supporting authority detract and divert attention from the stronger arguments.

(2) Rule of Law Presentation. Present the rule of law, whether it is enacted or case law, in a manner that supports your argument.

🔲 *For Example:*

Objective presentation:
The statute that g*overns oppressive conduct* is . . .

Persuasive presentation:
The statute that *prohibits* oppressive conduct by a majority shareholder is . . .
(The first example merely indicates that the statute governs the area. The
   second example persuasively emphasizes the prohibitory nature of the
   statute.)

🔲 *For Example:*

Objective presentation:
The courts of other states are split on what constitutes oppressive conduct.
   Most courts follow *Smith v. Jones,* which provides . . . . A minority of
   courts follow *Dave v. Roe* . . . . The majority view is based on the
   premise that the conduct need be either wrongful or improper . . . .

Persuasive presentation:
The majority of courts follow the definition of oppressive conduct presented
   in *Smith v. Jones.* In this case, the court defined oppressive conduct as . . . .
   This definition is based on the well-reasoned view that the conduct need
   only be wrongful or improper. A minority of courts follow . . .

In that example, the persuasive presentation is more forceful and introduces the majority view in a manner that indicates it is preferable.

The objective view is passive and treats both the majority and minority views equally. It does not emphasize one view as favorable. Refer to the discussion in "Issues—Persuasive Presentation" in Subsection 10.2 B when drafting the rule of law component of the argument section of a brief.

(3) **Case Presentation.**   When introducing case law, discuss the favorable case law first, followed by the unfavorable or opposing case law, then a response or rebuttal that emphasizes why the favorable case law should be followed. This is similar to the format followed in the facts statement: *placement of the unfavorable material in the middle of the presentation following the favorable material tends to minimize its importance.*

Discussion of the case law should emphasize the similarities and applicability of the case you rely on and the dissimilarities and inapplicability of the case relied on by the opposition.

> **For Example:**
>
> The term *oppressive conduct* is defined in the case of *Tyrone v. Blatt.* In *Tyrone,* the majority shareholder refused to authorize the issuance of dividends. He granted himself four major pay increases, quadrupling his salary during the period when dividends were not issued. In the holding, the court noted that there was no justification for the salary increases and ruled that his conduct was oppressive. The court stated that "oppressive conduct" occurs when there is wrongful conduct that inures to the benefit of the majority shareholder and to the detriment of the minority shareholders.
>
> In our case, just as in *Tyrone,* the majority shareholder refused to issue dividends. In our case, like *Tyrone,* the majority shareholder gave himself large salary increases. In both cases, there was no justification for the increases. Therefore, the court should apply the standard established in *Tyrone* and find that the defendant engaged in oppressive conduct.
>
> ***
>
> It is argued by the defendant that the court should apply the holding reached in *Wise v. Wind* and find that the defendant's conduct was not oppressive. The defendant's reliance on *Wise* is misplaced. In *Wise,* there was evidence that the salary increases were justified.
>
> Our situation is distinguishable. There is no evidence that the salary increases the defendant awarded himself and the refusal to issue dividends were justified. Therefore, the *Wise* opinion is not on point and is not applicable. The *Tyrone* opinion is on point and should be followed.

(4) **Argument Order.**   When interpreting and applying a rule of law, always introduce your arguments first, address the counterargument, then present your response. In addition, spend more time affirmatively stating your position than responding to the opponent's counterargument.

There are several reasons for this:

► As with the presentation of the facts statement and organization of the argument, the reader tends to remember and emphasize information presented at the beginning and end of a section or paragraph. You want to draw attention to and emphasize your argument; therefore, address it first.

► By introducing your argument first, you have an opportunity to soften the impact of the opposing argument through the strong presentation of your position.

► In a busy court, if you discuss your position or argument after the opponent's, you run the risk of it not being read or given equal attention to by the court.

► By following the counterargument with a response or rebuttal that sums up your position, you remove the counterargument further from the reader's attention. It is buried in the middle of the argument where its significance is downplayed and it is de-emphasized.

> ◘ *For Example:*
>
> It is appropriate for the court to allow the admission of the INDM test results. The court of appeals in *State v. Digo* ruled that scientific tests are admissible when the reliability and scientific basis of the test are recognized by competent authorities. The INDM test, developed in 1985, is universally accepted by all competent authorities as scientifically valid. *It is argued by the defendant that the test results should not be relied on by the court. Defendant relies on the case of* Ard v. State *to support this argument. Defendant's reliance on* Ard v. State *is misplaced. In this 1985 case, the court of appeals did not allow the admission of the INDM test results because the INDM was a new test not universally accepted.* The ruling in *Ard* is no longer applicable. The INDM test is no longer a new test and is universally used and accepted. (The defendant's position is italicized.)

(5) **Word Choice.**   Careful word selection is an invaluable aid in the crafting of a persuasive argument. The argument can be significantly enhanced by the use of forceful, positive, and confident language.

> ◘ *For Example:*
>
> **Ineffective:**
> We believe that the defendant engaged in oppressive conduct.
>
> **Effective:**
> The defendant engaged in oppressive conduct.
>
> **Ineffective:**
> It is the defendant's position that the search was illegal.
>
> **Effective:**
> The search was illegal.

Present the opposing position in a manner that de-emphasizes its importance or credibility.

> **For Example:**
>
> **Ineffective:**
> The defendant states . . .
>
> **Effective:**
> The defendant alleges . . .
>
> **Ineffective:**
> The defendant's position is . . .
>
> **Effective:**
> The defendant claims . . .

(6) Point Headings.   Point headings are a summary of the position *advocated in the argument*. They are presented at the beginning of the argument. Section 10.3 "Trial Court Briefs" in this chapter addresses the details of format, content, and presentation of point headings. It discusses the persuasive nature and presentation of point headings.

The persuasive role of a point heading is to focus the reader on the position advocated in the argument. Therefore, you should draft a point heading in a manner that provides a positive presentation of that position.

> **For Example:**
>
> **Not persuasive:**
> The court should not grant the motion to suppress.
> The photos of the victim were inflammatory and should not have been admitted into evidence by the trial court.
>
> **Persuasive:**
> The court should deny the motion to suppress.
> The inflammatory nature of the photographs of the victim outweighs their probative value. Their admission was highly prejudicial to the defendant and was improper.

The difference in those two presentations is that the persuasive presentation more affirmatively and positively characterizes the position argued. The previous discussions concerning word choice and active voice apply to point headings.

A checklist for use in the persuasive presentation of the argument in a court brief is presented in Exhibit 10-4.

10.3 TRIAL COURT BRIEFS

In many instances, when a trial court is in the process of ruling on a motion or an issue in a case, the judge requires the attorneys to submit a memorandum of law. This memorandum of law is often referred to as a memorandum of points and

Exhibit 10-4

◼ Argument—Persuasive Presentation—Checklist

Checklist to Use When Preparing the Argument Section

- ❑ Argument Organization—Follow the standard organizational format: rule of law followed by the interpretation of the law through case law followed by the application of the law to the issue.
  - ❑ Issue Presentation—If there is more than one issue, discuss the issue supported by the strongest argument first.
  - ❑ Rule of Law Presentation—Present the rule of law in a manner that supports your argument.
  - ❑ Case Presentation—Discuss favorable cases first, followed by unfavorable cases, then a rebuttal emphasizing why the favorable cases should be followed.
- ❑ Argument Order—When applying the rule of law, introduce your argument first, then the counterargument, and conclude with your response.
- ❑ Argument (Word Choice)—Present your argument with forceful, positive, and confident language.
- ❑ Argument (Point Headings)—Draft point headings persuasively.

authorities or a trial brief. The trial brief presents the legal authority and argument in support of the position advocated by the attorney.

A trial brief is similar to a research memorandum in many respects. Both are designed to inform the reader as to how the law applies to the issues raised by the facts of the case. Most of the considerations involved in the preparation of a research memorandum also apply to the preparation of a trial brief. Therefore, when preparing a trial brief, in addition to this chapter, refer to Chapter 9 for guidelines. As discussed in Section 10.2 B "Dissimilarities—Court Briefs and Legal Research Memorandums," the major difference between a research memorandum and a trial brief is that a trial brief is designed to persuade the reader to adopt the position advocated in the brief, whereas a research memorandum is designed to present an objective analysis of the law.

Guidelines for preparing a persuasive trial brief are discussed in the previous section. This section addresses other considerations involved in the preparation of a trial brief, such as the application of the writing process.

10.3 A   AUDIENCE

The audience for the trial brief is the judge assigned to the case. Trial court judges are usually busy with heavy caseloads and may rule on several motions a day. They may not have time to carefully read lengthy drawn-out briefs. Therefore, a judge appreciates a trial brief that consists of a short, well-organized, and concise presentation of the law.

10.3 B   CONSTRAINTS

Court rules are procedural rules that govern the litigation process. The major constraints on a trial brief are usually imposed by the local court rules. Many trial courts have local rules that govern various aspects of a trial brief, such as length, format, and style.

> ◧ *For Example:*
>
> A local rule may establish a maximum length of a trial brief and require the permission of the court before that length can be exceeded.

Local rules must always be consulted when preparing a trial brief.

Usually, there is a time constraint. The court or the local rules often require submission of a brief within a certain number of days. Become aware of the time deadline and allocate your time accordingly. Usually, but not always, upon request, extensions of time may be granted by the court.

10.3 C   FORMAT/CONTENT

The format of a trial brief varies from court to court and from jurisdiction to jurisdiction. In many instances, the local court rules establish a required format. Generally, a trial court brief includes some or all of the components presented in Exhibit 10-5.

If the brief is short, such as in the case of a single-issue brief, a table of contents, table of authorities, or preliminary statement may not be required. In many instances, it is clear from the motion what the issue is; therefore, the brief will consist only of a brief facts statement, an argument, and a conclusion. Trial court briefs often are informal in such situations.

Exhibit 10-5

◧ **Components of Trial Court Brief**

Some or All of the Components of a Trial Court Brief

Caption
Table of Contents
Table of Authorities
Preliminary Statement
Question(s) Presented—Issue(s)
Statement of the Case (Fact Statement)
Argument
Conclusion

> ### ❑ *For Example:*
>
> A motion to dismiss a complaint is filed for failure to include an indispensable party. The issue is clear from the motion, so the memorandum in support of the motion may consist simply of a brief summary of the facts, the legal argument, and a conclusion.

Each of the components in Exhibit 10-5 is briefly discussed in the following subsections. An example of a trial court brief showing the components discussed here is presented in Appendix C.

1. **Caption**   Every brief submitted to a trial court requires a caption. The format varies from court to court, but the caption usually includes the following:
   - name of the court
   - names and status of the parties
   - file number and type of case—civil or criminal
   - title of the document, such as BRIEF IN SUPPORT OF MOTION TO DISMISS
2. **Table of Contents**   When a table of contents is required, it follows the caption page. The table of contents lists each component of the brief and the page number. If point headings are used in the argument section, they are stated in full. The table of contents allows the reader to locate the various components of the brief.
3. **Table of Authorities**   When a table of authorities is required, it is presented after the table of contents page. A table of authorities lists all of the law used in the brief and the page on which the law is cited in the brief. This allows the reader to quickly locate where the authority is discussed in the brief. Present the case law and enacted law in separate sections. List the case law in alphabetical order by case name.
4. **Preliminary Statement**   The preliminary statement introduces the procedural posture of the case. It usually includes the following:
   - identification of the parties
   - procedural events in the case relevant to the matter the court is addressing
   - description of the matter being addressed by the court, such as "This matter is before the court on a motion to dismiss the complaint."
   - relief sought, such as "This memorandums is submitted in support of the motion to suppress the evidence seized during the search."

> ### ❑ *For Example:*
>
> **PRELIMINARY STATEMENT**
>
> Edna and Ida Tule, the plaintiffs, are minority shareholders in Tule, Inc. Their brother, Thomas Tule, is the defendant in this action, the majority shareholder, and president of Tule, Inc. On January 9 of this year, a request for the production of company records relating to salary increases and bonuses granted to Mr. Tule was delivered to him. Mr. Tule has refused to produce the company records. This memorandums is submitted in support of a motion to compel the production of those documents.

5. **Question(s) Presented**   This section of a brief discusses the legal issue(s) addressed in the brief. The issue(s) should include the rule of law, the legal question, and the key facts. When there is more than one issue, list the issues in the order in which they are discussed in the argument section of the brief. A research memorandum identifies the issue(s) objectively. In a trial brief, you should draft the issue(s) in a persuasive manner. "Issues—Persuasive Presentation" in Subsection 10.2 B discusses the techniques involved in the persuasive drafting of the issue. Chapter 9 addresses the presentation of the issue(s) in a research memorandum. Refer to that chapter when preparing the issue.

6. **Statement of the Case**   This section is often referred to as the statement of facts. It corresponds to the statement of facts section of a research memorandum. Its purpose is to explain the facts of the case. This section in a trial brief is different from that in a research memorandum because it is drafted in a persuasive manner designed to introduce the facts in a light that most favors the client's position. "Statement of Facts—Persuasive Presentation" in Subsection 10.2 B.2 discusses the persuasive nature of the facts section and provides examples of persuasive examples of fact. Also, see Appendix C. The facts section should be accurate and complete and should include background facts and key facts. For additional help when drafting the facts section, refer to "Statement of Facts" in Chapter 9.

7. **Argument**   The argument section of a trial brief, like the analysis section of a research memorandum, is the heart of the document. It is unlike the analysis section of a research memorandum in that it is not an objective legal analysis. Rather, it is designed to persuade the court to adopt one's interpretation of the law. "Argument—Persuasive Presentation" in Subsection 10.2 B.3 discusses the considerations involved in crafting an argument in a persuasive manner. This section addresses the basic organization of the argument and the components. The organization and components are presented in Exhibit 10-6.

Exhibit 10-6

Organization and Components of Argument Section of Trial Brief

Standard Organization and Components of the Argument Section of a Trial Court Brief

1. **Summary of argument**
2. **Point headings**
3. **Argument**
   Rule of law
   Case law (if necessary)—interpretation of rule of law
   Application of law to the issue being addressed
   > **Discussion of opposing position (similar to counteranalysis in office legal memorandums)**

The format in Exhibit 10-6 is recommended; it is not necessarily followed in every office, however, and a different format may be required by local court rule. In some instances, a summary of the argument may not be required and some local court rules and office formats do not require point headings. This is often the case when the brief is short and involves a single issue. All of the components of the argument section are presented here so you will be familiar with them when they are required.

a. ***Summary of Argument***—The argument section of a trial brief should begin with an introductory paragraph that summarizes the argument. It presents the context of the argument, the issues in the order in which they will be discussed, a summary of the conclusions on each issue, and the major reasons that support each conclusion.

> ◻ ***For Example:***
>
> On December 12, 2001, John Jones, the defendant, was arrested for possession of cocaine. On January 1, 2002, he was indicted for possession of four ounces of cocaine. The trial commenced on October 25, 2002. On November 11, 2002, he was found guilty by a jury and convicted of possession of four ounces of cocaine. This matter is before the court on Mr. Jones's motion for a new trial, filed March 7, 2003. Mr. Jones's motion is based on the claim that new evidence has been uncovered that shows the drugs belonged to a Mr. William Smith, a visitor in Mr. Jones's home. In order for a new trial to be granted on the basis of newly discovered evidence, the defendant must demonstrate that the newly discovered evidence was not available or discoverable at the time of trial. The information concerning Mr. Smith was available at the time of trial. The defense made no effort to interview Mr. Smith or in any way discover whether the drugs belonged to him. The evidence regarding Mr. Smith is not newly discovered evidence, and the motion should be denied.

The use of an argument summary is valuable when you believe the judge may not have time to read the entire brief. It may not be necessary when the brief is short or when a single issue is involved. It should be a complete summary; the reader should not have to refer to the body of the argument to understand the summary.

b. ***Point Headings***—Point headings are a summary of the position you are asking the court to adopt. They should be drafted persuasively. The guidelines for drafting persuasive point headings are addressed in "Argument—Persuasive Presentation" in Subsection 10.2 B.3.

Point headings are designed to do the following:

- ▶ organize, define, and emphasize the structure of an argument
- ▶ act as locators, allowing the reader to quickly find specific sections of an argument
- ▶ focus the court's attention on the outcome you advocate and provide an outline of your theory

Point headings may not be required in a trial brief, especially when the brief is short or addresses a single issue. In such instances, they are not needed as an organizational tool, nor are they needed to guide the reader. Check the court rules and office format to determine when they are required.

Keep the following guidelines in mind when using point headings.

▶ Place the point headings at the beginning of each section of the argument and include them in the table of contents.

▶ Divide the point headings into major and minor point headings. Include a major point heading for each issue presented. Use minor headings to introduce significant points supporting the major heading.

🔲 *For Example:*

ARGUMENT

I. THE TRIAL COURT ERRED WHEN IT RULED THAT MR. DELMONICO'S CONDUCT DID NOT CONSTITUTE BREACH OF CONTRACT BECAUSE THE GOODS WERE DEFECTIVE AND DELIVERED LATE.

    A. <u>Mr. Delmonico's delivery of the widgets ten days late constituted a breach of the contract.</u> (text of argument)

    B. <u>The delivery of the widgets with a five-pound spring instead of a ten-pound spring constituted a breach of the contract.</u> (text of argument)

▶ Use a complete sentence for each heading and subheading.

▶ Make sure each heading identifies the legal conclusion you want the court to adopt and the basic reasons for the conclusion.

🔲 *For Example:*

THE TESTIMONY OF DR. JENKINS IS PROBATIVE OF THE DEFENDANT'S INTENT AND THEREFORE IS ADMISSIBLE.

THE DISTRICT COURT'S SUPPRESSION OF THE EVIDENCE WAS IMPROPER BECAUSE THE SEARCH WARRANT WAS SUPPORTED BY PROBABLE CAUSE.

▶ Use minor headings only when there are two or more. The rules of outlining require more than one subheading when subheadings are used. Minor headings present aspects of a major point heading in the context of the specific facts of the case. Note that the minor point headings in the example in number 2 above present two aspects of the major point heading. The minor point headings are stated in the specific context of the facts of the case:

    A. <u>Mr. Delmonico's delivery of the widgets ten days late constituted a breach of the contract.</u>

    B. <u>The delivery of the widgets with a five-pound spring instead of a ten-pound spring constituted a breach of the contract.</u>

▶ Type major headings in all capital letters and minor headings in regular type. Minor headings may be underlined. Check the court rules for the proper format. The example in number 2 above illustrates the format for major and minor point headings.

   c. *Argument Format*—The argument section of the trial brief is similar to the analysis section of a research memorandums, and "Analysis" in Chapter 9 should be referred to in the preparation of a trial brief. The same basic IRAC format is followed:

    Rule of law

    Case law (if necessary)—interpretation of rule of law

       1. Name of case

       2. Facts of case—sufficient to demonstrate that case is on point

       3. Rule or legal principle from case that applies to issue being addressed

    Application of law to issue being addressed

       Discussion of opposing position (similar to counteranalysis in legal research memorandums)

   The major difference between the argument component of a research memorandum and that of a trial brief is that a trial brief introduces the argument in a persuasive rather than an objective manner. Refer to "Argument—Persuasive Presentation" in Subsection 10.2 B.3 for guidelines in organizing and preparing a persuasive argument.

8. Conclusion   The conclusion section of a trial brief presents the specific relief desired. Depending on the complexity of the brief, it may be a single sentence stating the requested relief or a summary of the entire argument.

> ■ *For Example:*
>
> For the foregoing reasons, the defendant requests that the motion to dismiss be granted.

A single sentence is appropriate when the trial brief is a simple, one- or two-issue brief and the argument section concludes with a summary of the analysis. When the trial brief is longer and more complicated, the conclusion may include an overall summary of the law presented in the argument section and end with a request for relief. That type of conclusion is similar to the conclusion section of a research memorandum discussed in Chapter 9. Refer to Chapter 9 when preparing that type of conclusion. Note that the conclusion should summarize the argument section and should reflect the persuasive nature of the argument.

10.4   APPELLATE COURT BRIEFS

An individual who disagrees with the decision of a trial or lower court may appeal the decision to a court of appeals. The individual who appeals is called the **appellant,** and the individual who opposes the appeal is called the **appellee.** On appeal, the appellant argues that the lower court made an error, the error affected the outcome of the case, and the appellant is entitled to relief. The appellee argues that the lower court did not commit an error that entitles the appellant to relief.

An appellate court brief is an external memorandum of law submitted to a court of appeals. It presents the legal analysis, authority, and argument in support of the position that a lower court's decision or ruling was either correct or incorrect. The format and style of the appellate brief is strictly governed by appellate court rules, and these rules must be consulted in the preparation of an appellate brief.

Preparation of an appellate brief is a complex undertaking, and a detailed discussion of the subject is beyond the scope of this chapter. Entire texts available at a local law library address the detailed considerations involved in preparing an appellate brief. You should refer to those texts when assigned the task of preparing an appellate brief.

Paralegals and law clerks are not usually required to draft appellate briefs. They may, however, be called upon to assist in the preparation of the brief and, therefore, should be familiar with its components. This section presents a summary of the format and basic components of an appellate brief.

An appellate brief, like a trial brief, is designed to advocate a legal position and to persuade the court to adopt the position argued in the brief. Therefore, you should draft the brief in a persuasive manner. The discussion of the persuasive nature of court briefs, presented in Section 10.2 "Dissimilarities—Court Briefs and Legal Research Memorandums," applies to the preparation of appellate briefs: an appellate brief should be crafted in a persuasive manner.

An appellate brief, like a trial brief, is similar to a research memorandum in many respects. For example, a writing process should be used when preparing both briefs. Therefore, in addition to this chapter, refer to Chapters 7 and 9 when undertaking an appellate brief assignment.

10.4 A   AUDIENCE

A trial court brief is submitted to a single judge, the trial judge assigned to the case. The audience for the appellate brief is usually a panel of three or more judges. In addition, the judge's law clerk usually reads the brief; on many occasions, the law clerk is the first to read the brief. Although you are writing to a wider audience, the same basic considerations are involved in the preparation of trial court and appellate court briefs. Appellate court judges, like trial court judges, are usually busy with substantial caseloads and appreciate an appellate brief that is a short, well-organized, and concise presentation of the law.

10.4 B   CONSTRAINTS

The major constraints on appellate briefs are similar to those on trial court briefs in that they are imposed by the court's rules. Appellate court rules differ from trial court rules in that they are usually more detailed: appellate court rules may establish

Exhibit 10-7

◼ Components of a Basic Appellate Court Brief

Components of a Basic Appellate Court Brief

Cover Page/Title Page
Table of Contents/Index
Table of Authorities
Opinions Below/Related Appeals
Jurisdictional Statement
Question(s) Presented—Issue(s)
Statement of the Case/Statement of Facts
Summary of Argument
Argument
Conclusion

the sections that must be included, the format of the sections, the type of paper, the citation form, and a maximum length for the briefs and a requirement that permission of the court be obtained before the length can be exceeded. Always consult the appellate court rules when preparing an appellate brief.

10.4 C   FORMAT/CONTENT

The format of an appellate brief varies from jurisdiction to jurisdiction. Generally, the basic appellate court brief includes some or all of the components presented in Exhibit 10-7. For examples of the components, refer to the appellate court brief presented in Appendix C.

The following subsections briefly discuss each of the components of the appellate brief presented in Exhibit 10-7.

1. **Cover Page/Title Page**   The court rules govern the format of the cover page, often called the title page. The cover page usually includes the following:
   - name of the appellate court
   - number assigned to the appeal
   - parties' names and appellate status (appellant and appellee or petitioner and respondent)
   - name of the lower court from which the appeal is taken
   - names and addresses of the attorney(s) submitting the brief

2. **Table of Contents/Index**   Sometimes referred to as an index, the table of contents lists the major sections of the brief and the page number of each section. The table of contents provides the reader with a reference tool for locating specific information within the brief. The table includes the point headings and subheadings. The point headings, when included in the table of

contents, provide the reader with an overview of the legal arguments and allow the reader to easily locate the discussion of the arguments in the brief.

3. **Table of Authorities**   The table of authorities lists all of the law cited in the brief. The authorities are listed by category, such as constitutional law, statutory law, regulations, and case law. The table includes the full citation of the authority and the page number or numbers on which the citation appears.

4. **Opinions Below/Related Appeals**   The brief may include a section that references any prior opinions on the case or related appeals.

> **For Example:**
>
> **From a Supreme Court brief:**
> The opinion of the Court of Appeals is reported at 580 F.2d 501. The order of the District Court is not reported.

5. **Jurisdictional Statement**   The brief usually includes a separate section that introduces, in a short statement, the subject matter jurisdiction of the appellate court.

> **For Example:**
>
> This court has jurisdiction under 42 U.S.C. 1983.

Some appellate rules do not require a jurisdictional statement. Some appellate rules require, in addition to the jurisdictional statement, a history of the case and an explanation of how the matter came before the court.

> **For Example:**
>
> The judgment of the trial court was entered on October 5, 2003. The notice of appeal was filed on October 26, 2003. The jurisdiction of the court is invoked under 42 U.S.C. 1983.

6. **Question(s) Presented**   This section is also referred to as legal issues or assignment of error. It lists the legal issues the party requests the court to consider. The issues should be listed in the order in which they were addressed in the argument section and written in a persuasive manner, as discussed earlier in this chapter. Also, refer to Chapter 9 when preparing the issue section of a brief.

7. **Statement of the Case/Statement of Facts**   The statement of the case section, often referred to as the statement of facts, is similar to the Statement of facts section of the trial brief, and the same considerations apply in the preparation of both.

The statement of the case in an appellate brief, however, differs from the statement of facts in a trial brief in that the statement of the case should also include a summary of the prior proceedings (what happened in the lower court) and appropriate references to the record. In the following example, *Tr.* refers to the pages in the transcript of the trial record and *Doc.* refers to documents included in the record on appeal.

> ❏ *For Example:*
>
> After the presentation of the key facts and background facts of the case,
> the information concerning the prior proceedings might read as
> follows:
>
> At the motion to suppress hearing, held on December 12, 2003, the trial
> court denied the motion to suppress. (Tr. at 37). At the hearing, Officer
> Ramirez, the officer conducting the search, testified . . . . (Tr. at 33).
> The trial court stated that there were sufficient exigent circumstances
> present at the scene to support the unannounced entry by the officers.
> (Tr. at 38).
>
> Trial was held on January 15, 2004. (Tr. at 201). On January 18, 2004, the
> jury found the defendant guilty of possession of an ounce of cocaine.
> (Tr. at 291). On January 28, 2004, the defendant filed a notice of ap-
> peal. (Doc. 44). On March 7, 2004, the defendant was sentenced to a
> term of imprisonment of five years. (Doc. 49).

8. **Summary of Argument**   This section may be optional under the appellate court rule. Rule 28 of the Federal Rules of Appellate Procedure states that the argument may be preceded by a summary. The content of an argument summary is discussed in "Argument" in Section 10.3 C.

9. **Argument**   The point headings and body of the argument section are addressed here.

   a. *Point Headings*—The considerations involved in preparing point headings are the same for appellate and trial court briefs. Refer to the discussion of point headings earlier in this chapter when preparing point headings for appellate briefs.

   b. *Body*—The argument section of an appellate brief is similar to the argument section of a trial brief. The format is the same as in a trial brief. Refer to "Argument" in Section 10.3 C when preparing this section of an appellate brief. Remember to present the argument section of an appellate brief in a persuasive manner. Review Subsection 10.2 B.3 "Argument—Persuasive Presentation" when preparing the argument.

10. **Conclusion**   Prepare the conclusion section of an appellate brief the same way as the conclusion of a trial brief. The content, structure, and considerations involved are the same for both. Refer to "Conclusion" in Section 10.3 C when preparing the conclusion.

✦ 10.5   KEY POINTS CHECKLIST: COURT BRIEF

❏ Trial and appellate briefs are similar to legal research memorandums in many respects. Refer to Chapter 9 when preparing them.

❏ Remember to craft the brief persuasively. Court briefs are designed to persuade the reader to adopt the position taken or recommended in the analysis. They are not supposed to present a purely objective analysis.

❏ De-emphasize the position taken by the opposition. Part of the persuasive nature of a court brief is to downplay and discredit the opponent's position. That is accomplished through use of passive voice, long sentences, and placement of the opposing argument in the middle of the analysis.

❏ Always check the court rules. The format, length, and style of court briefs are often governed by the rules of the court. Appellate court rules govern most aspects of appellate briefs.

❏ The required components of trial and appellate court briefs often vary from jurisdiction to jurisdiction. Some of the components discussed in this chapter may not be required or necessary, such as a table of contents, a table of authorities, and an argument summary. This is often the case when the analysis is brief.

Correspondence

Contents
A Example—Information Letter
B Example—Opinion Letter
C Example—Demand Letter
D Comments on Examples

Following are three examples of legal correspondence that illustrate the application of the principles discussed in Chapter 8: an information letter, an opinion letter, and a demand letter.

A   EXAMPLE—INFORMATION LETTER

In this example, the information letter is presented in full block format.

Law Offices of Alice Boardman
2100 Main Street
Friendly, New Washington 00065
(200) 267-7000 • FAX (200) 267-7001 • www.boardmanlaw.com

April 29, 2006
Mr. Nick Stevens
9100 Second Street
Friendly, NW 00065

Re: *Stevens v. Blue Sky Resort*
   Motion to dismiss for failure to state a claim

Dear Mr. Stevens:

The purpose of this letter is to inform you of the status of your case and to summarize the law with regard to the motion that will be heard on May 17, 2006.

As you know, on April 6, we filed your complaint against Blue Sky Resort. In the complaint, we claim that the resort was negligent for failing to post a sign warning skiers of the ice hazard you encountered. In order to prove a claim for negligence, one of the requirements we must establish is that the resort had a duty to warn skiers of the ice hazard.

On April 20, the resort filed a motion with the court, asking that the court dismiss the case. A motion is a request submitted to the court, asking the court to take some form of action. The court usually holds a hearing on a motion. At the hearing, the parties present their position on whether the request should be granted.

On May 17, 2006, the court will conduct a hearing on the resort's motion to dismiss. At that hearing, we anticipate the resort will claim that under the provisions of the Ski Safety Act, it does not have a duty to warn skiers of ice hazards. The resort will argue that ice hazards are the responsibility of skiers under the Act and, therefore, it cannot be sued for negligence since it had no duty to warn of the ice hazard.

In support of its argument that it does not have a duty to warn of ice hazards, the resort will rely on section 8B of the Act. This section states that skiers are responsible for injuries that result from snow and ice conditions. Our position is that the resort does have a duty to warn of this type of hazard under section 7A of the Act. That section provides that resorts have a duty to warn skiers of unusual conditions or hazards on ski runs.

It is unclear from the statute which section of the Act applies in a situation such as yours. The state court of appeals, in the case of *Aster v. White Mountain Resort,* interpreted the Act in a fact situation similar to yours. In this case, a skier, while skiing on a new ski run, hit a rock covered by snow. The court stated that resorts have a duty to warn of snow conditions if the conditions are unavoidable and present an unobvious or latent hazard.

At the motion hearing, we will argue that the resort's motion to dismiss should be denied because the ice condition you encountered was unavoidable and latent, just as the snow condition was in *Aster v. White Mountain Resort.* We will further argue that the rule of law stated in that case provides that resorts have a duty to warn of hazards such as the one you encountered. Therefore, the resort can be sued for its negligence in failing to post a warning of the ice hazard.

The resort will probably argue that the ruling of the court of appeals in *Karen v. High Mountain Pass* should apply. In that case, a skier broke his leg after failing to negotiate a series of moguls that were present in the middle of a turn on a ski run. The court stated that skiers are responsible for snow and ice hazards, and moguls, even though unavoidable, are snow hazards easily observable and routinely present on most ski runs. We believe the court will not apply the ruling in the *Karen* case because that case involved a snow hazard that was observable and routinely encountered by skiers. In your case, the snow hazard was unobservable, unavoidable, and not routinely encountered by skiers.

In conclusion, we are optimistic that the court will rule in our favor and deny the motion. The ice hazard you encountered was unavoidable and latent, just like the snow condition in *Aster v. White Mountain Resort*. This being the case, the court should follow the holding in that case and find that Blue Sky Resort had a duty to warn skiers of the hazard. You are not required to attend the hearing, but you may attend if you wish. Please let us know if you plan to attend.

If you have any questions, please call.

Sincerely,

Pam Hayes
Paralegal
PAH/wkk

◆ B   EXAMPLE—OPINION LETTER

The opinion letter is presented in modified block format.

Law Offices of Alice Boardman
2100 Main Street
Friendly, New Washington 00065
(200) 267-7000 • FAX (200) 267-7001 • www.boardman.com

January 18, 2006

Via Facsimile and U.S. Mail
Mr. David Duggan
5501 Glenview Avenue
Friendly, NW 00065

Re: Possibility of a lawsuit against Red Mountain Ski Resort for failure to warn
    of moguls

Dear Mr. Duggan:

On January 6, 2006, we met in my office to discuss the possibility of suing Red Mountain Ski Resort for the ski injury you suffered on December 7, 2005. This opinion is based on the facts outlined in the Facts section of this letter and the applicable law as of the date of the letter. This letter is solely for your benefit and limited to the facts discussed below. Please contact me if any of the facts are misstated or if you have additional information.

FACTS

On December 7, 2005, you were skiing on an expert run at Red Mountain Ski Resort. Near the top of the run, you encountered a series of moguls. The moguls were difficult to ski, and as a result, you lost control and broke your left arm. There were no signs posted on the run that warned skiers of the upcoming moguls.

ANSWER

Based on the above facts, you probably cannot successfully sue Red Mountain Ski Resort for its failure to warn of the moguls. The only possible theory under which you could sue is negligence. You would claim that the resort was negligent for failing to warn of the upcoming moguls. Under the applicable state statute and the court opinions that interpret that statute, the resort does not have a duty to warn of the presence of moguls.

EXPLANATION

Chapter 70 of the New Washington statutes, the Ski Safety Act, governs the operation of ski resorts and establishes the duties of skiers and resort operators. Section 7A of the Act requires resorts to warn of sections of trails "which present an unusual obstacle or hazard." Section 8B of the Act states that a skier "expressly assumes the risk and legal responsibility for any injury to a person or property which results from . . . surface or subsurface snow or ice conditions. . . ."

The Act does not discuss whether a mogul is a snow condition for which the skier is responsible. The state court of appeals, however, in the case of *Karen v. High Mountain Pass,* addressed the question of whether a resort has a duty to post a warning of the presence of moguls on a ski run. In this case, a skier broke his leg after failing to negotiate a series of moguls that were present in the middle of a turn on a ski run. The court stated that skiers are responsible for snow and ice hazards. The court noted that moguls, even though unavoidable, are snow hazards easily observable and routinely present on most ski runs. The court ruled that under the act, resorts have no duty to warn of snow hazards such as moguls.

The facts in your case are very similar to the facts in *Karen v. High Mountain Pass.* In your case, just as in that case, the injury occurred as a result of an encounter with moguls. It is apparent from section 8B of the statute, and the court's interpretation of that section in *Karen v. High Mountain Pass,* that skiers are responsible for injuries sustained as a result of encountering moguls on a ski run. Therefore, based on the statute and the court opinion in *Karen v. High Mountain Pass,* in my opinion, it is highly unlikely that a lawsuit against Red Mountain Ski Resort for the injuries you sustained would be successful.

I hope this information answers your question. I regret that I am not able to provide a more favorable answer. If you have additional information concerning the accident or if you have any other questions, please contact me.

Sincerely,

Alice Boardman
Attorney at Law
ALB/wkk

C EXAMPLE—DEMAND LETTER

The following demand letter is drafted in modified block style.

Law Offices of Alice Boardman
2100 Main Street
Friendly, New Washington 00065
(200) 267-7000 • FAX (200) 267-7001

April 25, 2006

Via Facsimile and U.S. Mail

Mr. Terry Spear
President
Inki Appliances, Co.
1001 Maple Drive
Friendly, NW 00065

Re: Mrs. Tatum
    File No. 97-131

Dear Mr. Spear:

Our office represents Mrs. Tatum with regard to her purchase of a microwave oven from Inki Appliances, Co. The purpose of this letter is to demand that Inki Appliances repair or replace the microwave or refund Mrs. Tatum the purchase price of the defective microwave.

On February 1, 2006, Mrs. Tatum purchased a new microwave from Inki Appliances, Co. One week after Mrs. Tatum purchased the microwave, it quit working. Three days later, on February 11, 2006, she returned it to your store.

Since that date, Inki Appliances has refused to repair or replace the microwave and has refused to refund Mrs. Tatum the purchase price.

Section 50-102-314 of the New Washington statutes creates an implied warranty of merchantability for goods sold by merchants. This means that there is a warranty for goods sold by merchants that the goods are merchantable; that is, the goods will work. The warranty of merchantability for the microwave Inki Appliances, Co. sold to Mrs. Tatum was breached because it stopped working after only one week.

In the case of *Smith v. Appliance City,* the New Washington supreme court ruled that the seller has three options when an implied warranty is breached: return the purchase price to the buyer, repair the merchandise, or replace the merchandise. Inki Appliances has refused to perform any of those options.

In light of the fact that the warranty of merchantability for the microwave has been breached, we demand that you comply with New Washington law and return the purchase price to Mrs. Tatum, repair the microwave, or replace the microwave. If Inki Appliances does not act in accordance with this letter within thirty days, we will take the appropriate steps necessary to obtain the relief provided by New Washington law.

Please contact us within the time provided to confirm your compliance with the terms of this letter.

Thank you for your consideration of this matter.

Sincerely,

Alice Boardman
Attorney at Law

AB/wkk

D COMMENTS ON EXAMPLES

Note that the preceding letters do the following:

- ▶ present the subject matter clearly through the use of short sentences rather than complex sentences, which are often more difficult to follow and understand
- ▶ present the law in an objective and professional manner
- ▶ avoid legalese and discuss the material in a simple and clear manner (Although there are references to statutes and case law, a summary of the law is provided rather than a technical discussion. The legal points are simply phrased in lay terms.)

In addition, the opinion letter clearly states at the outset that the opinion is limited to the current law and the facts provided by the client. Reference is made to the fact that the letter is intended solely for the benefit of the recipient.

Appendix **B**

Legal Research Memorandum

The following two examples of legal research memorandums illustrate application of the principles discussed in Chapter 9.

EXAMPLE 1

To: Supervisory Attorney
From: Paralegal
Re: *United States v. Eldon Canter*
            Armed bank robbery with a deadly weapon

STATEMENT OF ASSIGNMENT

I have been assigned the task of determining—within the meaning of the federal bank robbery statute—whether a crudely carved wooden replica of a handgun can be considered a "dangerous weapon" when it is used in a bank robbery and when the teller who was approached believed the replica was real.

ISSUE

Under the federal bank robbery statute, 18 U.S.C. § 2113 (a) and (d), is there sufficient evidence to support charges of bank robbery with a dangerous weapon when the weapon is a crudely carved wooden replica of a 9mm Beretta handgun and the teller approached by the robber believed it was a real handgun, but the only other witness did not believe it was real?

BRIEF ANSWER

Qualified yes. In the case of *U.S. v. Martinez-Jimenez,* the court held that a dangerous weapon includes a replica if it appears to be a genuine weapon to those present at the scene. In our case, the teller being robbed believed the replica was real and another teller, the only other witness, did not believe it was real. If the case is interpreted to provide that it is sufficient if any witness present believed that the replica was a real weapon, then the carved wooden replica was a dangerous weapon within the meaning of the statute.

FACTS

On January 5 of this year, Mr. Eldon Canter robbed the First State Bank. He entered the bank, approached a teller, pulled out a crudely carved wooden replica of a 9mm Beretta handgun, and robbed the bank. The replica was carved from pine, was stained with dark walnut wood stain, and had a hole drilled in the "barrel" to make it look real. The teller whom Mr. Canter approached believed it was a real Beretta. The teller at the next window was fairly certain that it was fake. No one else observed the replica.

ANALYSIS

Mr. Canter is charged with armed bank robbery with a dangerous weapon in violation of 18 U.S.C. Section 2113(a) and (d). The relevant portions of the statute provide:

> (a) Whoever, . . . by intimidation, . . . takes . . . any property or money or any other thing of value belonging to . . . a bank . . . .
>
> Shall be fined not more than $5,000 or imprisoned not more than twenty years, or both. (d) Whoever, in committing . . . any offense defined in subsections (a) . . . assaults any person, or puts in jeopardy the life of any person by use of a dangerous weapon or device, shall be fined not more than $10,000 or imprisoned not more than twenty-five years, or both.

The statute does not define what constitutes a "dangerous weapon." Therefore, it is necessary to consult case law to determine how the courts have defined the term in cases where the alleged "dangerous weapon" is not in fact an actual weapon.

A case on point is *U.S. v. Martinez-Jimenez,* 864 F.2d 664 (9th Cir. 1989). In this case, the defendant robbed a bank with a toy gun that eyewitnesses identified as a dark revolver. The defendant was convicted of armed bank robbery under Section 2113(d).

On appeal, the court addressed the question of whether a toy gun is a "dangerous weapon" within the meaning of Section 2113(d). The court noted that "The toy gun did not fit the statutory definition of a firearm under 18 U.S.C. § 921(a)(3). However, it did fall within the meaning of a 'dangerous weapon or device' under Section 2113(d)." *Id.* at 666. In support of this conclusion, the court referred to other cases where unloaded or inoperable guns were held to be dangerous weapons and stated, "These cases reflect a policy that the robber's creation of even the appearance of dangerousness is sufficient to subject him to enhanced punishment." *Id.* at 666. The court went on to note that "A robber who carries a toy gun during the commission of a bank robbery creates some of the same risk as those created by one who carries an unloaded or inoperable genuine gun." *Id.* at 666. The court concluded that:

> The values of justice, administrability, and deterrence require the rule that a robber's use of a replica or simulated weapon that appears to be a genuine weapon to those present at the scene of the crime, or to those charged with responsibility for responding to the crime, carries the same penalty as the use of a genuine weapon.

Id. at 668.

In applying the *U.S. v. Martinez-Jimenez* holding to our facts, it appears that there is sufficient evidence to support the charge of bank robbery with a dangerous weapon. Even though in our case the instrumentality was a wooden replica of a handgun rather than a toy replica, the result is the same: in both cases, the instrumentality was so sufficiently similar to a real handgun that a witness believed it was real, creating the appearance of dangerousness and the consequent risks. As the court noted in its conclusion, the use of a replica or simulated weapon that appears to be genuine subjects the robber to the penalty imposed by Section 2113(d) for use of a dangerous weapon.

A possible counterargument, however, is that the instrumentality cannot be considered a dangerous weapon if some of the witnesses believe that it is not a dangerous weapon. In *U.S. v. Martinez-Jimenez,* all of the witnesses believed the toy gun was a real handgun. The court did not address the question of whether all of the witnesses must believe the instrumentality is a real weapon in order for it to be considered a dangerous weapon. It should not, however, make a difference if some of the witnesses do not believe the instrumentality is real. In *U.S. v. Martinez-Jimenez,* the court focused on the increased risk to the physical security of those present at the scene created by the appearance of dangerousness. *Id.* at 667. As long as some of the witnesses believe the instrumentality is real, that risk is created. The goal of the court's holding was to eliminate or reduce that risk, and, therefore, the holding should apply whenever the risk is created, even if all of the witnesses do not believe the risk is present. See the Recommendation section below.

CONCLUSION

The federal bank robbery statute, 18 U.S.C. § 2113(a) and (d), establishes a criminal penalty for bank robbery with a "dangerous weapon." In *U.S. v. Martinez-Jimenez,* the Ninth Circuit Court of Appeals concluded that a replica that appears to be a genuine weapon to those present at the scene of the crime constitutes a "dangerous weapon" within the meaning of 18 U.S.C. Section 2113(d). In our case, Mr. Canter used a carved wooden replica of a handgun when he robbed the bank, and the teller he robbed believed it was a real handgun. In light of the holding in *U.S. v. Martinez-Jimenez,* it appears that there is a sufficient basis to support the charge that he committed bank robbery by use of a "dangerous weapon" in violation of Section 2113(d).

RECOMMENDATION

Additional case law should be researched to determine whether there are any cases that hold that all of the witnesses must believe the instrumentality is real in order for 18 U.S.C. Section 2113(d) to apply.

EXAMPLE 2

To: Supervisory Attorney
From: Paralegal
Re: Mr. Arturo Garcia—child support modification

STATEMENT OF ASSIGNMENT

This assignment addresses two questions:

1. Was Ms. Chavez's act of unilaterally reducing her child support obligation when the oldest child reached the age of majority permissible under New Mexico law?
2. Will a court grant a modification of child support when there is a voluntary change of occupation that substantially reduces the income of the obligor parent?

ISSUES

Issue I

In light of the provisions of the child support statute, NMSA §40-4-7 (Repl. Pamp. 1994), may the obligor parent unilaterally reduce an undivided child support obligation when one of the children reaches the age of majority and moves out?

Issue II

Under the provisions of the New Mexico Statute governing child support obligations, NMSA §40-4-11.4 (Repl. Pamp. 1994), will a material change in the financial circumstances of an obligor parent, resulting from a voluntary career change, warrant a reduction in that parent's support obligation when the parent has stated that the change was made because she "can't stand to pay that much money to my ex-husband"?

BRIEF ANSWER

Issue I

No. In the case of *Britton v. Britton,* the New Mexico Supreme Court ruled that modification of support obligations is strictly a matter to be determined by the courts and not by unilateral action of the obligor parent.

Issue II

Qualified no. NMSA Section 40-4-11.4A (Repl. Pamp. 1994) gives a court the authority to modify a child support obligation upon a material and substantial change in circumstances of the obligor parent. In the case of *Wolcott v. Wolcott,* the

New Mexico Court of Appeals stated that when a career change is not made in good faith, a reduction in child support is not warranted. If the trial court determines that Ms. Chavez's statement concerning why she changed her occupation is sufficient to constitute bad faith, the court will not reduce her child support obligation.

FACTS

Arturo Garcia and Mary Chavez were granted a divorce in May of 1997. Mr. Garcia was awarded primary custody of the three children from the marriage. Ms. Chavez, a brain surgeon at the time of the divorce, was ordered to pay $3,000 monthly in child support. The child support obligation was undivided; that is, it did not specify a "per child" amount.

Ms. Chavez recently quit her medical practice and enrolled in the legal assistant program at the community college. This career change resulted in a substantial reduction in her income. She has informed several individuals that she quit her practice because she "can't stand to pay that much money" to her ex-husband.

Four months ago when the oldest child turned eighteen and moved out of Mr. Garcia's house, Ms. Chavez reduced the amount of child support she was paying by one-third. She did not obtain a court order granting a reduction in her child support obligation. She informed Mr. Garcia that she did not have to pay the full amount because the oldest child had turned eighteen.

Two months ago she reduced her support payment to $500 per month. Again, she did not obtain a court order granting a reduction in the amount she owed. She informed Mr. Garcia, "That's all I can afford to pay now that I'm going to school."

ANALYSIS ISSUE I

Two New Mexico statutes are relevant to questions involving age of majority and child support orders issued by a court. The age of majority is established in NMSA Section 28-6-1 (Repl. Pamp. 1991). This section provides that the age of majority is reached when an individual turns eighteen years old. The statute governing child support obligations is NMSA Section 40-4-7F (Repl. Pamp. 1994) which in relevant part provides "[t]he court may modify and change any order in respect to the . . . maintenance . . . of the children whenever circumstances render such change proper. The district court shall have exclusive jurisdiction of all matters pertaining to the . . . maintenance . . . of the children so long as the children remain minors."

Although NMSA Section 40-4-7F clearly states that the court shall have exclusive jurisdiction over matters concerning the maintenance of children, the statute does not address the specific question of an obligor's power to unilaterally reduce a child support obligation when one of the children reaches the age of majority. This question, however, has been addressed by the New Mexico courts.

In the case of *Britton v. Britton,* 100 N.M. 424, 671 P.2d 1135 (1983), the custodial parent petitioned the court for a judgment for the accrued and unpaid child support arrearages of the obligor parent. The case involved an undivided child support order. The obligor parent had failed to make several child support payments when due. By his actions he had, in effect, unilaterally reduced his support obligations. The trial court entered a final judgment against the obligor parent in the amount of $7,900. He appealed the court's award of arrearages. The state supreme court focused on questions concerning the ambiguity of the original final decree entered by the trial court, the application of the statute of limitations to the collection of accrued arrearages, the Respondent's claim to offset against any arrearages, and other issues. In addressing those questions, the court noted that "[t]he well-established general rule is that an undivided support award directed at more than one child is presumed to continue in force for the full amount until the youngest child reaches majority." *Id.* at 426, 671 P.2d at 1137. With regard to the obligor parent's failure to meet his child support obligations, the court stated:

> Respondent, as the obligor parent, cannot by his actions unilaterally alter the support obligations set forth in the decree. As we stated in our discussion concerning the asserted ambiguity of the decree, Respondent properly should have petitioned to modify the child support terms of the decree in light of this asserted change in circumstances. Modification of support obligations is strictly a matter to be determined by the courts.

Id. at 430, 671 P.2d at 1141.

Although the court addressed different issues in *Britton,* the rules of law and legal principles discussed in the case also apply in our case. Ms. Chavez, the obligor parent, unilaterally reduced the undivided support obligation when the oldest child reached the age of eighteen, the age of majority under NMSA Section 28-6-1A (Repl. Pamp.1991). She did not petition the court for a modification of the terms of the child support order. As the court noted in *Britton,* a modification of a support obligation is a matter for the courts and cannot be accomplished by the unilateral act of the obligor parent. Therefore, it was not permissible for Ms. Chavez to unilaterally reduce her support payment by one-third when the oldest child reached the age of eighteen and moved out.

There does not appear to be any valid counterargument to this analysis. The statute and case law clearly require that any modification of a child support obligation must be made by the court and not by unilateral act of a party. It may be argued that *Britton* does not apply because the facts of the case and the issues the court addressed are somewhat different from those present in our case. Although there are some differences, the cases are fundamentally the same in that the obligor parent reduced an undivided child support obligation without petitioning the court for an order modifying the terms of the support decree. Therefore, the principles applied in *Britton* should apply in our case.

CONCLUSION ISSUE I

The age of majority in New Mexico is eighteen, NMSA §28-6-1 (Repl. Pamp.1991). Under NMSA Section 40-4-7F (Repl. Pamp. 1994), the district court has exclusive jurisdiction over and authority to modify any order pertaining to the maintenance of the children. The court in the *Britton* case stated that an undivided child support order continues until the youngest child reaches majority. The court noted that the modification of a support obligation is strictly a matter for the court and may not be accomplished by the unilateral act of the obligor parent. Ms. Chavez's unilateral act of reducing her child support obligation by one-third when her oldest child attained the age of eighteen is clearly not permissible under New Mexico statutory and case law.

ANALYSIS ISSUE II

The relevant rule of law governing the modification of child support orders due to a change in financial circumstances is NMSA Section 40-4-11.4A (Repl. Pamp. 1994). This section provides in relevant part "[a] court may modify a child support obligation upon a showing of material and substantial changes in circumstances subsequent to the adjudication of the pre-existing order." The section does not include provisions that answer the question of when a material change in circumstances resulting from a voluntary career change warrants a reduction in an obligor spouse's support obligation. The New Mexico Court of Appeals, however, has addressed this question.

A case on point is *Wolcott v. Wolcott,* 105 N.M. 608, 735 P.2d 326 (Ct. App. 1987). In this case, the husband was a physician specializing in obstetrics and gynecology at the time of the divorce in 1983. In 1985, he closed his office and began working in a psychiatric residency program. This career change resulted in a substantial reduction in his income. He unilaterally reduced his child support payments without judicial approval or without forewarning his former spouse. Subsequently, he petitioned the trial court for a reduction of his support obligation. The court denied his petition, finding that he did not act in good faith when he voluntarily made the career change.

The Court of Appeals upheld the trial court. The court, referring to decisions in other jurisdictions, stated:

> The common trend in various jurisdictions is that a good faith career change, resulting in a decreased income, may constitute a material change in circumstances that warrants a reduction in a spouse's support obligations. Likewise, where the career change is not made in good faith, a reduction in one's support obligations will not be warranted. (citations omitted)

Id. at 609, 735 P.2d at 327.

As the court noted in *Wolcott,* where a career change is not made in good faith, a reduction in the support obligation of an obligor parent is not warranted. If *Wolcott* is followed and the trial court determines that Ms. Chavez's career change was not made in good faith, she should not be granted a modification of her child support obligation.

A likely counterargument is that Ms. Chavez's statements that she quit her practice because she could not stand to pay Mr. Garcia "that much money" are insufficient to support a conclusion that the career change was made in bad faith. This argument should not prevail. In *Wolcott,* without any direct evidence or statement from the husband indicating his intent, the court concluded that he was acting in bad faith. The husband's bad faith was inferred from his disregard of financial obligations under the marital settlement, his failure to make full disclosure of his income and assets, and his self-indulgent lifestyle. In our case, Ms. Chavez's statement to several witnesses regarding the reason for her career change is direct evidence clearly indicating that the change was not made in good faith. If *Wolcott* is followed, the trial court has sufficient evidence to find bad faith and deny any petition by Ms. Chavez for a reduction in her support obligation.

CONCLUSION ISSUE II

The New Mexico law governing the modification of child support orders based on a change of circumstances requires a showing of a material and substantial change in circumstances subsequent to the initial court order. NMSA §40-4-11.4A (Repl. Pamp. 1994). In the *Wolcott* case, the Court of Appeals stated that a reduction in an obligor parent's support obligation is not warranted when a career change is not made in good faith. In our case, Ms. Chavez's statement that she quit her practice because she could not stand to pay her ex-husband "that much money" is clear evidence that her career change was not made in good faith. In light of the holding in *Wolcott,* Ms. Chavez is not entitled to a modification of her child support obligation.

RECOMMENDATIONS

Issue I

Since there are differences between the facts and issues discussed in *Britton* and our case, it may be advisable to conduct further research to determine whether there is another case that is more on point.

Issue II

Further investigation should be conducted to determine whether there is additional evidence indicating that Ms. Chavez's career change was made in bad faith.

Court Briefs

TRIAL COURT BRIEF

Following is an example of a trial court brief based on a hypothetical fact situation and the law of a hypothetical state—New Washington. Following the hypothetical are comments on the brief.

LINCOLN COUNTY DISTRICT COURT
STATE OF NEW WASHINGTON
NO. CIV. O3-601
NICK STEVENS
     Plaintiff,

vs.

BLUE SKY RESORT
     Defendant.

BRIEF IN OPPOSITION TO MOTION TO DISMISS
PRELIMINARY STATEMENT

On December 5, 2005, Nick Stevens, the plaintiff, was injured while skiing on a ski run at Blue Sky Resort. He was injured skiing on an ice hazard that the resort admits was not marked with any type of warning sign. Mr. Stevens filed a complaint against the resort for negligence in failing to warn of the hazard. The resort has filed a Rule 12(b)(6) motion to dismiss for failure to state a claim, alleging that it does not have a duty to warn of ice hazards. This memorandum is submitted in opposition to that motion.

QUESTION PRESENTED

Under the New Washington Ski Safety Act, sections 70-11-1 through 70-11-22, can a negligence claim be stated when a skier is injured on an unmarked ice hazard that is unavoidable and unobservable by the skier due to the sun glare?

STATEMENT OF THE CASE

On December 5, 2005, Mr. Stevens, an expert skier, was skiing on an intermediate ski run at Blue Sky Resort. Midway through the run, there is a slight uphill turn to the south. When Mr. Stevens encountered the turn, the sun was directly in his eyes, and the glare prevented him from seeing that the trail was entirely covered with ice. Due to the glare, he was unable to avoid the dangerous ice hazard. He immediately hit the ice and lost control. As a result, he slid into a tree and broke his left arm and leg. No signs warning of the ice hazard were present.

On April 6, 2006, Mr. Stevens filed a negligence complaint against Blue Sky Resort for the resort's negligent failure to warn of the unavoidable ice hazard. On April 20, 2006, the resort filed a motion to dismiss under Rule 12(b)(6), alleging that it does not have a duty to warn of ice hazards, and, therefore, as a matter of law, a claim for negligence cannot be stated.

ARGUMENT

MR. STEVENS' ARGUMENT THAT THE ICE HAZARD IS UNAVOIDABLE AND LATENT IS A SET OF FACTS THAT, IF PROVEN, WOULD ESTABLISH THE DEFENDANT'S DUTY TO WARN, AND, THEREFORE, A CLAIM CAN BE STATED AS TO DUTY.

This matter is before the court on a Rule 12(b)(6) motion to dismiss for failure to state a claim. In the case of *Myron v. Cox, Inc.,* 40 N. Wash. 210, 215, 740 N.E. 309, 314 (1989), the New Washington Supreme Court established the standard for the granting of a 12(b)(6) motion. The court stated, "A Rule 12(b)(6) motion to dismiss is properly granted only when it appears that there is no provable set of facts that entitles the plaintiff to relief." Blue Sky Resort's motion specifically alleges that a claim cannot be stated in this case with regard to duty. To survive this motion, Mr. Stevens must demonstrate that there is a provable set of facts that would establish the duty of Blue Sky to warn of the ice hazard in this case.

The Ski Safety Act establishes the duties of ski resorts and skiers. Section 70-11-7A sets out the duties of the resort; it provides, "The ski area operator shall have the duty to mark conspicuously with the appropriate symbol or sign those slopes, trails, or areas that are closed or that present an unusual obstacle or hazard."

Section 70-11-8B sets out the duties and responsibilities of the skier:

> A person who takes part in the sport of skiing accepts as a matter of law the dangers inherent in that sport, and each skier expressly assumes the risk and legal responsibility for any injury to a person or property which results from . . . surface or subsurface snow or ice conditions. . . .

The act does not define the terms "hazard" and "snow and ice conditions." The statute also does not provide guidance as to which duty applies in a fact situation such as the one presented in this case. New Washington case law, however, does provide guidance.

The controlling case is *Aster v. White Mountain Resort,* 55 N. Wash. 756, 866 N.E. 421 (Ct. App. 1994). In the *Aster* case, Mr. Aster was skiing on a newly opened run from which several fairly large rocks had not been removed. Usually, the rocks would be removed before the run was opened. The rocks were covered by approximately two and one-half feet of new snow and were not visible. The resort did not post a warning that the large rocks were present on the run. Mr. Aster hit a rock with the tip of his ski, lost control, and was injured. The court ruled that under NWSA § 70-11-7A, a resort has a duty to warn of hazardous snow conditions if they are unavoidable and latent. The court stated, "The statute will not be interpreted to reach an absurd result, and requiring a skier to be responsible for unavoidable latent hazards would lead to an absurd result. Skiers are responsible only for those unavoidable snow or ice conditions that are not latent or unobservable." *Id.* at 759.

Mr. Stevens' complaint, like the complaint in the *Aster* case, states that the ice condition encountered was an unavoidable latent hazard. Under *Aster,* the resort has the duty under § 70-11-7A to warn of such hazards. Under the rule adopted in *Aster,* Mr. Stevens' complaint does present a provable set of facts that establishes a claim as to duty and entitles him to relief. Therefore, the motion to dismiss should be denied.

It is contended by Blue Sky that they do not have a duty to warn of the ice hazard, and in support of this contention, they rely on *Karen v. High Mountain Pass,* 55 N. Wash. 462, 866 N.E. 995 (Ct. App. 1994). In this case, a skier broke his leg after failing to negotiate a series of moguls that were present in the middle of a sharp turn of a ski run. The moguls were obvious to the skier but unavoidable. The trial court granted the resort's motion to dismiss for failure to state a claim. On appeal, the court of appeals, in upholding the trial court, held that under the statute, the skier assumes the risk of snow and ice hazards that are easily observable and routinely present on ski runs.

Blue Sky's reliance on *Karen* is misplaced. The case is clearly distinguishable. The snow condition in *Karen,* though unavoidable, was clearly observable, and moguls are routinely present on ski runs. Skiers are aware that they will encounter moguls and know they must be able to navigate them. Ice conditions also may be encountered on ski runs. The ice condition Mr. Stevens encountered, however, was not a routine ice condition. It was unobservable, unavoidable, and extremely dangerous due to the glare of the sun. The *Karen* case involves observable, routine snow hazards. The present case involves unobservable ice hazards that are not routinely encountered. *Karen* is obviously not on point and is not controlling in this case.

The hazard encountered by Mr. Stevens was identical in nature to the hazard in the *Aster* case: the ice condition was an unavoidable, latent hazard. Under the holding in *Aster,* the resort has a duty under § 70-11-7A to warn of this type of hazard. Mr. Stevens' complaint argues that the hazard is an unavoidable and latent hazard. The complaint presents a provable set of facts with regard to duty upon which relief can be granted, and, therefore, a claim for duty can be stated and the motion to dismiss should be denied.

CONCLUSION

Blue Sky Resort's motion to dismiss for failure to state a claim should be denied. Mr. Stevens' argument that the ice condition constitutes a latent hazard is a provable set of facts that entitles him to relief.

COMMENTS

1. The preceding example of a trial brief does not have a table of contents or a table of authorities. When a trial brief is short or involves a single issue and few authorities, these tables may not be required. Be sure to check the local court rule.
2. The preliminary statement presented at the beginning of the brief is often called an introduction.
3. A summary of the Argument section is not included in this brief. A summary of the argument is usually included in an appellate brief, but not always in a trial brief. It is useful and may be necessary in a trial brief when there are several issues or the analysis is complex, but it is not necessary when the analysis involves a single issue or is not complex.
4. Note the persuasive tone of the brief:
   - The statement of the case introduces the facts with language that favors the client: *dangerous hazard; he immediately lost control.*
   - The Statement of the Case and Argument sections state the client's position in short, clear sentences using active voice. The opponent's position is presented in a long sentence using the passive voice: "It is contended by Blue Sky that it does not have a duty to warn of the ice hazard . . . ."
   - The Argument section downplays the opposition's position. It is placed in the middle of the argument and is immediately discounted after it is presented.
   - The conclusion is very short. In a brief that is short or does not involve a complex analysis, an abbreviated conclusion is appropriate.

APPELLATE COURT BRIEF

In the following example, the major components of an appellate court brief are presented. Due to its length (36 pages), it is not practicable to reprint the entire brief. Omitted material is indicated by three asterisks (*   *   *). The brief was prepared by Ms. Vicki W. Zelle. Prior to becoming an attorney, Ms. Zelle was a paralegal. She is currently an assistant appellate defender for the state of New Mexico.

IN THE SUPREME COURT OF THE STATE OF NEW MEXICO

STATE OF NEW MEXICO,
          Plaintiff-Petitioner,

          v.   No.   27,509

SHAWN VANDENBERG,
          Defendant-Respondent.

**DEFENDANT-RESPONDENT'S ANSWER BRIEF
ON WRIT OF CERTIORARI TO THE NEW MEXICO COURT
OF APPEALS**

**Appeal Originating from the Twelfth Judicial District Court, Otero County,
The Honorable Jerry H. Ritter, Presiding**

PHYLLIS H. SUBIN
Chief Public Defender

Vicki W. Zelle
Assistant Appellate Defender
Public Defender Department
301 N. Guadalupe Street
Santa Fe, N.M. 87501
(505) 827-3909

Attorneys for Defendant-Appellant

<u>TABLE OF CONTENTS</u>

*   *   *

*   *   *

TABLE OF AUTHORITIES

New Mexico Cases

*   *   *

Statutes, Rules, and Constitutional Provisions

Treatises

Other Authorities

I. <u>SUMMARY OF PROCEEDINGS</u>

A. NATURE OF THE CASE

Shawn Vandenberg and his companion, Jason Swanson, were subjected to two traffic stops in five minutes because of one deputy's hunch. The first stop that afternoon was based on a deputy's baseless impression that the car did not display a license plate. The deputy passed his suspicions along in a "suspicious vehicle" BOLO. Another officer responded within minutes, stopping the two for a second time, ostensibly for speeding. Despite all documentation twice having been shown to be in order and their full cooperation during both stops, the two were subjected to pat-downs at the conclusion of the second stop, when only Jason's signature on the warning citation prevented them from going on their way. The officer's safety concerns purportedly were based upon the BOLO and the young men's conduct that he observed when he was writing up the warning citation and running the second inquiry in minutes. The conduct: Jason was drumming his fingers on the top of the car; Shawn rolled his passenger window up and down several times; there was sporadic conversation between the two, who now were nervous and watching the officer in the car's rearview mirrors or by glances over their shoulders.

*   *   *

B. STATEMENT OF RELEVANT FACTS AND COURSE OF PROCEEDINGS

This Court must be informed of the totality of the circumstances in order to conduct a meaningful review of the Court of Appeals' legal conclusion based upon the analysis of those facts. In its brief, the state presents a sanitized version of the facts that fails to reveal the true contextual flavor of the events that occurred. For this Court to truly comprehend the alarming nature of the constitutional violations visited upon these private citizens, the following statement of facts is provided.

One hot summer day in July 1999, around five o'clock in the afternoon, Shawn Vandenberg, twenty-three years of age, was a passenger in a blue 1975 Monte Carlo. Jason Swanson, a young man with longer hair, was driving the car northbound on highway 54, the road between El Paso and Alamogordo, and was just a few miles outside of Alamogordo. (T. 1 /028-39; T. 2 /218-220) Being the "monsoon season," it was raining, off and on; the afternoon was not only hot, but humid too. (T. 2 /095-100; /375-80)

1. THE FIRST TRAFFIC STOP

Deputy Sheriff Benny House, observing the car and its occupants, made a U-turn and stopped the 1975 blue Monte Carlo that was traveling on highway 54 about five miles south of its junction with highway 70. (T. 1 /032-37, 486-88) House admitted that when he is on patrol, as he was that day, he will pull over a vehicle even if it is only one mile-per-hour (mph) over the speed limit. (T. 1 /074-80) However, House did not stop the car for speeding. Instead, House claimed that he had not seen a license plate on the Monte Carlo when it had passed him, going in the opposite direction. This is in spite of the fact that the car's license plate was displayed in the exact manner as was designed by the manufacturer. (T. 1 /452-55) In his pursuit of the vehicle, after making his U-turn, he had approached the car from behind. House admitted that once he had stopped the car, "pull[ing] right up on the vehicle," he realized that not only could he see the license plate, he observed that it was current and valid. However, in his opinion, where the license plate was displayed, it was "[h]ard to see." (T. 1 /040-44)

House approached the driver's side window and told the occupants the reason for the stop. He told the young men that "You need to get this plate up where it's visible." (T. 1 /045-50) House demanded Jason's driver's license as well as the car's registration/proof of insurance documentation. (T. 1 /040-43) It is House's practice to ask for the documentation at a traffic stop, even when an infraction is so minimal that he doesn't intend to cite the driver, as a form of follow-up. This is to ensure that they are "legitimate to be on the road" and to make sure the car wasn't stolen.[1] (T. 1 /042-44, 076-80) The driver, Jason, was completely cooperative and promptly complied. (T. 1 /163-65)

*　　*　　*

II.　<u>ARGUMENT</u>

A.　STANDARD OF REVIEW

The denial of a motion to suppress evidence is reviewed to determine "whether the law was correctly applied to the facts, viewing them in a manner most favorable to the prevailing party" and with "all reasonable inferences in support of the court's decision . . . indulged in." <u>State v. Chapman</u>, 1999-NMCA-106, ¶ 12, 127 N.M. 721, 986 P.2d 1122, (quoting <u>State v. Boeglin</u>, 100 N.M. 127, 132, 666 P.2d 1274, 1279 (Ct. App. 1983)). However, an error of law, such as the reasonableness of a weapons search, is reviewed *de novo*. <u>See</u> <u>id.</u>; <u>State v. Flores</u>, 1996-NMCA-059, ¶ 6, 122 N.M. 84, 920 P.2d 1038. "*De novo* review of such questions is necessary to *meaningfully discharge* [the appellate court's] *duty* . . . to shape the parameters of police conduct by placing the constitutional requirement of reasonableness in factual context . . . ." <u>State v. Arredondo</u>, 1997-NMCA-081, ¶ 9, 123 N.M. 628, 944 P.2d 276 (emphasis added) (quoting <u>State v. Attaway</u>, 117 N.M. 141, 145, 870 P.2d 103, 107 (1994)).

*　　*　　*

---

[1] House explained that, although he normally doesn't, sometimes he will pull drivers over for driving one mile per hour over the speed limit. Even though he would have no intention to cite them, he would take this opportunity to check the driver's documentation. (T. 1 /076-80)

B. **ISSUE I: THE COURT OF APPEALS CORRECTLY HELD THAT OFFICER HOUSE'S MISTAKE OF FACT DID NOT CONSTITUTE "REASONABLE SUSPICION" TO CONDUCT THE FIRST STOP, MAKING IT CONSTITUTIONALLY INVALID UNDER FOURTH AMENDMENT JURISPRUDENCE.**

In the case *sub judice,* House's stop was invalid, since the facts "available to the officer at the moment of the seizure . . . [would not have] 'warranted a man of reasonable caution in the belief'" that the action taken was appropriate[.]" See Terry, 392 U.S. at 21-22 (citation omitted); see also State v. Paul T., 1999-NMSC-037, ¶ 18, 128 N.M. 360, 993 P.2d 74 (same). There simply was *no display violation* on the Monte Carlo.[2] When House realized there was *no violation,* he nevertheless executed the stop and demanded that Jason, the driver, produce his driver's license and vehicle documentation. In so doing, House exceeded his authority. State v. Reynolds, 119 N.M. 383, 388, 890 P.2d 1315, 1320 (1995), allows officers to confirm that the driver is both licensed and driving a car that is registered and insured "whenever [that] officer is *reasonably* called upon to make contact with the driver." House was *not* reasonably called upon to make contact with the driver—an officer must be required to make a reasonable effort to confirm his initial, but mistaken, observation before conducting a baseless traffic stop.

The trial court erred in relying on the idea that "a reasonable suspicion can be a mistaken one" to legitimize House's stop. See State v. Brennan, 1998-NMCA-176, ¶ 12, 126 N.M. 389, 970 P.2d 161 (citing to earlier cases supporting this proposition). **In all the cases in which this idea has found voice, the "mistake" referred to a legal mistake, as a matter of interpretation of law, rather than a factual mistake. See id. (making the statement when discussing the argument that the suspicion of careless driving in a private parking lot could not be reasonable, as a matter of law, when the careless driving statute does not apply to private property); State v. Apodaca, 112 N.M. 302, 304, 814 P.2d 1030, 1032 (Ct. App. 1991) (same, but in context of argument that suspicion of seatbelt violation could not have been reasonable when officer could only see that the shoulder-harness was not in use); State v. Mann, 103 N.M. 660, 664, 712 P.2d 6, 10 (Ct. App. 1985) (same, but in context of discussing whether suspicion of impeding traffic by traveling 20 mph under the posted limit on the inside lane, despite no cars having been actually impeded, was reasonable basis for stop).** An officer cannot merely claim, without making any legitimate effort to confirm the perception, that he *thought* that he had observed a particular violation in order to make a valid traffic stop, even though a modest effort would have shown his fleeting perception to have been mistaken. Otherwise, all sorts of "hallucinated" violations would serve to justify stops—where absolutely nothing was actually wrong. This would remove any requirement of "objectiveness" from the analysis, which clearly is incorrect.

The state mischaracterizes the Court of Appeals' *de novo* application of the law to the facts of this first stop as a "revision of facts found by the

trial court," since the trial court found House "did not lie" about not seeing a license plate on the Monte Carlo. (BIC 8, 9) Quite to the contrary,
the Court of Appeals found the trial court's conclusion of law to be in error, finding that the deputy's subjective and fleeting impression was not
objectively reasonable. See Vandenberg, 2002-NMCA-066, ¶ 18 ("We
conclude that . . . the evidence . . . would not support a finding that
Deputy House's failure to notice the license plate was objectively reasonable.") In reviewing the facts with the required *objectivity,* the Court of
Appeals insisted that an "objective evidentiary justification" be made. In
finding it lacking, the Court of Appeals properly held the line against police conduct [that] "is overbearing or harassing, or which trenches upon
personal security." Terry, 392 U.S. at 9.

C. **ISSUE II:** THE COURT OF APPEALS RIGHTLY CONCLUDED THAT OF-
FICER ROBERTS' PURPORTED SAFETY CONCERNS WERE **NOT** OBJEC-
TIVELY REASONABLE UNDER FOURTH AMENDMENT JURISPRUDENCE.
THE FACTS DID NOT SUPPORT AN OBJECTIVELY REASONABLE BELIEF
THAT EITHER OCCUPANT OF THE CAR, STOPPED FOR A MINOR TRAFFIC
INFRACTION, WAS ARMED AND DANGEROUS OR INVOLVED IN ANY CRIM-
INAL ACTIVITY UNRELATED TO THE SPEEDING INFRACTION.

D. **ISSUE III:** THE FOURTH AMENDMENT TO THE UNITED STATES CON-
STITUTION AFFORDS MR. VANDENBERG THE PROTECTION HE SOUGHT.
THE COURT OF APPEALS CORRECTLY DECLINED TO EXAMINE HIS
STATE CONSTITUTIONAL CLAIM UNDER ARTICLE II, SECTION 10 OF THE
NEW MEXICO CONSTITUTION.

Citing to STATE V. VANDENBERG, 2002-NMCA-066, ¶ 25 n.3, 132 N.M.
354, the state asserts that "the Court of Appeals had no basis on which to
hold that the pat-downs violated both federal and state constitutions," and
berates that court for not conducting a separate reasonableness analysis under Article II, Section 10 of the New Mexico Constitution. (BIC 22-23)
However, this Court has made clear that if the federal Constitution affords a
citizen the protection sought, then the reviewing court will not examine the
state constitutional claim. See State v. Cardenas-Alvarez, 2001-NMSC-
017, 130 N.M. 386 (citing State v. Gomez, 1997-NMSC-006, ¶ 19, 122
N.M. 777). Mr. Vandenberg has consistently argued that his right to be free
from unreasonable governmental intrusions into his privacy was violated,
under both federal and state constitutions. (R.P. 39(A-E), 111-17) The de-
fense argued that the stops and the pat-downs were pretextual and unreasonable, citing both the Fourth Amendment and Article II, Section 10 of the
New Mexico Constitution, reminding the court that New Mexico has not followed lock-step with the federal interpretations of the Fourth Amendment or
the progeny of Terry v. Ohio, 392 U.S. 1. (Id., T. 2 /453-82; T. 3 /106-24,
127-29, 131-34, 138-42) Contrary to the state's assertion, Mr. Vandenberg's
state constitutional claim was clearly preserved for appellate review under

the less restrictive test applied to Article II, Section 10 claims. <u>Cf. Cardenas-Alvarez</u>, 2001-NMSC-017, ¶¶ 12-13.

*   *   *

III. <u>CONCLUSION</u>

Appellant, Shawn Vandenberg, asks that this Court reverse the trial court's denial of his suppression motion, vacate his guilty plea, and remand this matter to the trial court for further proceedings, and for such other relief as the Court deems proper.

Respectfully submitted,

PHYLLIS H. SUBIN
Chief Public Defender

____

Vicki W. Zelle
Assistant Appellate Defender
301 N. Guadalupe Street
Santa Fe, New Mexico 87501
(505) 827-3909

I hereby certify that a copy of the foregoing was served by hand delivery to the Attorney General's Box in the Court of Appeals this______16th______day of______February______, 2001.

____

Public Defender Department

Glossary

absolute phrase A group of words that modifies a clause in a sentence.

active voice See *voice.*

adjective A word that modifies a noun or pronoun. An adjective usually describes a noun or pronoun (a *red* car).

administrative law Rules, regulations, orders, and decisions adopted by administrative agencies that have the authority of law.

adverb A word used to modify a verb, an adjective, or another adverb.

advocacy The act or process of supporting or urging the adoption of a position through the use of an argument.

advocacy letter See *demand/advocacy letter.*

affect/effect *Affect* is a verb meaning "to influence." *Effect* is either a verb or noun. As a verb, *effect* means "to bring about or cause"; as a noun, it means "result."

affirm A decision of an appellate court that upholds the decision of the trial court.

agreement Correspondence between words in gender, number, case, or person. (e.g., *Workers* must wear *their* helmets. *Ereka* must wear *her* helmet).

antecedent A word, clause, or phrase referred to by a pronoun. In the following sentence, the word *workers* is the antecedent for the pronoun *their.* The *workers* put on *their* helmets.

apostrophe (') A mark that serves to indicate possession (Hara's hat) or to form a contraction (can't).

appeals court A court that reviews the decision of a trial court or another lower court to determine and correct any error that may have been made.

appellant The party who files an appeal. On appeal, the appellant argues that the lower court made an error that entitles the appellant to relief.

appellate court brief   An external memorandum of law submitted to a court of appeals. It presents the legal analysis, authority, and argument in support of a position that the lower court's decision or ruling was either correct or incorrect. It is often referred to as an appellate brief.

appellee   The party who opposes the appeal. On appeal, the appellee usually argues that the lower court did not make an error that entitles the appellant to relief.

appositive phrase   A phrase that describes or renames the noun it modifies.

authority   Anything a court may rely on when deciding an issue. It includes the law, such as constitutions and statutes, and nonlaw sources, such as legal encyclopedias and treatises.

background facts   Facts presented in a court opinion, case brief, or legal memorandum that put the key facts in context. They give an overview of a factual event and provide the reader with the overall context within which the key facts occurred.

brackets ([ ])   Marks used to show changes in or additions to quotations, usually for the purpose of providing clarification to the quotation or indicating an error in the original quotations. ("The privilege [against self-incrimination] allows an individual to remain silent.")

brief   See *appellate court brief; case brief; trial court brief.*

brief answer   A section of a memorandum of law that presents a brief, precise answer to the issue(s) addressed in the memo.

canons of construction   The rules and guidelines courts use when interpreting statutes.

caption   In an opinion, the names of the parties to a lawsuit and their court status (e.g., Eddie RAEL, Plaintiff-Appellee v. Emillio CADENA and Manuel Cadena, Defendants-Appellants).

case brief   A written summary identifying the essential components of a court opinion.

case law   See *common law/case law.*

cause of action   The legal basis upon which a lawsuit is based (e.g., negligence). To state a claim in a lawsuit means to allege facts in support of each element of the cause of action (e.g., in a negligence case, there must be facts alleged in support of each of the elements of negligence—duty, breach of duty, proximate cause, and damages).

certiorari   See *writ of certiorari.*

citation   Information that allows the reader to locate where a reference can be found. In case law, it refers to the volume number, page number, and name of the reporter where a case may be found.

cite   See *citation.*

clause   A group of words that includes a subject and a predicate. There are two types of clauses:

▶ Independent clause—Also referred to as a *main clause,* an independent clause can stand alone as a complete sentence. Every sentence has a main clause.

► Dependent clause—Also referred to as a *subordinate clause,* a dependent clause cannot stand alone as a sentence.

collective noun   A noun that refers to a group; e.g., *jury, family, crowd,* and *majority.*

colon (:)   A punctuation mark used to introduce or call attention to information that follows. (The statutory requirements are the following: the will must be witnessed by two witnesses . . . .)

comma (,)   The most frequently used punctuation mark. It is used to separate parts of a sentence.

common law/case law   The body of law created by courts. It is composed of the general legal rules, doctrines, and principles adopted by courts when interpreting existing law or when creating law in the absence of controlling enacted law.

complex sentence   A sentence composed of an independent clause and one or more dependent clauses.

■ *For Example:* Do not cross the bridge before you come to it. Although Irina was busy, she took time to help the courier.

compound sentence   A sentence composed of two or more independent clauses. The clauses are usually linked by a semicolon or a coordinating conjunction such as *and, but, or, nor, yet, for,* or *so.*

■ *For Example:* Carol played the flute, and Ann played the piano.

compound-complex sentence   A sentence composed of at least two independent clauses and one or more dependent clauses.

■ *For Example:* The dependent clause is italicized: Lenny hurried *whenever he was late,* and he often forgot to shave.

concurring opinion   A judicial opinion that agrees with the majority holding in a case but for different or additional reasons than those presented by the majority.

constitution   A governing document adopted by the people that establishes the framework for the operation of the government, defines the powers of the government, and guarantees the fundamental rights of the people.

contraction   A word formed by combining two words: *can't* (cannot); *isn't* (is not).

council/counsel   A deliberative or administrative body. A councilor is a member of the body. As a verb, *counsel* means "to give advice or guidance." As a noun, *counsel* is advice. A counselor is a person, such as a lawyer, who gives advice or guidance.

counteranalysis   The process of discovering and considering the counterargument to a legal position or argument; the process of anticipating the argument the opponent is likely to raise in response to the analysis of an issue.

It is the identification and objective evaluation of the strengths and weaknesses of a legal argument.

counterargument   The argument in opposition to a legal argument or position; the argument the opponent is likely to raise in response to the analysis of an issue.

court opinion   The statement of a court of its decision reached in a case, the rule that applies, and the reasons for the court's decision.

court rules   Procedural rules adopted by a court that govern the litigation process. Court rules often govern the format and style of documents submitted to the court.

dangling modifier   A modifier that does not modify any other part of a sentence.

dash (—)   A mark used in a sentence to emphasize something, to set off lists, to briefly summarize material containing commas, or to show an abrupt change of thought or direction. (The items located at the scene—the knife, the drugs, and the scarf—have disappeared from the evidence room.)

defendant   The party against whom a lawsuit is brought.

demand/advocacy letter   Correspondence designed to persuade someone to take action favorable to the interests of the client or to cease acting in a manner that is detrimental to the client.

dissenting opinion   A judicial opinion in a case that disagrees with the majority opinion.

district court   In many states, the trial court of general jurisdiction. See also *United States district court.*

element   An essential component of a law, rule, principle, or doctrine. In order for a law, rule, principle, or doctrine to apply, the requirements of each element must be met. (The elements of negligence are duty, breach of duty, proximate cause, and damages. For a claim of negligence to prevail, the plaintiff must establish that the defendant had a duty, the defendant breached the duty, the breach of duty was the cause of the incident, and the plaintiff was damaged as a result of the breach.)

ellipsis   The use of three dots to indicate the omission of part of a quotation (e.g., "The statute provides that contractors are responsible for . . . the preparation of work orders . . . .")

enacted law   The body of law adopted by the people or legislative bodies, including constitutions, statutes, ordinances, and administrative rules and regulations.

expanded outline   See *outline—expanded.*

external memorandum   A memorandum of law designed for use outside the law office (e.g., memorandums submitted to a court, such as briefs in support of motions; memorandums designed for other external use, such as for clients or opposing attorneys).

fact   Information concerning some thing, action, event, or circumstance.

general jurisdiction   A court that has the power, with few exceptions, to hear and decide any matter brought before it.

generic noun   A noun that represents a member of a group. Generic nouns are singular.

gerund   A verb ending in *-ing.*

gerund phrase   A phrase consisting of a gerund and accompanying words.

> ◘ *For Example:* Tom, *having finished his nap,* went back to work.

good/well   *Good* is an adjective (adjectives modify nouns and pronouns). It cannot be used as an adverb (adverbs modify verbs, adjectives, and adverbs). *Well* can act as an adverb or an adjective.

headnotes   Summaries of the points of law discussed in a court opinion prepared by the publisher of the opinion.

holding   The court's application of the rule of law to the legal question raised by the facts of a case; the court's answer to the legal issue in a case.

hyphen (-)   A mark used to form compound modifiers and compound nouns (e.g., well-known, ex-judge).

indefinite pronouns   Pronouns that do not refer to a specific person or thing; e.g., *anybody, each, either, everyone,* and *someone.*

infinitive   A verb form that functions as a noun or as an auxiliary verb (e.g., to argue, to leave); the word *to* followed by a verb. A *split infinitive* refers to the placement of an adverb between *to* and the verb in an infinitive (e.g., to *completely* understand).

infinitive phrase   A phrase consisting of an infinitive and accompanying words.

> ◘ *For Example:* It is important *to take continuing education classes.*

information letter   Correspondence that provides general legal information or background on a legal issue. It usually communicates the results of legal research and analysis to a client or third party.

in personam jurisdiction   See *personal jurisdiction.*

IRAC   An acronym commonly used in reference to the legal analysis process. It is composed of the first letter of the descriptive term for each step of the process—**I**ssue, **R**ule, **A**nalysis/Application, **C**onclusion. The standard legal analysis process is the identification of the issue, the presentation of the governing rule of law, the analysis/application of the rule of law, and the conclusion.

irrelevant facts   Those facts that are coincidental to an event but are not of significant legal importance in a case.

issue   The precise legal question raised by the specific facts of a dispute.

jurisdiction   The court's authority to hear and resolve specific disputes. Jurisdiction is usually composed of *personal jurisdiction* (authority over persons) and *subject matter jurisdiction* (authority over the types of cases a court may hear and decide).

key facts   The legally significant facts of a case that raise the legal question of how or whether the law governing the dispute applies; the facts upon which the outcome of the case is determined. They are the facts that establish or satisfy the elements of a cause of action and are necessary to prove or disprove a claim. (Key facts are so essential that if they were changed, the outcome of the case would probably change.)

key facts–groups Individual facts that, when considered as a group, are key facts; Individual facts that, when treated as a group, may determine the outcome of a case.

key facts–individual Key facts that, if they were changed, the outcome of the case would be affected or changed.

key number West Group has divided all areas of American law into various topics and subtopics. Each area is identified by a topic name, and each specific topic or subtopic is assigned a number called a key number.

law The enforceable rules that govern individual and group conduct in a society. The law establishes standards of conduct, the procedures governing standards of conduct, and the remedies available when the standards are not adhered to.

legal analysis The process of identifying the issue or issues presented by a client's facts and determining what law applies and how it applies; the process of applying the law to the facts of a case. It is an exploration of how and why a specific law does or does not apply.

legalese terms of art used in the legal profession that are not generally known outside the profession.

legal issue See *issue*.

legal research The process of identifying the law or legal authority that applies to the issue.

legal research memorandum A legal memorandum prepared for office use. It presents an objective legal analysis of the issue(s) raised by the facts of the client's case and usually includes the arguments in favor of and in opposition to the client's position. It is often referred to by other names: office legal research memorandum, office research memorandum, and interoffice memorandum of law.

legal writing process A systematic approach to legal writing; an organized approach to legal research, analysis, and writing. It is composed of three stages: prewriting, writing, and postwriting.

legislative history The record of legislation during the enactment process. It is composed of committee reports, transcripts of hearings, statements of legislators concerning the legislation, and any other material published for legislative use with regard to the legislation.

lie/lay *Lie* is an intransitive verb that means "to rest or recline." (An intransitive verb is verb that does not take a direct object.) Its forms are *lie, lay, lain* and *lying.*

limited jurisdiction A court that is limited in the types of cases it may hear and decide.

listserv An e-mail discussion group. A listserv links people with common interests to share information on a topic or area of expertise.

majority opinion The opinion in a court decision of the majority of judges.

mandatory authority Any authority or source of law that a court must rely on or follow when reaching a decision (e.g., a decision of a higher court in the jurisdiction on the same or a similar issue).

memorandum of law A written analysis of a legal problem. It is an informative document that summarizes the research and analysis of the legal issue or issues raised by the facts of a case. It contains a summary of what the law is and how the law applies in the case.

misplaced modifier   A word or phrase that is placed in the wrong location in a sentence. Because of its placement, it appears to modify one word or phrase when it is intended to modify another.

modifier   A word or phrase that provides a description of the subject, verb, or object in a sentence.

nominalization   A noun created from a verb (e.g., *realization* from the verb *realize*).

nouns   Words that refer to persons, places, things, or qualities.

on point   A term used to refer to a prior court opinion in which the facts are sufficiently similar to the facts of the client's case or the case before the court for the prior court opinion to apply as precedent. A case is on point if the similarity between the key facts and rule of law or legal principle of the court opinion and those of the client's case is sufficient for the court opinion to govern or provide guidance to a later court in deciding the outcome of the client's case.

opinion   The written statement by the court expressing the way it ruled in a case and the reasons for its ruling.

opinion letter   Correspondence, usually written to a client, that, in addition to informing the reader of how the law applies to a specific question, provides legal advice. It informs the reader about how the law applies and advises which steps should be taken.

outline   The skeletal structure and organizational framework of a writing.

outline–expanded   An outline that has been expanded so that it may be used in the prewriting stage. The use of an expanded outline allows the integration of all research, analysis, and ideas into an organized outline structure while research and analysis are being conducted. It facilitates the preparation of a rough draft.

paragraph   A group of sentences that address the same topic.

parallel citation   When a court opinion is printed in more than one reporter, the citations are referred to as parallel citations. Each citation is a parallel citation to the other citation or citations. (E.g., *Britton v. Britton,* **100 N.M. 424, 671 P.2d 1135 (1983).** [The parallel citations are in bold.])

parallel construction   Listed items that are similar in grammatical structure. In sentences that include a list, a group of activities, and so on, each of the items use the same grammatical form; (that is, all of the items or members of the group should agree in verb tense, number, and so on.)

parentheses ( )   Marks used to add to a sentence information that is outside the main idea of the sentence or is of lesser importance.

participial phrase   A phrase consisting of a participle and accompanying words. A participle is a verb that may be used as an adjective.

> ■ *For Example:* The paralegal, *hired to perform research,* was paid an excellent salary.

party   A plaintiff or defendant in a lawsuit.

passive voice   See *voice*.

personal jurisdiction   The authority of the court over the parties to resolve a legal dispute involving the parties.

persuasive authority   Any authority a court is not bound to consider or follow but may consider or follow when reaching a decision (e.g., a decision of a court in another state on the same or a similar issue, secondary authority, and so on).

phrase   A group of words that lacks a subject or predicate or both. Therefore, it is not a sentence. A phrase usually functions in a sentence as an adjective, an adverb, or a noun.

plain meaning rule   A canon of construction that provides that if the meaning of a statute is clear on its face, it will be interpreted according to its plain meaning and the other canons of construction will not be applied by the court.

plaintiff   The party who starts (files) a lawsuit.

point heading   A summary of the position advocated in the argument section of a trial or appellate brief.

postwriting stage   The stage in the legal writing process where an assignment is revised, edited, and assembled in final form.

precedent   An earlier court decision on an issue that applies to govern or guide a subsequent court in its determination of an identical or similar issue based on identical or similar facts. A court opinion is precedent when there is a sufficient similarity between the key facts and rule of law or legal principle of the court's opinion and the matter before the subsequent court.

predicate   A verb, its modifiers, and the object of the verb, such as a direct object (if necessary). The predicate of a sentence provides information concerning the subject of a sentence. (*E.g.,* Mazhar *ran to the store.*)

preposition   A word that expresses a relationship between the word or words that follow and other words in the sentence. Some common prepositions are *about, after, at, before, by, for, from, in, of, on, over, through, up,* and *with.*

prepositional phrase   A phrase that begins with a preposition and ends with a noun or noun substitute.

> ◼ *For Example: After Shelly completed the brief,* she went to lunch.

prewriting stage   The stage in the legal writing process where the assignment is organized, researched, and analyzed.

primary authority   Authority that is composed of the law (e.g., constitutions, statutes, and court opinions).

principal/principle   When used as a noun, *principal* means "the head of an organization or a school" or "a sum of money"; as an adjective, *principal* means "most important." *Principle* is a noun meaning "a rule of conduct or basic truth."

prior proceedings   The events that occurred in the litigation in a lower court or an administrative hearing.

proper nouns   The names of specific persons, places, or things.

punctuation   Marks or characters used in writing to make the meaning clear and easy to understand (e.g., period [.], comma [,], semicolon [;], and colon [:]).

purpose clause   A statutory section that includes the purpose the legislative body intended to accomplish when drafting the statute.

quotation marks (" ")   Marks used to identify and set off quoted material. (Courtney said, "I do not believe it is true.")

re   A term meaning "in the matter of, about, or concerning." It is usually placed at the beginning of the reference line in a memo or in other correspondence.

relative pronoun   A pronoun that refers to another noun in the sentence. *Which, who,* and *that* are examples of relative pronouns.

remand   A decision of an appellate court that sends the case back to the trial court for further action.

reverse   A decision of an appellate court that disagrees with the decision of the trial court.

salutation   The part of a letter that presents the greeting (Dear Ms. Nusbaun).

scope   A statutory section that specifically states what is and is not covered by the statute.

secondary authority   Any source of law a court may rely on that is not the law (e.g., legal treatises, restatements of the law, and legal encyclopedias).

semicolon (;)   A punctuation mark used to separate major elements of complex sentences or to separate items in a series when the items are long or when one of the items has internal commas. (The shareholders held their meeting at noon; the board of directors met immediately thereafter.)

sentence   The fundamental building block of writing. It is composed of a group of words that conveys a single thought. It is usually a statement in which the actor (subject) performs some action or describes a state of being (the predicate).

short title   The name by which a statute is known (e.g., Uniform Commercial Code—Sales).

simple sentence   A sentence that is composed of an independent clause and no subordinate clauses. It is composed of only one subject and verb structure.

For Example: Barb writes songs.

split infinitive   See *infinitive.*

squinting modifier   A modifier located in a sentence such that it is unclear whether the modifier refers to the word that precedes it or the word that follows it. (E.g., The report that was prepared *routinely* indicated that the structure was unsafe. [It is unclear whether *routinely* refers to the report being prepared routinely or the report routinely indicating the structure was unsafe.])

stare decisis   A basic principle of the common law system that requires a court to follow a previous decision of that court or a higher court when the current decision involves issues and facts similar to those involved in the previous decision; the doctrine that provides that precedent should be followed.

statement of facts   The section of a memorandum of law that presents the factual context of the issue(s) addressed in the memorandum.

statutes Laws passed by legislative bodies that declare rights and duties or that command or prohibit certain conduct.

statutory analysis The interpretation and application of statutory law; the process of determining whether a statute applies to a specific fact situation, how it applies, and what the effect is of that application.

statutory elements The specific conditions or components of a statute that must be met for the statute to apply.

statutory law The body of law composed of laws passed by legislative bodies. The term includes laws or ordinances passed by any legislative body.

subject A noun or pronoun that is the actor in a sentence. (E.g., *Devon* ran to the store.)

subject matter jurisdiction The types or kinds of cases the court has the authority to hear and decide.

topic sentence The sentence that identifies the subject of a paragraph. It introduces the subject and provides the focus of a paragraph.

trial court The court where the matter is heard and decided; testimony is taken, the evidence is presented, and the decision is reached.

trial court brief An external memorandum of law submitted to a trial court. It presents the legal authority and argument in support of a position advocated by an attorney, usually with regard to a motion or an issue being addressed by the court. It is often referred to as a trial brief.

United States district court The trial court of general jurisdiction in the federal judicial system.

United States Supreme Court The final court of appeals in the federal system and the highest court in the United States.

URLs Uniform resource locators; the addresses of Web sites.

verbs Words that express action, a state of being or feeling, or a relation between two things. (E.g., Devon *ran* to the store.)

verb tense The time in which a verb's action occurs. Events happening in the present use the present tense, events that occurred in the past use the past tense, and events that will take place in the future use the future tense.

voice The relationship of the subject to the action of the sentence. *Active voice*—the subject of the sentence is performing the action in the sentence. (The automobile hit the child.) *Passive voice*—the subject of the sentence is acted upon. (The child was hit by the automobile.)

writing stage The stage in the legal writing process where research, analysis, and ideas are assembled into a written product.

writ of certiorari A writ from a higher court asking a lower court for the record of a case. A petition for a writ of certiorari is a request filed by a party in a lawsuit that a higher court review the decision of a lower court.

Index